LAST FUTURES

LAST FUTURES

*Nature, Technology and the
End of Architecture*

Douglas Murphy

VERSO
London · New York

This paperback edition first published by Verso 2022
First published by Verso 2016
© Douglas Murphy 2016, 2022

1 3 5 7 9 10 8 6 4 2

Verso
UK: 6 Meard Street, London W1F 0EG
US: 388 Atlantic Avenue, Brooklyn, NY 11217
www.versobooks.com

Verso is the imprint of New Left Books

ISBN-13: 978-1-78168-982-0
eISBN-13: 978-1-78168-981-3 (US)
eISBN-13: 978-1-78168-980-6 (UK)

British Library Cataloguing in Publication Data
A catalogue record for this book is available from the British Library

The Library of Congress has cataloged the hardback edition as follows:
Murphy, Douglas, author.
 Last futures : nature, technology and the end of architecture / Douglas Murphy.
   pages cm
  ISBN 978-1-78168-975-2 (hardback)
1. Architectural design–History–20th century. 2. Architectural design–Social
aspects. 3. Architecture–Forecasting. I. Title.
 NA2750.M87 2016
 724'.6–dc23

2015031872

Typeset in Electra by MJ & N Gavan, Truro, Cornwall
Printed and bound by CPI Group (UK) Ltd, Croydon CR0 4YY

CONTENTS

INTRODUCTION

This book tells the story of the near futures of a past era and what became of them. The late 1960s and early 1970s were a time of rapid change, and last chances. How did this affect architecture, the form of cities and the lives of their citizens? It was a time when radicals of previous generations found themselves at the heart of the establishment, while a new generation challenged the foundations of that elite. What united them all, however, was a belief that the future was up for grabs, that changes in the very patterns of life were possible – in fact that it was inevitable that, the way things were going, life itself and its physical surroundings would soon be utterly different.

In those days of the Cold War and the space race, it was common to imagine the future in terms of visually striking advanced technology of a massive scale. This was the era of space rockets, giant satellite dishes, radio transmitters and TV towers, and these artefacts of high technology were reflected in the architectural predictions of the time. Innovations in construction led many to believe that buildings of the near future were going to be larger and more complex, with forms that would express the increased social complexity of the late twentieth-century world. Many designs of the era appear fantastic and implausible to our eyes now, yet at the time were often considered only a few years away from implementation, inevitable developments considering the speed of urban change at the time.

The world exhibitions and the culture surrounding them were some of the clearest examples of this way of thinking, and architects and planners were heavily involved. Nation states and corporate organisations invested enormous sums in promoting their values and ideologies through architecture and technology at these international events. Looking closely at this culture allows us to see not only the official stories that those in power told about themselves through architecture, but also the fears and struggles that quietly informed these pageants' political aesthetics.

The rate of social change then apparent influenced whole generations of architects and planners to imagine how the city could be made to be more responsive and flexible, in the process inventing a kind of anti-architecture, against monumentality and against permanence. In some ways the resulting investigations attempted to turn housing into another form of white goods, like refrigerators or washing machines, but in others they asked profound questions about how people might live in cities in the future, and about what relationship they might have with transience in their built environment. The image of the nomadic subject moving freely through a city constantly fine-tuned to their requirements was one that haunted the dreams of the age.

While many embraced the promise of change, the strains of this transforming world were everywhere apparent. One reaction in this time of upheaval, which encompassed the Vietnam War and other proxy battles of the Cold War, the nuclear age and the military-industrial complex, was to attempt to escape from modern society entirely. The communes and other countercultural movements of the era were forced to innovate architecturally in their attempts to create new forms of social organisation, and at the time their rudimentary experiments, often imitations of the most sophisticated contemporaneous technology, attracted great interest. They inspired many to consider ways in which the city of the future might be remade from scratch, in the service of completely new ideas of what constituted the good life.

This was also the era of first-wave environmentalism, when the global side-effects of the Industrial Revolution and the exploitation of hydro-carbons first began to enter public consciousness. Architecture found itself having to understand its role in the systems of the planet, the limits of which were becoming more apparent by the day. On the one hand this unleashed a flood of pessimism, as population growth, pollution and resource depletion all appeared to threaten the existence of human society, even long before climate change became an issue. On the other hand, the new sciences that had fed this environmentalism, the holis-tic studies of systemic behaviours known as cybernetics and ecology, inspired architecture to change. The apocalyptic rhetoric that took hold at the time had a profound effect on how people thought architecture would be made in the future.

Throughout the era, again and again the notion of the spherical envi-ronment, the dome or the bubble, came to represent the new-found sense of the earth as a small, vulnerable globe in the vastness of space, and the quest, for some, was to expand that protective interior zone to encompass ever-greater aspects of life. Over a century before, the first industrially produced buildings – the Crystal Palace of 1851, the arcades of Paris – had stirred the public imagination and suggested a future world under glass, where everything was comfortable and harmonious. The massive interior environments of the time, both imaginary and in some cases built in germinal form, were some of the purest architectural visions of social and natural harmony conceived in human history.

But these futures failed to arrive, and as time moved on, a different world of high technology coupled with social and aesthetic reaction set in. The city of the future went from being an imminent prospect to become instead a thing of the past. In the US and its sphere of influence, extreme economic liberalism combined with social conservatism, and facilitated by the development of computing and digital technology, the existing order began to ossify. By the time the Cold War ended, radical change of any sort began to seem ever more distant.

There are many reasons these futures didn't arrive as expected. As with all innovations, designers met with many problems when they attempted to incorporate major change rapidly, and a number of accidents and dis-asters, both isolated and system-wide, occurred when new technologies went badly wrong. The political reaction against futuristic architecture came on a number of levels, from designers and planners who became disillusioned with the optimistic rhetoric as the political context changed around them in the 1970s, to a public who grew weary and distrustful of so-called expert and professional opinion. Ideologically, many rejected the egalitarian impulses of these visions of the future, and with a rise in individualism, they reacted aesthetically and politically on a number of levels, with the purpose of obliterating the potential for architecture to be seen as a tool in the service of social change. In many cases, the boldness of the social vision of these last futures was matched by the severity of the reactions to them later.

After at least a generation of stasis, however, it now appears that we again stand at the edge of massive transformations in human society. Rapid climate change, however severe, and however we are able to avoid or mitigate its effects, is likely to have – at the very least – a profoundly negative effect upon agriculture and thus the human food supply, while also rendering some parts of the world practically uninhabitable. As a result, mass migration at a level never before seen, and a concomitant increase in political and social instability, war and famine, seem inevitable. Apocalyptic rhetoric in the public sphere has reached a point not seen since the oil crisis of the early 1970s, but this time the signals are less a forewarning than first symptoms of a catastrophe already occurring.

For some, as before, technology offers an escape route out of the crisis. Rapid developments in energy production (including renewable and zero-carbon energy production), medical technology, finance and telecommunications media all seem to offer glimpses of some kind of route through the unfolding crisis. Unlike in the past, however, many of these routes simply offer the preservation of current wealthy lifestyles for as long as possible, rather than the possibility of remaking human relations entirely.

Once again, great powers are moving against each other in a multipolar world, while a massive wave of popular disgust at elites continues to unfold. As global economic inequality widens, revolutions and unrest have erupted against establishments across the world. After generations of being told 'there is no alternative', it seems that change – of one kind or another – is definitely coming.

In the experiments in architecture and urbanism of the post-war era, we see that many of the abandoned and defeated futures that the era dreamed resonate strongly with our current experience, at times giving us a sense of political déjà vu. These previous attempts to deal with the various challenges caused by technological, environmental and social change, the paths suggested but untrodden, deserve our attention, since they may offer us ways of working through current crises.

Many of the subjects in this book are familiar from architectural histories of the period, but many have quietly been dismissed as germinal forms of what led inexorably to present conditions, or as failures whose flaws are self-evident from today's perspective. Others have been understood as radical in formal and expressive content, but with their social implications considered naive or irrelevant. By situating them within a context of architectural radicalism on a longer timescale, I hope to show that there are still glimmers of potential and that by looking to the past, strategies for the present might become clearer.

The attitude of this book, however, is generally anti-utopian. Against common interpretations, many of the architectural experiments and proposals of the time are poorly understood by stories of human and social perfectibility. Much that I will discuss often appears to today's eyes to be part of a period of naive utopianism – a belief that good design would improve its users and that ordinary human beings were material to be moulded in the service of a grand vision. This is largely myth, retroactively applied, and in the following chapters I hope to provide a more sophisticated view of various cultures who understood that they were going through a period of rapid change, with a great many serious challenges to be addressed which could not be ignored, and the ambitious ways that they attempted to work through them.

This book does not presuppose expert knowledge of architectural history, and it is not a comprehensive historical guide to the architecture or literature of the era in question. Indeed, like many germinal forms, much of the design discussed within is often of dubious quality when evaluated according to established standards. But what shines through is the fact that the experiments and visions of this period were far more sober attempts to address the challenges of the times than the apparently more sensible world that came afterwards, a world whose continued existence since the last decade's upheavals has raised the ominous prospect that it may well be too late to change.

In short, this book is an attempt to contribute to the understanding of some of the most vital and difficult challenges that humanity faces in general, not by making a direct argument about today's world, but by looking back a few generations and telling a story of what we can only hope were not the last futures.

Chapter 1

The Museum of the Future

A visitor stepping out of Jean-Drapeau metro station in Montreal, Canada, is confronted with one of the oddest sights in all of architecture. Through the branches of the trees in this island park rises a strange silvery object. It is transparent, dissolving against the sky, a fuzzy haze that hardens towards its perfectly circular profile. If the visitor walks towards this odd vision, the beautiful and delicate lattice of its construction is revealed, along with the platforms and buildings within its spherical shell. A closer look shows that this filigree dome is welded together from innumerable short steel bars, as plain as scaffolding poles. Surrounded by greenery in summer and encrusted with icicles in the winter, the dome seems to melt into the sky, a huge object with almost no presence.

Approaching the dome along a pathway bordered by shallow ponds, the visitor will find that there is a small gap at the very bottom of the dome through which they can enter, and in passing through the threshold, a remarkable thing happens. Although the external world remains completely visible, all of a sudden the dome seems to vanish, its boundaries disappearing as the visitor moves inward. At the same time, the entire sky becomes marked with the grid of fine elements, in every direction; the triangles and hexagons of the structure seem as far away as the

The geodesic dome of Buckminster Fuller's USA Pavilion

stars, ethereally etched against the sky above. The visitor feels as though they are both inside and outside at the same time, and that there is the most featherweight of protective boundaries around them at an almost indeterminate distance.

This remarkable structure was once the USA Pavilion at Expo 67, one of the most iconic works of Richard Buckminster Fuller, the Cold War world's most visionary designer.

Expo 67 was one of the most popular world exhibitions in the entire 150-year history of the cultural form. Awarded to Quebec in the early 1960s by the Bureau Internationale des Expositions, in part to mark the Canadian Centennial, over fifty nations took part and many millions of people passed through the park in the six months that it was open. It was situated on two artificially constructed islands in the St Lawrence River and linked to the rest of the city by new metro lines, bridges and a monorail. It involved the construction of hundreds of buildings, gardens and amusements, most of them temporary, some permanent, and some that were among the most important works of architecture of the 1960s.

It's easy to forget now that world's fairs were once highly significant events, pageants of progress, displays of industrial, technical and cultural power. Stranger still, they were entertaining, the sort of event where half a million people could pass through in a single day, with families travelling across countries, even from around the world, just to attend. Odd relics from an age where material culture was still the scene of the greatest achievements of progress and development, where new technology was large, visible and worth travelling to see, expos were a cross between amusement parks, political rallies and museums – museums of the near future.

The history of world's fairs is inextricably tied into the history of global capitalism. Distant relatives of the old trade fairs that occurred throughout pre-industrial history, world's fairs appeared almost fully formed with the Great Exhibition of 1851 in London. This was the very first event in the world with a self-proclaimed global scope, inviting the nations of the world to come together and celebrate the new cultures of industrial production. Conceived in a genuine spirit of optimistic fraternity, but also as a spectacular patriotic event designed to help alleviate the social pressures that had led to revolutions all over the world in preceding years, it attempted to show that all people had a stake in the new world of capitalism and global trade.

It was also in the less noble interests of the UK to host the Great Exhibition as a demonstration of their might, given that at this point they still dominated the global economy, indeed were at the very zenith of their power. But there was also a chance for the USA and other countries to demonstrate their own achievements, which in many ways were beginning to threaten British supremacy. Within the exhibition the workings of industrial capitalism were put on public display. Arranged as a series of exhibits divided thematically and geographically, the millions of visitors who passed through encountered displays of raw materials, machinery and industrial equipment, and a bewildering range of products and manufactures. From furniture to textiles, from sculpture to the brand new media technology of photography, the Great Exhibition was a comprehensive introduction to the modern capitalist world.

The success of the Great Exhibition led to reiterations of the event in New York in 1853, Paris in 1855 and London again in 1862, before expositions spread across the world over the next fifty years. Early on, a pattern was established regarding the conventions of an expo, a pattern that involved massive, overwhelming collections of industrial machinery, raw materials, products, design, craftwork and fine art. Each World's Fair was intended to display the achievements of industrial capitalism and give prominence to the power of global trade. Thus the nineteenth-century crowds who attended these events were educated in the world of commodities and exchange, as every conceivable object (including human beings) was on show, subject to the same regime of examination and economic comparison.

Fairs were dreamlike events, in many cases the visitors' first experience of the fantastic qualities of capitalism, its aspirations and its tendency to abstract objects, processes and labour into an intangible realm. Furthermore, over the first half century, as the expositions became larger, they reflected growing waves of nationalism. In the process they became 'safe' spaces, akin to the Olympic Games, in which national tensions could be worked out visually and spatially, and where different ideologies would compete to stake their claim to offer the best future for humanity.

Architecture was absolutely integral to world's fairs from the very beginning. From the fragile sublime of the Crystal Palace in 1851, the resounding entry of industrial engineering into an architectural world that was groaning under the weight of academic traditions, a pattern was set up of gigantic iron and glass palaces, vast single internal rooms filled with exhibits, veritable cornucopias of objects. This format – the giant hall stuffed with displays – reached its apotheosis with the 1889 Universal Exposition in Paris, where the Eiffel Tower and Galerie des Machines created technical achievements in industrial architecture that remained unsurpassed for another forty years afterwards.

By the start of the twentieth century, expositions became so large that they spread across a selection of pavilions, each one assigned to a country or industrial corporation. This had the effect of multiplying the different voices expressed through architecture and allowed for the statements to become more complete. For example, Le Corbusier's Esprit Nouveau pavilion in Paris's 1925 L'Exposition internationale des arts décoratifs et industriels modernes displayed his polemical proposals for high-rise living in Paris. The Plan Voisin was one of the most infamous architectural proposals ever made, with its depiction of a series of gigantic tower blocks smashed through the centre of Paris, for better or worse one of the most influential urban visions of all time.

At the same exposition, Konstantin Melnikov built the Soviet pavilion, a bold timber structure arranged across a diagonal axis, which today is one of the best known works of Russian constructivism, eulogised for its expression of the dynamic and hopeful energy of the early Soviet Union before Stalinism. The 1929 exhibition in Barcelona saw the construction of Mies van der Rohe's German Pavilion, a deliciously refined series of polished steel columns and walls made of waxy travertine, demonstrating his vision of a luxury avant-garde – austere, technocratic, universal, yet classically minded – which would eventually evolve into the American post-war corporate style. At the 1937 Paris expo, Le Corbusier's Pavillon des Temps Nouveaux casually introduced a technologically advanced steel-framed aesthetic that would go on to become incredibly influential for following generations, but this achievement was completely overwhelmed by the Soviet and German pavilions, both totalitarian, both classical, both headbangingly regressive.

The last expo before World War II, the New York World's Fair in 1939, marked the transition from displays of industrial and cultural achievement to loud proclamations of the direction the future would take. Entitled 'Dawn of a New Day', it featured *Futurama*, an immersive exhibit created by titans of American industry General Motors, where visitors endured massive queues to be taken on a kind of futuristic ghost train. Inside, they sat in cars and were carried through a model environment depicting a near-future America of superfast highways, industrialised agriculture and bucolic super-suburbs. Today, *Futurama* appears something like a cross between Fritz Lang's *Metropolis* and a fairly quotidian depiction of the skyscrapers and motorways that would later become so utterly familiar. It offered a corporate future based entirely around the motor car, with a germinal splash of the aesthetics of the atomic age. For the American visitors of the time, still smarting from the Great Depression and aware of – if not yet involved in – WWII, it presented an attractive image of the American future.

The primary architectural vision of the New York fair was a variation on the moderne style: streamlined and industrial but not too avant-garde. Its defining images were the Trylon and Perisphere, which were an obelisk and globe, white, near featureless and poised in such a way that they made for fantastic photographs, icons of their time. The Perisphere contained an exhibit, *Democracity*, which was another immersive vision of the future, conceived by Edward Bernays, nephew of Sigmund Freud and 'father' of public relations. Again, behind this gently optimistic view of the future was the power of the American corporations, who were subtly but aggressively attempting to stake a claim on the hearts and minds of the public as the politics of the New Deal threatened to sideline them from power.

It was not until thirteen years after WWII that there was another official world's exhibition, Expo 58 in Brussels. At this point, one of the conceptual problems that would beset futuristic architecture over the second half of the twentieth century was already becoming apparent: in a world of atomic manipulation, of increasingly miniaturised electronic technologies, how best to display these new forms of technology in a spatial setting? This first post-war expo offered one the most blindingly obvious attempts to work this problem out. The Atomium, built for Expo 58 and still standing today, rises over 100 meters above Brussels and is a literal, inhabitable representation of an iron molecule. Nine large spheres – the atoms – are linked by structures representing the atomic bonds, which hold lifts and elevators that carry visitors to a viewing platform on the top floor.

A more successful attempt to deal with the new world of mass consumption and multimedia once again came from the studio of Le Corbusier. The Philips Pavilion, built for the electronics manufacturer, was almost completely unlike any other building in Le Corbusier's oeuvre. This is due to it being largely the work of Iannis Xenakis, a Greek engineer working for Le Corbusier who, after an acrimonious split with the master relating to credit for the pavilion's authorship, went on to become a renowned composer of experimental and stochastic music. For the pavilion, Le Corbusier (occupied somewhat with the building of the city of Chandigarh in India) sketched out a floor-plan that was a vague diagram of a stomach with two narrow entrances at either end. On top of this Xenakis set a series of hyperbolic paraboloids, saddle-shaped surfaces that curve in two directions, meeting at the edges to create a tent-like enclosure, which were realised as pre-fabricated concrete panels held in place partially by cables tied across the ruled surface.

Inside the Philips Pavilion, hundreds of loudspeakers and projectors were embedded into the walls for the purposes of displaying *Poème électronique*, a multimedia display featuring electroacoustic music by Edgar Varèse and a short film by Le Corbusier. Visitors were brought into the darkened hall before music and images emanated from all directions. Varèse's composition is a near-collage of synthesised and recorded music, with samples of industrial, musical and vocal noises and a variety of abstract and more tonal electronic sounds. It is mostly sparse in texture, with long silences, although there are moments of high intensity. The accompanying film was also a collage, with images ranging from European avant-garde staples such as tribal masks and ancient sculpture to animals, roads, cities (including several buildings by Le Corbusier) and images of nuclear explosions and starving concentration camp inmates. The Philips Pavilion was a deeply modernist multimedia experience, a corporate-sponsored experience whose every aspect was avant-garde. Although immersive multimedia technology would become ever more prevalent in expo culture, it would never again be so uncompromisingly experimental.

The New York World's Fair of 1964 was dampened by conflicts within the Bureau Internationale des Expositions (BIE), meaning that few international exhibitors took part. Instead it offered a vivid portrait of the United States' self-image at the height of its own world power. The theme of 'Peace Through Understanding' paid the traditional lip-service to fraternity while also making a blatant point about the Cold War. Meanwhile the dedication 'Man's Achievement on a Shrinking Globe in an Expanding Universe' was obviously born of the space programme, developments in cosmology and the race to the moon. The fair was held on the same land, Flushing Meadows Park, as the 1939 fair had been, and Robert Moses the arch-planner, who had reclaimed the land for the earlier expo, was given the job of delivering the later one. General Motors reprised their *Futurama* exhibit from a quarter century before, but this time the future they presented was less about life in an ordinary city and far more focused on frontier conditions: moon bases, orbital colonies, Antarctic research centres, underwater hotels, jungle cities and so on. *Futurama II* was dominated by a blasé feeling of American capitalism's technological dominance over adversarial natural conditions, seeking out resources and new frontiers wherever they could be found. Elsewhere at the 1964 fair, and perhaps most significantly, IBM laid on a spectacle of new digital technologies that was the very first encounter with a computer for many of the millions who passed through.

Of all the world's fairs, Expo 67 had one of the strongest claims on the future as a conceptual vision, but it also marked the point at which a backlash against the uncritical celebration of technology began to make itself felt in establishment consciousness. It occurred at the point in the twentieth century when accelerating progress was at its strongest, but this spirit was met with an emerging wave of self-criticism and social experiment that had perhaps not been seen before that century. The Vietnam War, the civil rights movement, the student revolts, the New Left and the counterculture were either already prominent or on the rise. The Apollo programme was nearing its successful attempt to land humans on the moon. Along with these major changes, Expo 67 was a point almost at the zenith of architecture's power as a vehicle for dreams of new social and technical organisation, but also where a perceived irrelevance of architecture began, gradually, to become apparent.

The title of Expo 67, 'Man and His World' (Terre des Hommes), is taken from Antoine de Saint-Exupéry, the author of *The Little Prince*. It is the name of a 1939 book that contains a passage wherein the author looks out from an aeroplane at night and becomes startlingly aware of the fragility of human existence on the earth below. This awakened global consciousness was in tune with the growing public awareness of sciences such as ecology and cybernetics, as well as the recent expeditions into outer space that were so prominent in the public imagination.

The motif was carried through the entire expo with pavilions devoted to various sub-themes such as 'Man the Explorer', 'Man the Creator',

'Man the Producer' and so on. This unreconstructed notion of 'man', which might sound strange to contemporary ears, is particularly significant for two reasons: one, the expo was notable for the involvement of many recently decolonized African countries such as Algeria, Ghana, Kenya and others, who were attempting to use the prominence of the expo as an opportunity to solidify public acceptance of their arrival as independent nations. On the other hand, 'man' becomes a word that universalises humanity through a sense of cosmic distance, where divisions are indistinguishable and patterns of behaviour common to all. In both these cases the word 'man' takes on a conspicuousness for its stressing of a (not unproblematic) universality, a world beyond struggle and conflict. Indeed, the fact that visitors were given a 'passport' instead of a ticket emphasises the notion of the expo as a zone apart from the political problems of the world.

Architecturally, Expo 67 was an exciting prospect. Gone were the overt science fiction conceits of previous years, in favour of a number of variations of a more genuinely technical design language. By this point, the architectural language of modernism that was formed out of the European avant-garde between the wars was at its most popular, with brutalism – that heavy, expressive, formally exuberant method – at its historic peak. Developed out of a fusion of Le Corbusier's post-war austerity buildings and the 'as-found' obsessions of pop art, brutalism was probably the boldest mode of building available to architects at the time, and although it was current, it didn't embody any particular vision of the future. Much of the time, brutalism tended to express a sense of confidence in the modernity of the present, and it was enthusiastically adopted by clients for civic, commercial and residential buildings across the world.

Montreal was a city that was booming in the 1960s, yet to be overshadowed within the Canadian economy by Toronto, and much of its downtown buildings and infrastructure, including many of the metro lines built for the expo, were created in a confident, stylish North American brutalism. Across the river at the expo, however, concrete was not the most prominent material. Instead of the heaviness and solidity of the concrete mode, the dominant architectural style of Expo 67 was light, repetitive and technical. Drawing visual cues from the simple, seemingly fragile engineering of radio transmitters, support towers for rockets and other space-age facilities, not to mention factories and warehouses, and taking advantage of new advances in material and structural research, the expo offered up a visual language of efficiency that hadn't been seen since the iron and glass boom of the late nineteenth century. This way of building didn't have a simple name, like 'brutalism', as it never became a dominant style of architecture, even though fragments of it are to be found in all kinds of buildings that followed in subsequent years. It is one of the principal sources for the architectural style known as 'high-tech' that developed in Britain in the late 1970s, but came far too early to be considered part of that world.

If the architecture of Expo 67 were to be defined by any particular motif, it would be that of cellular arrangements of blocks or of space frames; spindly fields of narrow struts, stacked in seemingly crystalline structures. Many buildings at the expo took advantage of these new structures, such as the Gyrotron, another expo attraction based on a ghost train ride, which was a pyramid of white painted steel struts – a thread-like web holding a sealed interior – and combined a visit to outer space with an encounter with a lava-crusted monster of the deep. Elsewhere, the Carrefour corporate pavilion, as well as the Canadian Pavilion, the Ontario Pavilion and many others, all relied on a triangulated steel-frame system; indeed, the Netherlands Pavilion was a collection of matchstick aluminium struts, etching out the form of some rudimentarily boxy spaces, but intangible, almost edgeless, like a cloud.

Perhaps the most consummately executed of the space-frame pavilions at Expo 67 was the one entitled 'Man the Producer'. It was one of the theme pavilions, produced by the organisers of the expo rather than a country or corporation, and was designed as an exhibition of natural resources and the way humanity extracts, processes and utilises them. Architecturally, it took the constructional system of the triangulated space frame to ridiculous lengths. The design was based upon a tetrahedron, a few metres in dimension, whose repetition would define an infinite three-dimensional grid. Real spaces and structures were aligned to this grid by constructing small steel units that welded together to create a space frame. These

Frei Otto's West German Pavilion, Expo 67

could be tightly packed, creating beam, column or array-like structures, but they could also define platforms, caverns and other spatial forms. A loose-fitting envelope of panels helped to delimit an interior space, but the overall effect of the thousands of rustily welded units reminded people of the Eiffel Tower in a state of collapse. There was definitely something ugly about the pavilion; irregular, scaleless and with its obsessive triangulations, it was basically impractical. But it was also very popular, both with the public and the architectural community as well.

There was something about the open-endedness of the pavilions that was particularly attractive. The fact that the simple three-dimensional grid suggested a potential extension in all directions was a hint that a building constructed in this way might be responsive to change. The over-provision of space, the loosely fitting infrastructure, suggested that different functions and activities could take place within the pavilion, that its particular contents were provisional. In short, the pavilion was a diagram of a flexible, dynamic, universal architecture of the future, one suited to conditions of rapid social and technological change. Indeed, connections with more radical ideas of the time were not lost on the critic Reyner Banham, who stated that 'in "Man the Producer" there were nothing but alternative routes, to be selected at conscious will or simply at random – the Situationist's psycho-geographical drift'.[1] What is significant here is that the conditions of indeterminacy that were to become so important to radical notions of the city could also be discerned in an establishment building celebrating raw materials and their production.

But space frames were not the only architectural innovations at work at Expo 67. A brief walk from Man the Producer would bring the visitor to the pavilion of the Federal Republic of Germany, with a roof designed by legendary German engineer Frei Otto. He had trained in architecture before WWII but came to prominence in the late 1950s thanks to his experiments in light-weight structures. Otto's specialty was the development of tensile structures that were at that point far too complicated to calculate mathematically, but which he could resolve through extremely precise form-finding and model-making, testing them through photographing their deflection due to added weights. These experiments won him many admirers in the late 1960s, when their twin themes of material efficiency and technological boldness were at their most popular, helped by his combination of high technical sophistication and slightly mystical pronouncements on human destiny.

Otto had already suggested that the entire Expo 67 site could be contained under a single tensile structure, although this was well beyond his brief. Instead, he developed a structure that would cover just the West German pavilion, itself no mean feat. The pavilion was approached by a bridge and occupied a space where the ground level had been removed; indeed, a large part of the pavilion stretched out over the river. Across its area the interior was divided into various platforms at different heights. This 'terrace landscape' was a variation of the *bürolandschaft*, the 'office landscape', which was an idea current at the time, a more humane attempt to deal with the open-plan efficiencies which were coming into fashion in workplace design of the post-war era.

The West German pavilion spread its exhibits, which included examples of the products of scientific research and technical innovation,

---

1   Reyner Banham, *Megastructures*, p. 116.

throughout the terrace landscape in a display designed to communicate the message that West Germany was a new, technologically sophisticated and, more importantly, friendly country. It also included a large model of Mies van der Rohe's pavilion from Barcelona, which was yet to be rebuilt, tying the new FRG to the Weimar Republic's associations with design and futurity. The terrace platforms were rudimentary structures to the point of near-blankness, which along with the pavilion having no 'ground' to speak of, meant that there was a sense of abstraction to the inside – as if this irregular collection of spaces, perhaps for work but potentially for any function, could be extended out infinitely.

However, what really gave the West German pavilion a visual identity was Otto's roof. Puncturing the pavilion at odd angles were eight cigar-shaped steel columns, between which was stretched a large field of steel mesh, drooped into an irregular tent shape. Acrylic panels created the envelope, and the building was turned into an 'interior' through glazed windows and doors towards the outside. The overall visual effect was that of a strange, oversized desert tent, complete with stay cables and sagging skin, but constructed in the very latest, most futuristic materials. The acrylic roof gave a milky, diffuse quality to the light inside, eliminating direct sunlight and softening shadows within, which contributed to the abstract spatial effect of the internal landscape. Like Antoni Gaudí before him, and Buckminster Fuller as his contemporary, Otto's combination of the most sophisticated technical resources and a highly intuitive approach was something that would become a common feature in the counterculture's architectural experiments of the following years.

The roof of the West German pavilion was just one of the many experiments in radical structures that Frei Otto was to undertake, and his dedication to the 'doing more with less' ethos appealed to designers in a time of growing concern for resource depletion and ecological disruption. A few years later, Otto would design the roof structures above the stadia for the Munich Olympics in 1972, which still stand today. Expanded versions of the Expo 67 pavilion set in parkland, they give off a very bucolic impression of high technology being deployed into an ecologically gentle context, a vision, perhaps rarely equalled, of a future city in 'harmony' with nature.

Alongside the theme of light-weight, increasingly immaterial architecture, Expo 67 saw the construction of one of the most remarkable
experiments in housing of the entire era, one which would influence
a whole generation of designers. On a narrow spit of land to the west of
the main expo islands, across the docks from Montreal's gigantic and
world-famous grain elevators (which, through their depiction in European avant-garde publications, played such an important role in the
development of the modernist architecture of the international style), a
most peculiar and seemingly unprecedented building was constructed.
Entitled 'Habitat', it was the work of Moshe Safdie, an Israeli-Canadian
architect who had only recently graduated from McGill University. It
was actually based upon Safdie's own diploma project, 'A Three-Dimensional Modular Building System', and to make the short hop from his
studies to such a prominent project was a remarkable achievement for
such a young designer.

As the thesis title suggests, Habitat was an attempt to create a system
of modular, pre-fabricated housing, which would both combine the
advantages and avoid the problems of suburban sprawl and high-density
modern housing, with Safdie arguing that 'we had to find new forms of
housing that would re-create, in a high density environment, the relationships and the amenities of the house and the village'.[2] Inspired by Safdie's
experiences of the communality of socialist kibbutzes, Habitat 67 was
commissioned primarily as a demonstration of the 'housing of the future'
but is all the more remarkable for the fact that its futurity was thought of
in terms of years, even months, rather than decades or centuries.

Across the industrially developed world at that time, the dominant attitude to housing was that it was imperative to speed up and rationalise the
process of construction. In a technological world changing as much as
it was by the 1960s, the hope, held by architects, contractors, developers
and governments alike, was that the introduction of factory techniques,
in particular innovations from the car industry, into the building process
would allow for greater numbers of houses to be built more quickly, more
cheaply, and in greater number than ever before. By the middle of the

2 Moshe Safdie, *Beyond Habitat*, p. 53.

Moshe Safdie's Habitat 67: A new system of living

1960s the process was in full swing in Europe, the USSR and the United States, with contractors utilising new 'system building' methods to create vast numbers of new houses.

Safdie explained the ethos behind Habitat: 'I didn't want to do a building, I wanted to do a system that could be applied to any site.'[3] What Habitat brought was a sophistication and formal experimentalism that was a world removed from the tower blocks going up elsewhere in the world. Basing his system upon a simple formal unit, one block, its length roughly double its width, Safdie designed a system of interlocking houses, ranging from one-bed apartments to family homes, sometimes on one floor, often on two, occasionally with double-height spaces inside, and with all units having access to an outside garden space above another unit. The units were stacked in an ingenious arrangement, symmetrically leaning against the circulation cores which brought people up to their flats, but in such a way that it was very difficult to read the system from the outside – rather the collected housing looks jumbled, irregular, without logic. Because the stepping arrangements created the roof

---

3   Ibid.

terraces, the whole Habitat complex leaned backwards, resulting in seem-ingly impossible overhangs and voids, adding to a composition of almost Piranesian intensity, the simple modules making up a complex and diverse whole.

The housing complex was not only a formal tour de force of sculptural daring and complexity, but it was an attempt to achieve two contradictory things at once, as Safdie's own experience of living in the building during the expo explains: 'Everything about it gave me the feeling of *house* and yet it gave me all the other things I had always wanted in a house but never found in the isolation of the anonymous suburb.'[4]

The flats had gardens that were closed off and private, yet over the balcony were thousands and thousands of people passing through the expo. Safdie's concept accepted the argument that people found tower blocks and other modern forms potentially alienating, but instead of retreating, Habitat was an attempt to show that the experience of homeli-ness could be abstracted and recreated without having to fall back into a false sense of tradition.

A small factory was built on-site for the construction of Habitat, and while Safdie's original thesis involved thousands of houses, and the origi-nal plan was to construct many hundreds, the scheme as it was built included just over 158 units of housing. The drawback was that as a demonstration of mass-fabrication techniques, construction was far too expensive, suggesting that the model was not necessarily deployable at that point. However, despite the complications and the perhaps inad-equate technical achievements of the project, Habitat remains one of the most significant housing estates in the world, imitated to a greater or lesser extent all throughout the next decade. The extreme modularity of the design can be understood as a cellular or perhaps crystalline form, but significantly it also has a flattened hierarchy of elements. Differences in sizes of house are almost imperceptible from the outside; everything remains at the level of the individual box unit, creating a complexity that is also a strongly expressed visual demonstration of an egalitarian political attitude to housing. Habitat was always intended to be a model

4   Ibid., p. 12

for state provision of housing, and it is interesting to note that it is now co-operatively owned by its residents, but the stacks of thousands of units blossoming like tiny crystals on the models of the scheme were never attempted at the originally suggested scale.

If Habitat demonstrated some of the problems of architecture's near-future housing scenarios, then another pavilion at the expo pointed to a more subtle but nonetheless significant problem that faced architecture in the coming decades. Labyrinth was a pavilion constructed for the National Film Board of Canada, just a short walk from Habitat, and was, ostensibly, a cinema theatre. A windowless and blank-surfaced concrete box topped with a steel crown, it presented nothing particularly interesting in the way of architecture. The Labyrinth pavilion was instead designed inside out as a series of multimedia experiences, based allegorically upon the myth of Theseus and the Minotaur. Visitors (who frequently subjected themselves to queues lasting a number of hours) were ushered inside and led to the first auditorium, which was a tall, elongated lozenge-shaped room with a series of balconies. Two large screens, one vertical against the narrow wall and one flat on the ground, played a split-screen film telling a story of childhood and youth. After this section, visitors were led through a maze, which was mirrored and dimly lit, and with specific acoustic effects adding to a sense of disorientation. The third part of the experience was another film, *Death/Metamorphosis*, which was projected onto five different massive screens in cruciform arrangement, viewed from another series of balconies. The entire experience lasted forty-five minutes from entry to exit.

Labyrinth was one of the most popular attractions at Expo 67, even though it was only one among numerous cinematic displays encountered throughout the expo grounds. It was also one of the most aesthetically radical of the attractions, but rather than being a spatial innovation through new construction technology or light-weight materials, what was radical about Labyrinth was the overwhelming multimedia quality of the experience. Compared to the Philips Pavilion of 1958, with its experimental architecture and rudimentary electronic art, the media technology in Labyrinth almost ten years later had become much more advanced, while architecture had begun to take a more circumspect role in the ensemble.

This began to become a concern for architecture at the time: as audio and visual technologies became more powerful, the very structural fabric that surrounded them seemed to become less significant, and over the course of the next decade this would lead to various arguments to the effect that it was in architecture's own interest to vanish behind these mediated skins and screens. Another attitude that was very much in the air at the time was a new taste for immersive experience: the world of the countercultures and youth cultures, of hallucinogenics and drug taking, if not often frequently experienced by the general public, were at least prominently discussed in culture. In the fine arts, various ways of creating new, overwhelming sensory experiences were frequently being experimented with, and as a result some forms of art were tending to blur into each other by this point. A certain synaesthesia was apparent, and Labyrinth represented a more establishment form of the trend for multi-sensory stimulation embodied by the 'happenings' of the era.

At the time of Expo 67, however, despite the emergence of computers, there was no hint of cyberspace or any other of the electronic notions of immersion that turned out to be so important a few decades later. Instead, at this point, everyone seemed to be in agreement it was necessary for a large space, albeit one of minimal architectural import, to play its role in these new sensory environments, which by extension were experienced communally. But we can see that the Labyrinth pavilion was, right among the most exuberant displays of future architecture, a step on a gradual process leading to the spatial disconnection and physical isolation of media experience.

Despite the plethora of architectural and spatial views of the future that were apparent at Expo 67, there is one particular object that has persisted in the public consciousness to this day. The United States Pavilion, a massive geodesic dome seventy-six metres in diameter, translucent by day and glowing resonantly at night, is a powerful symbol not just of the optimistic futurity of the era, of the ability of human ingenuity to mimic, control and improve upon the natural world, but also of the very fragility of this world, its increasingly apparent finitude, and the newly compre-hended dangers that it faced.

Richard Buckminster Fuller was one of the twentieth century's most intriguing characters. During the Cold War he was a loveable eccentric boffin shining in a world of sinister, faceless technocrats. A slight man, bald, who wore glasses so thick his eyes seemed as big as dinner plates, his utterly unique career brought together engineering, physics, cosmology, ecology, architecture, the arts, even mysticism, forming them into a syn-cretic stew of concepts that managed to touch all parts of the culture of his times. An optimist who did more than almost anyone to make human-ity conscious of its cosmic potential, he was also one of the first public thinkers to really warn just how tenuous modern human civilisation had become.

Born in 1895, he was of the same New England family as Margaret Fuller, the pioneering American feminist and transcendentalist writer and in many ways his vision of the world was similar in its cosmic scope, philosophical adventurousness, concerned morality and thoroughly American romanticism. At home everywhere and nowhere, Fuller spent most of his later life incessantly travelling around the world, giving lectures to a global network of students who – at best – treated him as a visionary, a prophet who pointed the way forward to a technologi-cally advanced society freed from conflict and repressive institutions, and more cynically as an eccentric old crackpot with a line in silly neologisms, and a tendency to lecture for four hours without taking a break.

Like many prophets before him, Fuller had experienced an epiphany: he would later tell of how in 1927, at a low ebb after being kicked out of Harvard, failing in business and still mourning the early death of a child, he found himself on the verge of taking his own life. Instead, he claimed, a vision told him that he had 'a blind date with principle' and had to devote his energies to the whole of humanity, dedicating himself to improving life for everyone. Soon afterwards he found himself hanging out in Greenwich Village, encountering artists, designing interiors and lecturing on the principles of light-weight construction that he had originally developed for a failed housing business.

What he now added to this rather dry knowledge was a cosmic dimension: influenced by syntheses of nature and mathematics such as D'Arcy Wentworth Thompson's *On Growth and Form*, the legendary 1917 book that explained natural forms in terms of processes of geometric variation and which influenced generations of artists, architects and other designers, Fuller explained that he had discovered the underlying structure of nature, specifically the tetrahedron, the simplest possible rigid three-dimensional form.

> I think all nature's structuring, associating and patterning must be based on triangles, because there is not structural validity otherwise. *This is nature's basic structure, and it is modellable.*[5]

From this infinitesimal position, Fuller's vision stretched out all the way to the cosmic scale: he described himself as a 'citizen of the universe'. Indeed, one of the recurring themes of his thought was the attempt to situate knowledge in as wide a context as possible. Fuller was a universalist in a world that was becoming more specialised, and never finding himself at home in any official scientific sphere, he instead always relied upon the patronage of social scientists, engineers, artists and architects.

By the time of World War II, Fuller had made his way into academia, becoming involved with Black Mountain College, the visionary institution which sought to synthesise the education of arts and sciences, before gradually building a teaching career travelling across the US and the world, conducting lectures and workshops in a variety of different departments. From the outset, he taught that the world was a fragile and delicate environment. Coining the term 'Spaceship Earth' to convey the sense of the planet as a closed system, he felt that the institutions of the world paid scant heed to the fact that the world was not infinitely abundant, that there was a limited amount of all materials, and that efficiency was therefore key to all human endeavour. His term 'doing more

---

5   As quoted in Hays and Miller (eds), *Buckminster Fuller: Starting with the Universe*, p. 189.

with less' was associated with his lifelong quest to encourage the reduction of waste and inefficiency, in the service of humanity, considered over the length of hundreds, thousands, millions of years.

Fuller was a lifelong anti-institutionalist, blaming almost all the ills of humanity on the short-sightedness of politicians and institutions of all kinds. The Cold War battle of ideologies was for him a distraction from the real processes of change that were occurring all around:

> There is a new idea aloft in our era, one in which we do not think of our great world dilemmas in terms of politics. For years we have been telling the politicians to solve our problems, and yet the crises continually multiply and accelerate in both magnitude and speed of recurrence.[6]

Fuller believed that developments in technology were on their way to eliminating labour, claiming that 'within a century the word "worker" will have no current meaning'.[7] This sudden relaxation of drudgery, combined with the rapid increase in education, led him to believe that a revolution in consciousness was just around the corner: 'As automation eliminates physical drudgery, we will spend more time in the future in intellectual activity. The great industry of tomorrow will be the university, and everyone will be going to school.'[8]

This explains why Fuller spent so much time travelling across the world teaching. He saw it as his mission to communicate a new way of looking at the world to the young generation, who were potentially the ones to surpass antagonistic, warlike, resource-hungry human society:

> This generation *knows* that man can do anything he wants, you see. These people know that wealth is not money – that it's a combination of physical energy and human intellect – and they know that energy can be neither created nor destroyed and that intellectual knowledge can only increase. They also know that they can generate far more wealth by cooperation on

---

6 Buckminster Fuller, *Ideas and Integrities*, p. 302.

7 Ibid., p. 54.

8 Ibid., p. 302.

a global scale than by cooperation with each other. And they realize – or
at least they sense – that utopia is possible now, for the first time in history.[9]

A more optimistic view of the world is hard to imagine, and Fuller's
political naivety is clearly something to behold. But lurking behind every
hopeful declaration of the imminence of a better world was a clear sense
that he thought it might not be enough, as encapsulated by his famous
answer to the question of whether humanity had a future: 'I think it's
absolutely touch and go whether we're going to make it.'

He was an early advocate of the transition away from a carbon-based
energy system, arguing that the energy that had gone into making coal
and oil over millions of years was drastically wasted if it were to be completely depleted in just a few hundred years. A ceaseless promoter of
himself and his ideas, it was his obsession with irreducible geometry
(encapsulated in his trademarked word 'Dymaxion', a portmanteau of
'dynamic maximum tension'), that led him in the years after WWII to
develop and patent, if not invent, the design of the geodesic dome, a
structure in which the surface of an abstract sphere is approximated by
interlocking triangles. In the years after the war, Fuller built a great many
geodesic domes, and in spite of his peace-loving rhetoric, one of his main
clients was the US military, who utilised the dome for efficient shelters
that could be rapidly deployed, with the sight of a dome lashed to the
underside of a helicopter becoming one of the most enduring images of
his work.

The firm he founded, Synergetics, also designed domes for industrial purposes, such as the Union Tank Car Dome of 1958, in which
railway tankers for the oil industry could be repaired, and for businesses
such as the headquarters of the American Society of Metals of 1959, or
the Climatron of 1960, a geodesic greenhouse in St Louis, Missouri.
Before Expo 67, Fuller's domes had been built at other fairs: one of
his early, prominent domes was built for a trade fair in Kabul in 1957;
there was one at the 1962 fair in Seattle; and the main auditorium at the
1964 World's Fair in New York, which was christened as the Churchill

9   *Starting with the Universe*, p. 209.

Pavilion when the ex–prime minister died, was also covered in one of his shallow geodesic domes.

Fuller's original response to the brief for the American Pavilion at Expo 67 was to suggest a geodesic dome twice the size of that eventually built. Inside this shell, a second structure, a geodesic sphere, was to be suspended. This inner sphere would be the setting for what Fuller called 'The World Game', which was a proposal he had been working on for a number of years. The World Game was an interactive map of the earth, upon which players were able to see information about raw materials, shipping routes, energy consumption, population growth and other geographical and technical facts. The players would then be able to make decisions based upon this data, in the interests of the entire globe, which reciprocally affected the system as it developed.

For Fuller, the World Game was part of an educational project to encourage the public to see the world as an interrelated system, one which required careful stewardship if it was to continue being hospitable. He had previously proposed the 'Geoscope' as a purely educational tool, as it was his conviction that the rising tide of education, leading to a greater awareness of the world and its systems, would eliminate many of the problems that bedevilled it. Politicians only held the world back, thought Fuller, whereas inventors and designers like him were the people who would be able to change the world for the better. The Geoscope was to have been a map of the world displayed upon the inside of a sphere, the rationale being that one can see an entire sphere from the inside, just by turning your head, whereas the exterior of a sphere can only be viewed by orbiting around it. The World Game, in the expo context, would have involved the visitor, in a playful and gentle way, in the detailed planning and strategic thinking that Fuller preached was necessary for the survival of humanity on the planet.

The organising committee were not interested in Fuller's proposal for the interior, however, and constrained his responsibility to the design of the dome itself. Nevertheless, his stress upon a vision of a fragile and interconnected world was still communicated by the design as it was constructed. The dome was spherical and truncated below the equator, at three-quarter level, thus appearing far more like a submerged sphere than if it had been purely hemispherical, like most previous domes had been. The structure was rationalised as two spheres, one just inside the other. The inner sphere consisted of various hexagonal and pentagonal forms, which were connected to a triangular grid on the outer sphere. This space between the two spheres gave the structural depth required for a dome of such size, but also somewhat roughened the surface of the sphere, giving it a satisfyingly rich texture when viewed from a distance.

There was also innovation in the materials used for the dome. A newly developed acrylic material called Oroglas was used for the skin: it was lighter than glass and allowed less direct light in, which helped to mitigate the greenhouse effect within the dome. Another climate control mechanism was developed whereby at various points around the dome, fabric 'petals' mechanically extended to provide sun shading at different points in the day, thus helping to regulate the internal temperature.

The lead designers for the pavilion were the Cambridge Seven, a US architectural practice. Their response to the brief 'Creative USA', was to create a series of platforms perched within the massive dome, arranged asymmetrically, not unlike those of the West German pavilion, and described as being somewhat like 'lily pads'. An escalator, the world's largest at that point, took the visitors slowly to the very uppermost level. This was a similar architectural device that had been used eighteen years previously in New York, where the largest escalator at that point in history

Inside the Dome: 'Creative USA'

carried visitors up to the *Democracity* exhibit. In 1967, once arriving at the very top level of the exhibit, which was barely more than half-way up into the dome, the visitors started to follow a route back downwards via more escalators and staircases.

The first platform was devoted to the space race, and in particular the moon. On a mocked-up lunar landscape, visitors could encounter a full-size model of one of the Apollo lunar modules that was to make it to the moon two years later, while suspended high up within the globe was a lunar re-entry module with its parachutes deployed, seemingly frozen in space. After this display of space technology (which had a counterpart in the otherwise architecturally conventional USSR pavilion), visitors travelled downwards past displays of contemporary American life and culture.

Massive artworks by the new heroes of pop art (including a Jasper Johns painting based upon Fuller's Dymaxion map of the earth) were suspended around the next platform, while further down there were portraits of movie stars, nostalgic collections of Hollywood memorabilia, and displays of music, arts and crafts. The selection was an attempt to capture the breadth of creativity in American society, with an unsurprising lack of any mention of military misadventure, social struggle or other form of conflict whatsoever. America, in this exhibit, was displaying its technical dominance but also putting forward a vision of its cultural freedoms and sophistication, as a contrast to its supposedly culturally monolithic enemy in the Cold War.

Threading through all of these platforms and suspended exhibits was the monorail that took visitors on an elevated tour around the whole expo. Plunging in and out through a specially created gap in the structure of the dome, it allowed the visitors to experience the thrill of approaching this gigantic sphere at pace, along a track curved as if in orbit, watching as it grew in sight like a translucent orb, the light glinting off the acrylic panels, before the train passed through the wall and entered a completely different environment, if only for a few seconds. It was a metaphorical journey that couldn't help but have connotations of space travel.

After more than a century had elapsed, the USA pavilion marked a return to a quality of architectural experience that had first been encountered at the Great Exhibition. In 1851, a container of almost non-existent presence had surrounded a massive collection of objects, intended to display the entire capabilities of industrial society at the time. But the blankness of the container, this vast, featureless, repetitive shed, encouraged the formation of a dream of space that was universal, that reduced architecture down to merely the slightest of boundaries capable of accommodating a level of freedom that had never been experienced before. The Crystal Palace, as a metaphor, became both a symbol of the harshness of technological world, where everyone and everything was the same, where scientific rationality destroyed the very possibility of human nature and thus life, but it also gave birth to a dream of a technologically sophisticated world where the barest of infrastructure would protect humanity, giving them the space and freedom to create a new world of leisure, creativity and love.

Despite the banality of its internal exhibitions, the US pavilion, with its vast frame etching out a grid across the entire sky, overwhelmingly enveloping the buildings and people within it, created the same impression of a minimal technology designed to accommodate the full potential of humanity within. But what the US pavilion added to this was a global metaphor. The simple fact of its shape was a visual metaphor for an ecological consciousness, of a planet which had been shrunk to the size of a day's travel, where the sky was no longer the limit, a world which could now be seen from the outside. And although the Crystal Palace itself had a structure which had been inspired by the ridges of a pond lily, and although the Atomium from the Brussels World Fair of 1958 was a literal depiction of a molecule, Buckminster Fuller let absolutely no one forget that his structures were intrinsically based on the very fundamental building units of nature, and that their deployment at human scale was part of a universal strategy for expanding consciousness of structure and space. Furthermore, the responsive shading in the US Pavilion gave the impression that the entire building itself was some kind of organism, responding to changes in stimulus and conditions through feedback mechanisms, and playing its part in the cybernetic regulation of the environment. Indeed, Fuller's dome was a concrete example of almost every futuristic metaphor that was at that point drifting through world culture.

Chapter 2

The City out of History

Outside of the world of expositions and fairs – the temporary pavilions shouting for attention, the pageants of new technologies, the ideological demonstrations – architecture generally was not quite so outlandish. By the 1960s, various modern methods of building had asserted themselves and had been established in the mainstream of global construction.

By far the most influential architect of the age was Le Corbusier, who had not only been fortunate and canny enough to see his ideas of high-rise residential buildings set in parkland both experimented with and then heartily taken up by governments across the world, but had also almost single-handedly created a pattern book of forms and details for the younger generation of architects to experiment with. Concrete, his favoured material, was by this point *the* matter from which modernist architecture was formed, while motifs such as shallow concrete vaults, abstracted gargoyles, odd L-shaped windows and irregular fenestration banding had become commonplace in the younger generation. Meanwhile, there was a simultaneous vogue for a more refined, more corporate mode of building that was developed and pioneered by Mies van der Rohe and had been taken up by American firms such as Skidmore, Owings and Merrill. As a result the architectural world of the early

1960s was perhaps more unified in its collectively understood forms of expression than it had been for hundreds of years.

Another development by the middle of the 1960s was the scale upon which architects were now called to design. Le Corbusier's 1950s work in Chandigarh, the administrative centre of the Indian Punjab, was commissioned after the partition of India in 1947. The project involved working on a plan for the entire city and the design of its central collection of administrative buildings. Elsewhere, in Brazil, the planning for the new capital city Brasilia involved the work of Lúcio Costa and Oscar Niemeyer, who also designed a central collection of monumental civic buildings as part of a brand new city. In both cases, what is notable is not just the sheer size of the commissions, for although planned settlements existed before this era, none were built at anything even remotely approaching the same scale, but also the fact that unprecedentedly large areas were put completely under the detailed design control of single groups of architects and planners.

In war-ravaged Europe, Asia and North Africa, cities had been rebuilt at high speed: bomb damage and population growth had exacerbated already existing housing shortages, a situation that led to the construction of whole areas accommodating tens of thousands of residents. In some cases, such as the New Towns of the United Kingdom, entire cities for well over 100,000 citizens were built, although not in such homogenous fashion. The tendency at the advanced end of architecture was to bring all of the various functions of the city together into interconnected complexes. Thus town centres, new settlements, university campuses and manufacturing plants were all created with this trend in mind. What linked them all was, first of all, the political belief that planning for the future was a vital function of human endeavour, as well as the confidence and determination to execute that planned vision. The inherent pride in which huge developments could display a singular architectural identity is testament to that.

This pride in the creation of new, planned settlements coincided with a particular attitude to the past. The first half of the twentieth century had seen two world wars; meanwhile the institutions of the nineteenth-century had been found entirely lacking. The built fabric of the world of

the previous generations, from rudimentary worker's housing to grandilo-
quent government buildings, became viewed as a set of suspicious wrecks
from a less civilised age of huge inequalities, social strife and imperialism.

Most importantly, the fabric of the nineteenth-century city was not
considered sacrosanct, and in the name of progress (a progress which we
should never forget was always away from real horror), it was at that point
acceptable to call for the destruction of the older built environment if it
was considered beneficial for long-term social goals. This attitude might
seem strange and cold today, after the rise of conservationism and generations of political attack against large-scale planning, but it is nevertheless
important to stress how common-sensical and uncontroversial a set of
opinions this once was.

Amid all the construction – of new towns, of new houses and of parts of
cities that had been destroyed – the growth in vehicle traffic was clearly
becoming unmanageable. City centres were gridlocked, while well over
300,000 injuries and 7,000 deaths were caused each year in traffic accidents, with that number increasing every year. If predictions were true,
then it appeared that the UK was heading for a crisis unless something
urgent was done to improve its ragged infrastructure.

A committee made up of a team of planners, sociologists and municipal leaders was formed to report on the problem, chaired by Lord
Buchanan. The report they produced was such an extremely important
moment in urban planning that due to popular demand it was published
as a book in 1963 called *Traffic in Towns*. It claimed that 'if we are to
have any chance of living at peace with the motor car, we shall need a
different sort of city'.[1]

Traffic in Towns is a perfect example of how the establishment viewed
the urban landscape with which they had to work, and the methods that
they used to guide their decision making. After analysing statistics and
trends relating to population and vehicle traffic growth, the committee
concluded that the UK's urban fabric and infrastructure was entirely
inadequate to accommodate these increases, and that the economic and

---

1 *Traffic in Towns*, 'Introduction', item 35.

social life of the country was at risk as a result. In comparison to the technologically advancing US, the UK, though still one of the most advanced
economies, faced ongoing decline in its Victorian fabric and needed
drastic measures.

The report put forward numerous solutions to these problems on different scales, ranging from small interventions in historic town centres
such as multi-storey car parks, street widening or pedestrianisation, all
the way up to 'comprehensive redevelopment'. These could include the
demolition of large areas of a city in order to completely overhaul traffic
and other infrastructure, and create a safer and more pleasant environment for pedestrians. The authors noted:

> It is clear that any attempt to implement these ideas would result in a gigantic
> programme of urban reconstruction. We see no reason to be frightened of
> this. The central sections of most of our cities were very largely built in a few
> decades of the nineteenth century, and the rebuilding necessary to imple-
> ment the ideas of the Buchanan Report – which would be not very much less
> than total reconstruction – should not be beyond the powers of a few decades
> of our century.[2]

The authors of the report were not advocating the destruction of cities out
of wanton disregard for their functions, but the upgrading of their infrastructure as part of what they saw as a desperate need to avoid an urban
crisis. In addition to that anxiety, there was an opportunity to deploy the
latest thinking in planning and urbanism, making space for new uses and
activities in the city as well as creating 'new environments of the most
interesting and stimulating kind'.[3]

The most dramatic (and infamous) part of *Traffic in Towns* was its study
of the comprehensive redevelopment of parts of central London. After
looking at approaches to various sizes of settlement and different levels
of intervention, the committee let their designers off the leash for a carte
blanche hypothetical redevelopment. They suggested that demolishing a

number of blocks of Victorian houses and offices (many of which would be replaced anyway by the end of the twentieth century) could create a large opening in the centre of the city, into which a network of new roads could be placed at the lowest level. These roads could be laid out on a hexagonal grid, allowing for simplified traffic interchanges compared to a standard orthogonal junction, thus streamlining intersections and traffic flow.

Above this vehicular layer, a deck was proposed which would provide uninterrupted access for pedestrians to move around between the various housing, offices and shopping buildings that would be built in the gaps between the roads. The benefits of the deck were not just to separate pedestrians from the smog and danger of cars, but also to effectively multiply the usable space: by splitting the ground level into two planes, there was far more space for different uses, creating a denser, more three-dimensional, sophisticated and efficient city. Being a pedestrian would be a much more pleasant experience, with more light and space, cleaner air and less risk.

The report had predicted and recommended many typical elements of the post-war city: over- and underpasses, sunken motorways, pedestrianised shopping centres and housing estates with their circulation raised up above moats of parking. These hints of the three-dimensional city of the future are now frequently the most neglected elements in city centres, gradually being demolished after years of neglect and the gradual rejection of car-dominated urbanism.

Another government report came out of this project, involving the work of many of the same members of the design team as *Traffic in Towns*. This was the proposal for the New Town of Hook, Hampshire, to the southwest of London. Hook was to be part of a second wave of British New Towns, and was to accommodate 100,000 people, but it was eventually passed over by the government in favour of another site.

Despite the project itself going nowhere, the work that had gone into Hook lived on as a book, *The Planning of a New Town*,[4] published in 1965. Filled with statistics, diagrams and rather abstract zoning plans,

---

4   John R. Gold, *The Planning of a New Town*.

A vision of a New Town: Hook

the book demonstrated the principles that were eventually to go into the design. The idea was for a compact, high-density settlement with strictly separated pedestrians and vehicles. At the very core of the plan was a large multi-purpose civic centre, containing the main shopping, entertainment, business and civic functions of the town in one massive complex, built directly over the traffic infrastructure. Spreading outwards from the centre was a field of high-density modernist housing, interspersed with greenery and pedestrian pathways that allowed for travel around the town without having to share space with cars and other vehicles. Accompanying the diagrams were seductive illustrations of a verdant, multilayered and modern planned town, with tower blocks looking out over lakes and parkland and cosy green pathways leading down through the houses towards the markets at the centre.

The Planning of a New Town proved very influential, being widely discussed across the world. Perhaps the most powerful albeit unexpected impact of the British establishment putting forth ideas of such ambition was that it gave encouragement to more experimental voices at the sidelines. These younger radicals saw, rightly, that the government was open to suggestion regarding how to proceed with urban planning. Around this time, ideas for buildings and structures barely off the university drawing boards were enthusiastically taken up and built within a few years, a situation which is almost unimaginable today. In Canada the young Safdie had been entrusted with Habitat 67, but elsewhere, such as in housing projects like Park Hill in Sheffield, built in the mid-1950s, or the fertile creative environment of Camden Council Architects' Department, young men and women were frequently able to apply their theoretical training directly into practice.

Conceived and planned at the same time as Hook, Cumbernauld, near Glasgow, deployed many of the new methods for separating cars and pedestrians advocated by *Traffic in Towns*. But what drew global attention towards Cumbernauld was its town centre, designed at the beginning of the '60s, with the first phase completed by 1967. Cumbernauld town centre, primarily the work of the architect Geoffrey Copcutt (who is mostly known for this building and not much besides), was a radical approach to the notion of what a town centre could and should be. Then-current thinking advocated a traffic-free area in the centre of a settlement that contained most of the shopping functions. But what set Cumbernauld apart was the stacking of almost all of the town's functions into a single interconnected complex: shopping, libraries, government, hotels,

Designed incompleteness: Cambernauld Town Centre

flats, even a bus interchange. The building itself was designed to be the focal point of the whole town, sitting at the top of a hill, and it straddled a main road that linked Cumbernauld to Glasgow in one direction and the north-east of Scotland in another.

As it was developed, the multi-purpose character of the town centre was expressed in a form that broke up into its constituent parts. In order to incorporate residential land use within the town centre, a spine containing penthouse flats ran across the building at its highest point, perched on concrete columns at wide intervals. On the level beneath this were municipal functions expressed within a different structure more suitable for office uses. Underneath all this again was the shopping centre, the very first in the UK (the Austrian socialist Victor Gruen had pioneered the utopian glimmers of the American indoor mall in the mid-1950s, as Cumbernauld was being planned), and the car parks and hotel were again designed in a slightly different mode. All of these different functions were tied together by a series of walkways and ramps, including bridges that led across the main road where shoppers could look down on the cars racing past below them. As conceived and constructed, Cumbernauld town centre appeared as a massive agglomeration of different objects and spaces, irregular, even unfinished. The penthouses stretched out above the shops below as if they were simply waiting for the space beneath them to be filled up, the entire complex seemingly uncomposed.

As the concrete was poured and the structure began to take shape on the crest of its hill, Cumbernauld town centre embodied many of the very latest ideas about how cities ought to be built. It was massive, complicated and technically advanced, but it also seemed to express a sense of freedom about what a city could be. Instead of the pristine perfection of many of the architectural dreams of the previous decades, with their white walls and perfect towers set down regularly in parkland, Cumbernauld town centre seemed to be able to accommodate change within its very structure, apparently capable of physically adapting in a changing world.

This sense of incompleteness was in tune with what many young designers were advocating at this point. As the '60s went on, they saw an increase in affluence, the development of youth and consumer culture, a rise in political antagonisms and an ever more rapid development of technology. It began to seem to this new generation that the modern architecture of the housing estates and new towns was not quite radical enough to create the urban environments that were required in a time of such change. As a result, younger designers across the world were trying to find ways to push architecture into a new era. The superdense packing together of functions and activities into single accreted complexes, exemplified by Cumbernauld, was one of the most promising developments.

Another part of the social landscape that was changing rapidly after WWII was higher education, due to a greater demand for social scientists to implement policies of state provision and for better trained graduates overall, commensurate with increasing technological sophistication in industry and higher expectations from a more affluent population. All of this contributed to an explosion in the higher education sector across advanced economies, and in many developing countries as well. This was the impetus behind the creation of a new kind of urbanism, a radical approach to the campus, and a model for future change in cities themselves.

In the UK, faced with the increasing demand for higher education, the Robbins Committee of 1961–63 recommended the formation of a number of new universities. Up until then, a higher education had been very much a way for the elite of the UK to perpetuate itself, but by the 1960s 'the launching of the Sputnik, and the realisation that an historic past counted for less than a scientific future, directed attention to the national need for educated men'.[5] But beyond issues of global competition or profit, in this era of welfarist consensus it was also generally seen as an inherent good to educate the people as highly as possible, with natural benefits that would affect everyone.

The new universities (which had been in planning through previous years) arrived soon after the Robbins Report and were, in a manner with echoes of Oxford and Cambridge, built in or around historic English cathedral towns. The 1950s had seen various new college buildings built

---

5   Michael Beloff, *The Plateglass Universities*, p. 23.

by young architects according to modernist principles, but the newly built 'plateglass' universities were mostly designed as single complexes without any existing context and thus were startling in their novelty. These included the University of East Anglia (Norwich) by Denys Lasdun, the University of Essex (Colchester) by Architects' Co-Partnership, Sussex University (Brighton) by Basil Spence, and the University of York by RMJM.

The development of the University of Essex was an attempt to mimic the success of technical universities in the United States such as MIT. As America pulled ahead in the technological race, the traditional British higher education system seemed inadequately poised to reduce that gap, and the UoE was conceived to compete on the American level. Like many of the new universities, its programme was experimental; accepted boundaries between disciplines were to be eliminated, and the students who entered the university were to be trained not as specialists but as thorough all-rounders, destined to enter a new technocratic elite for the scientific world. Furthermore, the students were to be treated as responsible adults in a way that was almost unprecedented in universities, and were to be given freedom not only in the way that their academic lives were structured, but also in the form of the environment in which they would learn.

Albert Sloman, the highly ambitious university vice-chancellor, worked closely with Kenneth Capon of the Architects' Co-Partnership on developing the design of UoE. Situated in the rolling grounds of Wivenhoe House, outside of Colchester, the master plan was highly radical. A series of residential towers were to be built, each one accommodating both male and female students, only marginally segregated across alternate floors but including communal social areas. Walkways through the landscape led the students towards the centre of the campus, where an entire new ground-level of squares and terraces was created, slowly stepping down the hill. Instruction would take place in raised teaching blocks sitting across the landscape, zigzagging back and forth over the terraces and enclosing social spaces on top of the decks, with the all-important library building at the top of the terraces. Hidden beneath the feet of the students would be the access for vehicles and services, almost invisible to those using the building.

The first stage of this remarkable architectural arrangement was complete by 1967, although it was never conceived as a finished structure. The original plan was for the complex to continue expanding until there were 20,000 students all living in the single aggregated complex, and much like Cumbernauld town centre it was specifically designed without a sense of completeness. The rugged concrete centre and the dark brick residential towers are set off against the bucolic quality of the countryside in which the university sits – an unapologetic part of the original concept – with Capon stating, 'The English love softening everything up and making things shaggy. We wanted to give them something fierce to work within.'[6] It was an uncompromisingly modern architectural environment for an ambitious modern world.

The architect for the new University of East Anglia campus in Norwich was Denys Lasdun, an English modernist who had previously built social housing in London and educational buildings for the Royal College of Physicians, as well as college buildings in Cambridge and, eventually, the National Theatre in central London. At UEA the two typologies of housing and educational buildings also merged, but on a scale way beyond anything that had been done before. The design concept was for a campus organised around a kilometre-long 'teaching wall' that meandered across the site, following the topography. All of the academic functions – again an experimentally mixed set of subjects diverging from the traditional methods of study – were to be contained in this 'spine' building, which was connected to the student accommodation by means of raised walkways that kept pedestrians away from vehicle traffic and services below.

Unlike the accommodation at Essex that were, despite their programmatic innovations, recognisable as modernist tower blocks, the buildings in which Lasdun accommodated the thousands of students and staff on campus at UEA were strange pyramid structures, in the original models looking like mineral encrustations growing out from the spine of the teaching wall. These structures were very similar to Safdie's ideas of housing in Montreal. which would be developed later that decade. The

---

6 As quoted in the exhibition, *Something Fierce*, University of Essex, 2014.

Denys Lasdun's ziggurats at the University of East Anglia

organisational idea was that these ziggurats, formed from pre-fabricated concrete panels, would cluster the living spaces together around communal facilities, with each room having its view out over the landscape.

Lasdun also worked closely with the university's vice-chancellor, Frank Thistlethwaite, who supported the architect to pursue a visionary, experimental approach that would embody the modernity of the new institution. UEA was therefore designed in a form that attempted to provide educational space appropriate for a generation of independent, critical young men and women. The way in which the functions and buildings were distributed was almost non-hierarchical, its arrangement dynamic and informal. The extent to which the design was broken down into repeated elements meant that it could be added to, if necessary; there were plans for further phases to be built in the same way as the university grew, and it appeared almost as though it could expand organically.

UEA's design can be seen to be a remarkably consistent embodiment of the ethos that had brought it into being. The state was creating the new universities in a climate of optimism, and the ambition of the UEA design – creating a consistent urban prototype from the geographical scale down to the individual component – was a testament to this confidence in their abilities. 'Lasdun was thinking of the university not as a series of isolated objects dotted around the fields, or as an ersatz Oxbridge of courtyard buildings stranded in a vacuum, but as a continuous range of urban landscape.'[7]

Lasdun was a great architect, and the UEA buildings are far more sophisticated than those at Essex, but on the whole the designs were fundamentally similar. Lasdun, Capon and many of their generation were working at a time when the avant-garde functionalist architecture of the inter-war years was no longer radical or subversive but had become the style of the progressive welfarist establishment. The lack of decoration suited a culture that was still in conscious rejection of the aesthetics and political values of the nineteenth century, the same values that had eventually led the world into unimaginable carnage, while the pre-fabricated elements were in accordance with the technocratic, progressive attitudes of the time. Furthermore, the effort to consider the buildings as part of rather than set within that landscape reflected the growing environmental consciousness of the period.

The spatial quality of UEA is remarkable. A visitor entering the university campus at the highest point of the site discovers that there is no formal entrance, no grand monumental building to define the public face of the institution, as would be expected in a more historic model. This is completely deliberate; instead of a monumental gateway leading into cloisters, it's as though the visitor enters directly into the workings of a large system of buildings, rather than being drawn in through hierarchical spatial presentations of power. Staircases and ramps set within grass bring the visitor to the centre of the campus: some shops around a square, the students' union, the library. This area, which was completed somewhat later than the majority of the campus, has a hint of the town square from one of the New Towns of the era, but the buildings are executed in a bold, confident style, in a well-poured grey concrete that has been looked after over the years.

Subtly it becomes apparent that what up until this point had appeared to be the ground level, following the terrain, is actually a terrace, and

7   William J. R. Curtis, *Denys Lasdun: Architecture, City, Landscape*, p. 92.

that stretching off in different directions are several raised walkways. A full two storeys below are areas for parking and deliveries, with many of the buildings folding away under the walkway level, there revealing their structural frame and their hard-wearing service spaces. The raised levels are just for students and staff to walk among the centre, their houses and the various departments along the teaching wall, and as the walkways stretch off in various directions, students in the distance seem to float along on thin concrete decks, with open space above and below.

The walkways are at the level of the canopies of mature trees, many of them sandy-soiled pines, their branches over the edges of the balustrades like some kind of tree-top walk or nature trail. To one side of the main walkway is the teaching wall, a long, horizontal building punctuated by lift shafts, with sleek bronze-tinted glass in its banded windows. To the other side are the backs of the housing units, with their own narrow walkways and front doors, again with tall lift-towers marking out the crown of each pyramid. The elevated level of the walkways gives a wider view of the landscape beyond, which due to the density of the architecture is left wide open, with the lake and forests becoming part of an ensemble with the ziggurats. It's a thrillingly three-dimensional experience, where the pedestrian is the priority.

Despite their modernity, the ziggurats themselves were conceived as an updated version of the collegiate 'staircase' system of housing traditionally encountered at Oxford and Cambridge. The top floor is where the dons or on-site academics live, and on the lower floors students have their own rooms, with a large shared kitchen and shared bathrooms. But this typological similarity is almost totally obscured by the level of abstraction and formal exuberance displayed by the housing, with its projecting concrete gargoyles and the seemingly detachable appearance of the rooms themselves. At the far reaches of the complex, the forms relax, the walkways become wider and narrower at different points, the staircases and other functional details are given prominence as part of an ensemble of parts.

From the meadow in front, pocked with rabbit holes and clumps of trees, as well as a selection of bronzes by such mid-century modern artists as Henry Moore, the visitor is immersed in a world that now seems long

gone, a post-war future urban landscape of popular modernist architecture and art, of new institutions for a changing social landscape. It
is a bucolic late 1960s world of concrete and trees, of a future faced
expectantly. Despite half a century passing since their construction, this
sense of institutions formed out of humanist ambition and more than a
little hope is still completely tangible. Reyner Banham noted that 'the
concept of the university as a mini-city or a sample city neighbourhood
was remarkably persistent',[8] and indeed the new universities were locations where these early 1960s ideas of the city of the future found their
fullest expression.

But just over a decade after the new campuses began admitting students
in 1967, the dreams of that era had all but vanished. New Universities
such as UEA, Essex, Warwick and others abroad, such as the University
of Nanterre, a similarly conceived new campus on the outskirts of Paris,
were to find themselves at the centre of the student movements of 1968,
with demonstrations quickly filling up the new concrete courtyards and
occupations taking over the lecture theatres. In the turmoil of the era, it
was thought that not only the radical new curricula but also the radical
new architecture might have played a role in enraging the students. It
was even argued that

> some of the planning of the New Universities appeared to provide the perfect
> frame for the rebellious students. Totally unexpected to the planners of the
> 1960s, it became clear that the more residential and dense the campus, the
> easier it was for the militants to organise themselves.[9]

The New Universities embodied not only the dreams of their era,
but also the ways in which these dreams turned sour. Initial enthusiasm
turned into dismay, and in a time of panic the same optimistic modernity
that was so initially attractive about the new universities became a stick to
beat them with. The new experimental forms of teaching didn't last long,
reverting to conventional systems, while the initial growth estimates were

8   Reyner Banham, *Megastructures*, p. 132.
9   Stefan Muthesius, *The Postwar University*, p. 181.

nearly all hopelessly optimistic. In fact, by the late 1970s many of the new universities faced closure.

Today, the New Universities are part of academic convention. For example, the campus at UEA has been enlarged on a number of occasions, in subsequent periods of expansion. These new buildings are also in keeping with the attitudes of their time, and as a result most of them are of very little consequence architecturally, and often are very poor indeed. Dramatic university buildings nowadays are frequently subject to the laws of 'iconicness', being organisationally conventional but formally whimsical, competing for students through branded images rather than their sense of modernity. However this decline in ambition still doesn't break the overall impression that UEA and others like it are the few consummately built examples of the architecture of the near-future as it was understood at that time.

One of the most obvious ways in which to push the boundaries of architecture was scale. It is true that all through history, there have been massive planned cities, frequently despotic, military or religious in character. Antiquity gives us a number of examples of theoretical cities and urban organisations, frequently described in terms of their social and political organisation rather than the form and methods of their construction. Since the Renaissance, it became common for artists and architects to design ideal cities that would better reflect the order of society than the conflicted metropolis that truly existed. Since the Industrial Revolution, indeed, since the Crystal Palace at the Great Exhibition, the dream of a technologically extended city became a common endeavour, whether through proposals to cover huge areas of cities in a single arcade or the more abstract dreams of future worlds under glass.

The turn of twentieth century was a golden age of imaginary cities: the Garden Cities of Ebenezer Howard, the Industrial Cities of Tony Garnier, the Futurist Cities of Sant'Elia, Le Corbusier's Radiant City, Frank Lloyd Wright's Broadacre City – a plethora of visions of how the city might be changed in future. These intensified right up to WWII, although not all were quite so forward-looking, as they reached an apocalyptic nadir in Albert Speer's plan for Germania, whose implementation would have seen the demolition of much of Berlin in the service of a backwards neoclassicism of utterly dumbfounding scale.

After the war, with much of Europe's cities flattened, reconstruction became urgent. These massive ruins, the pent-up energy that had been waiting for so long for a chance at reform, and the technological means being finally available meant that experimental or visionary schemes stood a greater chance than ever of making their way into the real world.

Post-war urbanism was based upon strict segregation of uses. Looking at a nineteenth-century industrial town, with factories crowding the centre of the city and slum dwellings in the shadow of the chimneys and smoke, it was clear to many observers that great improvements would result from separating off the filthy and dangerous aspects of the city from where people actually lived, giving them greater space and light, and a healthier, happier environment. This became the orthodoxy of architects and planners, dominating their research.

But by the end of the 1950s it was clear that a lot was being lost by splitting the city so neatly into its functional zones. A new generation of architects and planners sought ways to bring existing patterns of human life into new developments, combining the social complexity of historic urban patterns with new, more technically advanced forms. The city was now seen more as a complex, dynamic thing, a process rather than an object, and one result was the determined attempt to design for the intensification of urban uses within a single project.

The construction industry was also in need of revolution. By the later 1960s, electricity could be generated from nuclear reactors, rockets could make it to the moon, automobiles could be produced on endless, increasingly automated production lines, new forms of media were being introduced all the time, but buildings were still constructed by gangs of men carting wet materials around a building site – all cement, concrete, and mud. With such large demand for housing and new buildings, it was a travesty that things were still being done in such a backward and expensive manner. The earliest modernist architects between the wars had advocated industrial building methods but were thwarted both by the germinal state of the technologies available to them and a lack of political backing. But now, in the more advanced industrial economies of the mid-twentieth century, there was the opportunity for a serious attempt at introducing mass production and factory techniques into architecture.

After the war, various contractors set to work on 'system building' techniques: large concrete panels could be constructed in a factory, brought onto site and then put together with a minimal workforce and only the slightest amount of 'wet' construction. It promised to revolutionise the production of housing, and in the UK for example, various governments, who had successively outbid each other on the number of houses they were going to build each year, enthusiastically took to these new methods, offering subsidies to contractors for the height and swiftness with which they could complete them.

Any student architect, engineer or planner at the turn of the 1960s was entirely comfortable with the notion that the buildings they might be working on in the near future could be factory built, pre-fabricated, making use of the very latest materials. The taste for expressive concrete was at its peak, but new high-performance, light-weight materials such as aluminium, asbestos (whose dangers were yet to be fully understood) and the ever-increasing range of acrylics and plastics, used in everything from panels to insulation to the seals around the edges of windows, were all waiting to be picked up by a new generation.

In addition to changing technical capabilities and construction techniques, the most inspiring and challenging transformation was in the way people wanted to live in a city. Emerging from the dreary struggles of austerity and wartime degradation, people all over the world were looking to the American way of life – consumerism, pop culture, the sheer glamour of the world's most advanced country. American cultural forms, its films and its music, were dominant like never before, even when they were being sold back to the Americans by Brits such as the Beatles.

However, there was a fundamental mismatch between the future as represented by rock music or, say, the miniskirt (which caused a stir at Expo 67 when it was sported by the female staff at the British Pavilion), and by the slabs and blocks of council housing that were being lifted into the sky all over the UK at this point. It would be another generation before concrete housing was portrayed as something threatening and oppressive, but the enthusiasm of the turn of the decade was already being tempered. And in 1960s London, a movement started within architecture that began to look for a way to resolve this contradiction.

On 20 September 1964, in a section entitled 'Design for Living', the *Sunday Times* colour supplement ran a feature on a new idea for how cities should be built. Entitled 'The Plug-In City', this concept was the work of a group of young architects named Warren Chalk, Dennis Crompton and (primarily) Peter Cook, who had recently started working together in a practice by the name of Archigram. Although some of them (Chalk and Crompton in particular) had worked for developers such as Taylor Woodrow and had been part of the LCC team for the Southbank Centre, their new firm was less concerned about building and more about making waves within a still remarkably strait-laced profession. Their impact was to come through publication and teaching rather than built inspiration.

The primary illustration in the *Sunday Times* depicted a distant bird's-eye view, drawn and coloured in ink, following the conventions of architectural draughtsmanship. Its content, however, was mysterious, showing of a series of odd structures arranged along winding paths. Some

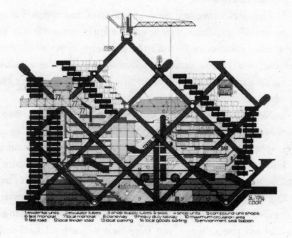

Archigram's Plug-In City

of these structures were cylindrical and recognisable as some kind of tower block, while others gave the impression of shards of coral, or a kind of mineral encrustation. Another drawing, this time a recognisably architectural section, gave more detail and put the first drawing in context.

Dominating the image was a grid, set diagonally at forty-five degrees, that appeared to show a triangulated structure. At the very top of this structure was a construction crane, which gave the first proper indication of the size of the ensemble: its scale suggested that the entire construction was around one hundred metres tall, about twenty-five storeys or the height of a large tower block. On this more detailed drawing, the encrustations were revealed to be houses, or more accurately, residential units. Each one was separate from the next, but they were all connected together and attached to the grid, sometimes vertically, sometimes leaning backwards along with the structure itself. Interspersed with the housing were yellow boxes that, according to the annotations, showed 'shop units' (one of them on the drawing is labelled 'bar'), while threading through everything else were platforms and escalators, car parks and monorails. A closer examination of the drawing revealed cars driving through a raised box tunnel, and even a few human figures wandering around the circulation zone.

Plug-In City was a proposal for a new kind of city, offered as a novel form of omni-infrastructure that would be built alongside the existing city. It intended all at once to solve the problems of population growth, the backwardness of the construction industry and the challenge of responding to a rapidly changing world in which products and lifestyles became obsolete at an ever-increasing rate.

The centrepiece of the design was a gigantic steel structure into which all the other elements were attached. The cranes at the top ran on rails and were able to move around the ensemble, carrying any and all elements. This included the monorails that carried people through and between the new cities, to the shops, houses and roads that constituted its human environment. Most importantly, its premise was that the solution to the housing problem was a reduction in permanence and a rise in industrialised production. 'You might choose a Ford bathroom and Vauxhall kitchen, and as you rise in the world you can trade in your

Hillman living room for a Bentley',[10] explained Warren Chalk in one quote, highlighting the awe in which the automobile industry was held. It also demonstrated the sense of increasing wealth that was apparent at this point. The cranes at the top of the structure would not only build the city but would replace or even remove components and parts when they were no longer required.

The drawings of Plug-In City were vague but had enough detail on them to give a certain sense of the concept. Priscilla Chapman, the author of the article, stated:

> [Archigram] find it hard to say exactly what it will be like to step out of your front door in Plug-In City, but it sounds as though it will be a mixture of a theatre (balconies, aisles and stairs) and Montmartre (passages and stairs connecting different levels): in any event, there will be lots of well-travelled, busy catwalks and streets honeycombing the grid system, all connected by the lifts and escalators.[11]

Plug-In City presented an intensification of the processes that were already changing architecture at that point. We can see the influence of the industrialised housing estates then under construction, with their pre-fabricated panels being hoisted into place by cranes; we can read the growth of the affluent society with its leisure (the *Sunday Times* article repeats the then-ubiquitous expectation that in the future, most people would have a three-day working week) and its new-found levels of consumption. Even the urban strategies of separating out the vehicle and traffic areas were taken up without much elaboration. Indeed, here we can even see much of what was innovative in Hook and Cumbernauld repeating itself on a much larger scale.

Eventually Archigram would become one of the most influential architecture practices of the period, despite building almost nothing apart from a children's play centre and a rapidly dated kitchen and swimming pool extension to Rod Stewart's mansion. Instead, Archigram became

---

10   Archigram, *Plug-In City*.

11   Ibid.

prominent through a series of magazines that they self-published, in the process creating a scene around themselves very much in the mood of 'Swinging London'. Their magazines, of which there were nine (and one further half-issue) published between 1961 and 1974, were dedicated to showing off not just their own work but the work of their heroes, such as Buckminster Fuller and Cedric Price, their contemporaries, as well as that of their students, many of whom would later go on to become some of the most established names in global architecture.

An often embarrassingly 'groovy' mix of science fiction, comics, appropriated imagery from fashion and advertising, DIY-zine aesthetics and all manner of ludicrous typefaces, the Archigram magazines deliberately blurred the line between serious proposals and speculations, and repeatedly stressed their main design concerns: indeterminacy, social freedom, new technologies and typologies, experimental forms of architecture. Their interests ranged from large-scale solutions to urban problems, such as the Plug-In Cities, to the space of the individual and their interface with the world. As documents of the architectural issues of the time they are unsurpassed, but they are also notoriously silent on politics despite the social milieu in which they were created, their ethos that of a rather uncritical awe of American economic and cultural dominance.

The interest in radical architecture that Archigram fostered blossomed all over the world. In Japan around the turn of 1960s, a group of young architects, around the same age as the Brits in Archigram, started working on similar themes. Influenced heavily by the wartime experience, especially the devastation that occurred after the US nuclear attacks, these young designers took the opportunities presented by post-war rebuilding as an opportunity to question what cities ought to be like. Calling their theoretical approach 'Metabolism', they imagined cities that were responsive, that could grow organically and were replaceable.

Schemes by the Metabolists frequently included similar concepts to Archigram – massive structures into which the population could attach their homes. They are now mainly known for their speculative projects, such as Arata Isozaki's Space City, which depicted service towers with cantilevered wings stretching outwards, towering over the existing city and sprouting houses directly from the walls. Unlike Archigram, the

Metabolists were quick to take to building, and in early years they frequently struggled to develop their architecture beyond a Japanese take
on Le Corbusier's concrete aesthetic. Later, architects such as Kenzo
Tange, Isozaki and Kisho Kurukawa would take their own place as global
architects, their youthful experiments long behind them.

Elsewhere, 1960s Vienna produced its own generation of architectural radicals, including two groups with the unwieldy titles of Coop
Himmelb(l)au, and Haus-Rucker-Co. Inhabiting a similar milieu of publications and European lectures, these groups were less interested in pure
novelty than in how the architecture of the future might interact with
the bourgeois city as it already existed. Their proposals were frequently
constructed as architectural interventions or 'happenings', with ties to
performance art and other forms of conceptualism.

The Viennese architectural radicals were especially fond of working
with inflatable structures and other gadgets, creating works such as
Haus-Rucker-Co's Oase No. 7, created for Documenta 5 in 1972, which
was a space-frame structure upon which a hammock had been strung
between two fake palm trees, all of which was cantilevered out from the
walls of a neoclassical building, contained within an inflatable plastic
bubble. This demonstrated the themes of environmental manipulation
and temporariness that were current in other groups, but the Viennese
experiments were clearly steeped in the intellectual history of Vienna,
dealing with notions of sexuality and the ways it broke through the tightly
controlled decorum of the spatial environment. From today's view-point
the early work of the Viennese groups had much more in common with
experimental fine art than architecture, although they too would end
up running successful global practices with only shades of their former
experiments detectable.

These groups, and others such as Ant Farm in the USA, whose work
frequently reckoned with the violent crushing of America's student movement, would for a time move away from trying to steer the establishment,
instead becoming more attached to politically radical countercultural
movements that were rising at this point.

Chapter 3

Megastructure Visions

Many of the architectural proposals and experiments of the early 1960s were eventually gathered under the umbrella term of 'megastructure'. This word evoked not only the sheer size of the new architecture but also the method in which a single initial construction would serve as a frame, augmented by infrastructure such as transport and electricity and capable of being added to or dismantled. Once all this was in place, the population would be given freedom to create their own living environment, moveable and ready for its own obsolescence, while commercial units and workplaces could come and go as needed.

The first coining of the term 'megastructure' was attributed to the Japanese Metabolist architect Fumihiko Maki, from a text of 1964, but the subject was to a large extent given its definition in Reyner Banham's book *Megastructures: Urban Futures of the Recent Past*, 1976, written in hindsight when the author's interests and enthusiasms had greatly changed. Thanks mainly to Banham's efforts, 'megastructure' became defined as a methodological approach to architecture which conformed to a number of criteria: a megastructure had to be modular, built from repeated components; it had to be capable of extension, of being made larger or smaller after its initial construction; it had to have a structural framework into which smaller elements could be 'plugged'; and this structure had to be more durable than the elements that would be plugged into it.

But megastructure also referred to an architectural aesthetic – massive, disparate structures combining strict artificial forms with an organic growth of spaces within. It was a serious attempt at developing the ongoing practice of addressing large urban problems through planning while simultaneously incorporating the rapidly changing lifestyles of the post-war era. The alienation that people reported feeling in social housing, where they had no opportunity to customise and make the space their own, the flowering of pop music, fashion and youth culture, the sudden proliferation of white goods and other consumer items all pointed towards a demand for differentiation and choice in the urban environment.

During the 1960s these desires manifested themselves in a set of formal motifs. The first of these was the giant frame. In Plug-In City this was absolutely massive, of a size that had never actually been built before, with entire buildings capable of fitting into the space between its diagonal beams. The giant frame would show up again and again throughout the 1960s: it was in the background of many of Archigram's proposals, Buckminster Fuller used it again and again, and it was clearly in evidence at Expo 67. Furthermore, this overarching frame was visible in innumerable student projects of the era, and before too long it would become a visual cliché, partially explaining Banham's weary evaluations.

The frame motif, as depicted, was almost always a space frame, formed by the connection of short members into a lattice that is both strong and very light but can cover or occupy a substantial volume. Its first development has been generally attributed to Alexander Graham Bell's experiments with tetrahedral kites in the early twentieth century, but the populariser of the form in architecture was an engineer called Konrad Wachsmann, who developed systems for the creation of space frames while working at the Illinois Institute of Technology after WWII. In his memorable proposals for aircraft hangars for the US Air Force, tiny figures are dwarfed by a massive roof consisting of millions of extremely thin steel members. Wachsmann's designs touched a nerve, suggesting the sublimity that came from the best work of nineteenth-century engineers, and which had been such an important part of the influence of the Crystal Palace.

As space frames developed further and became commercially available, they grew into a symbol of the new age, appearing in all manner of radical proposals of the period. Mies van der Rohe, in a more theoretical moment, created images of what he called 'universal space', giant space-frame structures under which the architectural needs of the population could be rearranged and adapted. Buckminster Fuller depicted them wrapping into spherical forms to create the structure for his larger domes. At the same time, a proposal for Coventry Cathedral by Colin St John Wilson directly deployed Wachsmann's aesthetic to suggest a giant numinous space. Compared to the general heaviness of concrete construction, the space frame, especially when scaled up to become a form in which a person could move around and inhabit, became a potent symbol of new technology, efficiency and adaptability.

At another scale, megastructure was represented by the unit. If the frame was the infrastructure, then what went into that frame expressed the freedom of the system. Safdie's Habitat 67 was an agglomeration of democratically scaled units, and in this and other works, the irregular stacking of dwellings and the inability to tell which ones were larger or smaller began to imply a certain egalitarianism. At a more experimental level, Archigram's earlier proposals usually involved some kind of colourful vessel, frequently modelled on the new plastic gaskets which had been introduced into architecture, or space capsules, or the more quotidian caravan, all of which could be moulded in a factory, brought on-site and plugged in accordingly. When stacked up together, units created a cellular format suggestive of biological processes, and the metaphors of growth and evolution that went along with it were very attractive. The Japanese Metabolists in particular were taken by this idea, and by the end of the 1960s there was a race to build the first genuine example of a capsule-type project.

Another more abstract element of the megastructural aesthetic was a new focus on the diagonal. Here Buckminster Fuller, with his obsession with the tetrahedron, showed his influence most clearly. Where Wachsmann's space frames alluded to rocket launch pads, radar dishes and other space technology, already imbued with a certain technological frisson, it was Fuller's quasi-mystical emphasis on triangulated geometry that encouraged other designers to develop it into a fetish.

Plug-In City was dominated by its diagonal frame, as were the pavilions at Montreal. Safdie's next experiments after Habitat involved a hexagonal grid which would be more neatly stackable, while the Israeli architect Zvi Hecker built housing towards the edge of Jerusalem that was also based upon stacked tetrahedrons; his results were formally exciting but ludicrously impractical. The diagonal in space could, in the eyes of theorist-architects Claude Parent and Paul Virilio in France, come to be seen as an experimental symbol of breaking down orthogonal – which implied fixed, hierarchical and thus oppressive – structures, a refrain which later found an echo in Deleuze and Guattari's *Mille plateaux*.

In Buckminster Fuller's own hands the diagonal became a symbol as powerful as an ancient pyramid. This could be seen in his Tetrahedral City of 1966, which was designed so that as the population grew, the structure could be built from the ground up and eventually reach a height of several kilometres. A collage showed it looming blankly above San Francisco, an image that resonated with the engravings of Étienne Boulleé, whose imaginary proposals for gargantuan neoclassical buildings were architecturally symbolic of the rationalist ambitions of revolutionary France.

At a less extreme level, the diagonal manifested itself in a new passion for ziggurats, or buildings set deliberately off the vertical. One possible origin for this has been traced to a 1928 throw-away design by Walter Gropius for an A-framed housing typology called a 'Wohnberg'. Here the flats would step backwards over the one beneath to increase exposure to the sun, while other structures such as roads could be hidden in the space underneath the lean. Later, other architects such as Alison and Peter Smithson examined the potential for this kind of housing in speculative projects. Meanwhile Kenzo Tange's Boston Harbour project of 1959, developed with students, was the first case of a large-scale ziggurat worked out in full detail.

In the megastructural imagination, the leaning ziggurat not only provided gardens to houses stacked vertically as flats, but also enclosed transport and other infrastructure in such a way that it could be placed up close to the housing without affecting it, making the city itself more dense and efficient. This was a practice visible in many actually existing buildings, especially those built according to the North American legal phenomenon of 'air rights', where buildings could be built above land owned by others, but it could also be seen in the enclosed roadways, monorails and other transport of Plug-In City. The ziggurat represented an extension and intensification of the split-level separation of pedestrians and traffic recommended by *Traffic in Towns*.

One prominent example of the ziggurat tendency came from the pen of Paul Rudolph, the virtuosic American brutalist, an exemplary performer of that typical American manoeuvre of defanging a politicised European aesthetic movement and turning it into something palatable for American capitalism. At the time his work was deeply frowned upon by more radical critics for being excessively formal and corporate, but he was not immune to the more intellectual currents of megastructure. In the late 1960s, working for the Ford Foundation, Rudolph developed a scheme for LOMEX, or the Lower Manhattan Expressway. This was one of Robert Moses's most extreme comprehensive redevelopment schemes, which would have demolished much of SoHo, Little Italy and other then-poor neighbourhoods, before laying a partly raised, partly sunken highway across the island, all connected to the Manhattan and Williamsburg bridges.

Famously the LOMEX scheme was defeated in 1962 by a community campaign led by Jane Jacobs, whose vociferous assaults on top-down planning and modernist urbanism ended up playing a huge role in changing the intellectual climate around city building. Rudolph was commissioned later in the decade to work on a further study of the scheme, and drew up a tantalisingly megastructural concept. Rudolph proposed that over a section of buried expressway a repeatable precast concrete housing module could be stacked up in various ways. A number of these units, when leaning against each other, could enclose the road beneath and create a long, linear structure of houses, hiding the expressway completely, creating light and quiet pedestrian areas overlooked by flats.

Rudolph's proposal for LOMEX was only ever speculative, however engineers at the time were attempting to put these ideas into practice, in the hope of unlocking the potential of building above unfriendly infrastructure. A decade later, in 1982, in a leafy suburb of West Berlin near the Freie Universität, a remarkable ziggurat-shaped social housing scheme more than half a kilometre long was built, containing more than a thousand homes and a shopping street. The complex was a demonstration of one possible solution to the problems of land density posed by West Berlin's encirclement by the GDR, which left very little room for the city to expand.

The complex was designed by Georg Heinrichs, who built a large A-frame structure directly over a newly constructed section of Autobahn. The upper structure was completely isolated from the road to eliminate vibration transfer between the two structures, meaning that the thousands of vehicles are almost indiscernible from inside the flats. As the housing grows higher above the road, it steps backwards at each level, thus creating an open garden space for each flat, much like Habitat, before on top it becomes a conventional slab block. Known locally as 'The Snake', it is remarkably similar to Rudolph's vision, and as one of the largest single housing blocks in all of Europe it is one of the clearest built examples of the megastructure concept.

By the time that Banham was writing his study on megastructures, he was firmly of the opinion that the moment had very much passed, and he described his subject matter as 'dinosaurs', relics of the past. But to what extent did megastructure actually take over the city?

Despite the predictions, and in spite of the more progressive architectural press of the late 1960s being full of tantalising glimpses of new forms of architecture, there were few examples of megastructural innovations actually being created. It was almost entirely in Japan, in fact, that anything was built which seriously attempted to achieve the interchangeability of function and units that was such an important aspect of megastructural thinking. While a number of large concrete buildings completed during the '60s give an aesthetic taste of megastructure, with overextended service cores and empty spaces where new units could be built – like in the UK, it was almost always for show, suggestive of ephemerality.

One example was the Shinjuku bus-body building by Yoji Watanabe of 1970. Watanabe was a Japanese architect a generation older than the Metabolists, whose apartment block achieves an apparently capsule-like arrangement through the use of a serrated facade in which each room appears to be completely separate from the next. This idiosyncratic design looked almost as if a set of aluminium Airstream caravans had been stuck onto the central funnel of a battleship, and created only slight interest in the architectural media outside Japan. After a number of years of being left to rot, however, it has recently been refurbished and continues to exist as an apartment block.

Nakagin Capsule Tower, Kisho Kurokawa

The nearest achievement and the most celebrated of any of the Japanese Metabolist projects is the Nakagin Capsule Tower, designed by Kisho Kurokawa, one of the most successful young architects of his generation, and completed in 1972. Occupying a corner site, the capsule tower consists of two service cores over ten storeys each, which have doors and service connections rising up the sides. Plugged into these cores via four large steel bolts are small, rectilinear boxes with a porthole window at one side, resembling something half-way between a washing machine and a space capsule.

Each of the tiny boxes was conceived as a self-contained living unit, divided into two rooms, with a corner cubicle given over to a shower and W.C. Towards the portal window was a bed, and along one wall ran an ingenious furniture unit containing a fold-out desk, sink, refrigerator and plastic modules for various appliances and media devices. The aesthetic of the interior was of cold, clean surfaces, something akin to the inside of an aeroplane or spaceship, and the tiny size was aimed at the Japanese 'salaryman' market.

On the exterior, the capsules are clearly staggered as they rise around the building, and some of them face in different directions, which along with occasional missing capsules creates formal interest and emphasises the adaptability of the structure. Rudimentary but visionary, with hints of both Habitat 67 and the ziggurats at UEA, the Capsule Tower was one possible first step towards a more flexible system of planning, but tellingly none of the original capsules have ever been replaced, and at the time of writing it faces demolition as it stands on land too valuable for its current use.

It was thus in Britain that the next development would occur: by the end of the 1960s the UK had already been building huge amounts of system-built housing, some of the most experimental large-scale architecture in the world. Because there was a strong culture of encouraging young architects to take charge of projects soon after leaving university, and since the aims of the radical architects, the demands of the establishment and the expertise of the construction industry seemed to converge, commentators assumed that it was just a matter of time before a fully articulated British megastructural project would make it off the drawing boards and out into the world.[1]

Archigram would continue working on the Plug-In City concept for a few years, until getting bored and moving on to other interests such as 'Instant Cities', which were partially inspired by the new phenomenon of music festivals – settlements that would appear from nowhere, last a few days and promptly vanish. The later studies that they worked on for Plug-In City are of interest, however, because they show the idea being worked at a closer level of detail than before, and they thus provided a further link that ties the flamboyant experimentalism of the Plug-In City to the actually existing system-built housing of the time.

A housing study that Peter Cook completed while teaching at Hornsey College of Art shows a step towards the execution of the megastructural method. It proposed a steel frame, with a grid about eight metres wide, reaching up a number of storeys into the sky. Every ten metres, or three storeys, there was a shallow space-frame deck which ran along the length of the structure, from which all the other units could be suspended. The houses were to be installed into the large gaps created within this frame, and Cook developed these in some detail, creating plans for various sizes of units made out of moulded plastic, which could be connected into the frame as desired.

These flats, as drawn, were garish and groovily coloured, had the rounded windows which were then fashionable, and featured light-weight furniture and odd, organic-looking media entertainment devices. Balconies could be extended out from the building, suspended from the frame immediately above, while pedestrian and vehicular access could run along within the frame at intervals. In this study (which apparently came close to having a small prototype made), we can see all the different megastructural ingredients, all of which already existed, coming together: there is raised deck access like so much housing of the time, a space-frame infrastructure, manufacturable units of varying sizes, and all the while, lurking in the background of the drawings, was the gigantic space frame from the original plug-in study.

---

1   See the 'New Directions in [...] Architecture' series of books from the 1960s, whose British edition by Royston Landau is by far the most futuristic.

Although it seems fantastic, and although its architectural merit was dubious at best, upon closer inspection everything depicted in the Plug-In City was something that already existed. The proposal seemed to suggest a housing estate that would have been a cross between the densely stacked clusters of units of Habitat, UEA or the Nakagin Capsule Tower, with a plastic aesthetic recognisable from old airport terminal buildings or perhaps the offices on a building site, pre-fabricated units set on steel frames, ready to be moved at a moment's notice. If it sounds ugly, there's every reason to believe it would have been, but the implication was that in a future of greater freedom, the static house itself and all of its social and historic meanings would become less and less important, and the more nomadic lives of the affluent society would no longer demand such frippery.

At around the same time, another germinal example of plug-in architecture was being built in the UK. In an area of nineteenth-century housing in Paddington, London, a series of townhouses were combined into halls of residence for international students. The existing buildings were almost completely inflexible, and space was at such a premium that it was necessary for the toilet facilities to be built as an extension to the back of the buildings. The two young architects of the Farrell/Grimshaw Partnership were hired to design these facilities.

Nick Grimshaw was a recent student of Archigram's Peter Cook and thus was steeped in the ethos of megastructure. He and Terry Farrell came up with an ingenious solution to the design problem that is still to this day quite unique. Due to the awkward levels of the floors within the nineteenth-century buildings, it wasn't practical to arrange the extension in a standard fashion, so instead a micro-megastructure was constructed. The bathroom tower was constructed around a central steel core that was the primary structure and also contained the electrical, ventilation and plumbing services. Attached to this core were the bathroom units, each one created from four seamlessly moulded, glass-reinforced plastic parts and into which the plumbing and fixtures were connected. These units were attached helically, in a spiral, and a ramp was fixed to the outside that managed to line up properly with the openings in the existing building. The whole construction then had a glass skin attached to the edge to create an interior space.

In this small project, now long since demolished, we see all the elements of megastructure: a central structural unit that contains all the services and to which more ephemeral units were attached, with the potential to be replaced at a later date. Indeed, the pods themselves, with their rounded corners and moulded forms, were seriously evocative of the housing units sketched out in the Plug-In City. This humdrum project, now clearly but a small moment of possibility, was at the time seen as just a simple next step in the radical change that was occurring to cities all over the world.

Megastructure, and its vision of the future, reached its peak at the universal exposition held in Osaka, Japan, in 1970, an event at which both its potentials and limitations became clearly apparent. It was the first world expo since Montreal and was the very last of the 'big expos' of the twentieth century that would capture the imagination of the public so readily, with visitor figures exceeding 64 million. Osaka 1970 was intended as a triumphant celebration of the exceptional economic and industrial growth of Japan, and visits beyond the expo site dazzled many Westerners with the speed and scale of ongoing development. It contested the idea that America was the sole vanguard of technological modernity, and where the architecture of Expo 67 began to define the new high-tech, immersive architecture being developed at the time, Osaka 1970 would be the triumph of this form.

The expo, situated within its own park, was planned by Kenzo Tange, and as usual, alongside a selection of global architecture, there were various theme buildings and attractions by Japanese architects. Expo 1970 had the banal theme of 'Progress and Harmony for Mankind', providing the typical glossy, heartwarming message seemingly devoid of politics or ideology. Dominating the expo park was a massive space-frame roof, nearly half a kilometre long and fifty metres high. This roof was designed to hark back to the immersive qualities of the Crystal Palace at the Great Exhibition.[2] In addition, it created a focal space in the centre of the expo site while also allowing for a diversity of architectural styles in

---

2   Udo Kultermann (ed.), *Kenzo Tange*, p. 286.

The inhabited space frame: Expo 1970 Theme Pavilion, Kenzo Tange

the pavilions, expressed in a hyper-modern form according to the technological dreams of the day. As Tange put it, 'the problem … is to evolve spatial harmony and order within diversity',[3] which is an almost perfect expression of the megastructural impulse.

The space-frame roof covered much of the public space of the expo and was fully inhabitable at upper levels. While functioning as a plaza, there was also a defined route through the structure that took visitors through a series of exhibitions, beginning in the basement, which represented the history of humanity, up onto the plaza, which depicted the present, and then up into the space frame, which – naturally – represented the future. Embedded into the space frame, perhaps one of the closest actual attempts to build a Spatial City like that of Yona Friedman, were various different installations and experiences (including one by Archigram).

The Osaka expo was the apotheosis of the space frame as a symbol of a future world. Along with the roof over the plaza, there was an abundance of geodesic domes, such as the Expo Tower, which contained a Japanese tea room, or the West German pavilion (in which Karlheinz

---

3   Ibid.

Stockhausen performed daily), and all manner of space-frame structures, ranging from the pragmatically experimental, like the Takara Pavilion, to the frighteningly mantis-like Toshiba Pavilion, all spikes and claws, both of which were designed by Kisho Kurokawa.

Almost every high-tech architectural idea of the time was in evidence: Arata Isozaki's 'robots' – ten-metre-high mobile structures containing stage equipment – crawled around the plaza, while many of the individual pavilions were modular, plastic, plug-in and gadget-like. It was here that inflatable architecture made its most prominent appearance: the USA built an inflatable pavilion, one of the largest experiments in pneumatic architecture attempted at that point. Pepsi built an inflatable pavilion which was entirely mirrored on the inside, while Fuji Group built the largest inflatable yet constructed, which for all the world resembled a curved, rather too bodily version of the already biological Philips Pavilion of 1958, and which also contained an experimental audio and cinema experience.

If Expo 67 prominently displayed new film and media technology within its pavilions, the Osaka expo took the focus on immersive media experience to a whole new level. Almost all of the pavilions were filled with video projections, displays, computers and new media, to the extent that this began to completely eclipse the architecture surrounding them. This discrepancy was clearly noted by the architectural press who attended; for example the reviewer for *Architectural Design* said:

> The inside of almost all the pavilions is a wonderland of complex communications, visual and aural effects; a series of comprehensive images of knowledge, wealth and life in the future. The outside of all the pavilions – the Expo site itself – is a huge grazing area for strange national dinosaurs, three or four years in gestation with a six month life ahead of them. These bizarre mutations are the least inspiring, least futuristic aspects of Expo 70.[4]

There is a certain irony that just a year after the moon landing, the grandest, most exuberant display of futuristic architecture there had

---

4   *Architectural Design*, June 1970, p. 271.

yet been had fallen in love with immaterial technologies – computers, video, sound, etc. It appeared that, due to its ever-so-laborious design and construction processes, even the most advanced and experimental architecture was being left behind. Some felt that the Japanese Metabolists who were so prominent at the expo had run out of ideas and were reduced to copying the British tendency. But the most troubling sign that the expo revealed was the realisation that megastructure as a response to technological change may have been a false promise. Martin Pawley, again in *AD*, explained the problem in the following way:

> If the environment of the future is going to be created according to the principles governing perception rather than those of construction; if the exhausting tramp over acres of concrete is to be avoided; if the monster space frame or geodesic dome is soon to master acres of previously open exhibition or townscape; then the design of that environment, with its accompanying software, is going to become the de facto province of systems and media men, electronics and computer experts, film directors and editors, photographers and yes, shopfitters.[5]

If the megastructural tendency was to be pushed much further, then there was every chance that architecture itself might soon become obsolete. If any environmental experience could be created by a few slide projectors in a darkened room, what was the point in ever more adventurous architecture? If the superstructure of the future was to be as blank and anonymous as a giant space frame or dome, then the only 'design' required would be that of the individual's multimedia experience within that frame, which would be an entirely new field of work, a kind of ever-more-personalised interior design.

This warning was also a promise: Expo 70 might have shown that there were clear limits to what was possible when attempting to build the architecture of the future, but at the same time it vindicated one of the earliest dreams of modern architecture – that the future of urban space would be an envelope at a massive scale, encompassing a completely

---

5   Ibid, p. 292.

free and pliable interior, the creation of an internal environment of such comfort, freedom and scale that it could effectively replace the 'outside' completely.

After the Osaka expo, the enthusiasm for such global spatial pageants as the expo waned. The next official exposition, in Spokane in the US, would be another four years away, and coming as it did after the oil crisis, and with ecology and environmental degradation now firmly on the agenda, it was a much smaller, much less triumphant affair. The theme for Spokane was 'Tomorrow's Fresh New Environment', and it is clear now just how differently the future was beginning to be seen, with the expo given over to conferences on 'planetary ecomanagement' and other such post–*Limits to Growth* themes. Over the next few decades, expos gradually receded from the public consciousness, as economic crisis, globalisation, the intimacy of technological advance, and the gradual thawing of the Cold War made many of its reasons for existence become less pertinent.

In concert with the decline of the expo, megastructure came increasingly to be seen as lacking credibility. One reason for this was found in a fundamental discrepancy between the stated ethos – a changing, dynamic city, adapting to radical changes in society through high technology systems, and the actual architecture that was being built – often a stylish, romantic brutalism, heroic but inflexible. Put simply, megastructure was such a powerful 'look' that it all too often remained as aesthetic dressing.

'Everywhere around were signs of a process that made architecture ever more ephemeral. Plastics were making their impact upon construction, not only finding their way into components but being used as experimental cladding for new tower blocks in the UK, to construct temporary buildings, art installations, the interiors of shops and other commercial spaces. Plastics could be seen in other early projects by Grimshaw, or in the late 1960s work of James Stirling, which combined a concrete ruggedness with new multicoloured plastic skins. They can be seen, in particular, in Stirling's training centre for Olivetti in the Hampshire countryside, or his remarkable Southgate housing estate in the new town of Runcorn, long since demolished.

Another direction taken was more pragmatic, similar to the practical studies of the Plug-In City. Nikolaas Habraken, a Dutch academic, spent much of the 1960s and early '70s working on a plausible infrastructural scheme of 'supports' that allowed the state to build structures into which the public could insert their own personalised buildings. His motivation was what he saw as the obvious and inevitable failure of mass housing. Attempts at mass production of housing were creating cities of crushing uniformity that poisoned social life and broke what he called the 'natural relationship' between humans and their dwellings, meaning the ability for people to make their mark and assert ownership of where they lived.

Furthermore, mass housing, for Habraken, meant that whole areas of cities were consigned to obsolescence at the same time, causing ghettoisation and choking the life from the urban environment. Habraken was attempting to resolve these urban problems by allowing people more control over their dwellings and their design but avoiding the American problem of endless suburban sprawl of detached houses, while in the process making it more practical to use new industrial technologies within the building industry.

His support cities were based upon the idea that the state would build multilevel structures with services and circulation, and the people would purchase industrially produced, customisable dwellings which could be placed into these external structures – essentially the Plug-In City. What set Habraken apart was his avoidance of aestheticising the process. Instead, he suggested that his system would allow for proper research and development, more freedom and individuality, the differentiation of varied neighbourhoods, without the need for comprehensive redevelopment.

> Our task therefore is to find a solution to the great problem of society: to find a formula for a housing process that allows comfort and human dignity to exist hand-in-hand, while maintaining the town as an aggregate of compact building.[6]

---

6   Nikolaas Habraken, *Supports*, p. 72.

Habraken's support city was free of the flamboyance and extremity of other proposals and tended to describe a streets-in-the-sky, three-dimensional city into which people built their own plug-in houses. Without supporting images, the focus was on the political and technical questions of how the people might benefit from this kind of change in procurement: Habraken thought that 'a new relationship between citizens and authority could develop'.[7]

At the other end of the scale, megastructure flew off into the realms of fantasy. Buckminster Fuller had always claimed that even his most fanciful notions – such as huge geodesic domes whose internal pressure could be reduced enough to allow them to float like bubbles, or the previously mentioned pyramid cities a kilometre high – were based on principles of pragmatic and sound engineering. Despite this, there were plenty of others whose flights of fancy took a leap into the ludicrous. Paulo Soleri, an Italian who had worked for Frank Lloyd Wright, took megastructure off into a mystical realm when he began publishing his series of 'arcology' designs. 'Arcology' was his term for ultra-dense cities containing millions if not billions of people, all packed into huge individual structures. Drawn exquisitely, these speculations were framed by long, meandering texts filled with talk of ecology and urbanism, man in harmony with nature, but they all seemed to depict quasi-organic structures like vast termite mounds or ornate cathedrals, drawn as much for the sheer joy of it than any serious intentions to build.

However, Soleri did – like many from the counterculture – start his own eco-community out in the Arizona desert. Called Arcosanti, it was to be a working model for an arcology, but over his life it grew only to the extent that it represented 0.01 per cent of the scale of the city he had in mind. Like Wright before him, he accommodated various apprentices who wanted to live there and build the future with him, but their primary source of income was to sell the products of a small bell foundry they built on-site, the proceeds of which were of course not quite enough to remake the entire world.

---

7   Ibid., p. 106.

As the '70s progressed, other architects tried to juxtapose megastructural thinking with the rising ecological consciousness. In 1960 Buckminster Fuller, in one of his most famous conceptual designs, had suggested that it would be both possible and economical to build a single geodesic dome structure over the middle of Manhattan, saving a fortune on air conditioning and protecting the inhabitants from pollution and nuclear fallout. Now, architect Glen Small designed his Biomorphic Biosphere, which took the aesthetics of space frames and domes and plastered them in plants and forests, like some kind of vast winter garden stretched out over hundreds of kilometres. But like many others, Small portrayed his work at such a grandiose scale that it just couldn't be taken seriously without some kind of transitional proposal.

In these and other projects, the line between what was intended to be built and what was merely visionary speculation became blurred. In the new climate of suspicion of bureaucratic solutions and the rise of conservation and community activism, large-scale proposals for remaking urbanism fell out of favour. Indeed, by 1976 Banham could make the accusation that much megastructural design was only ever just a self-indulgent excuse for architects to build big, satisfyingly complicated architectural models.[8]

So much of the energy that went into megastructure design was driven by the need, both real or perceived, to find more space for human occupation: to alleviate congestion, to solve the housing crisis or simply to achieve personal freedom. Throughout the 1950s and '60s, the space race was giving new energy to old ideas of expansion, as embodied by Star Trek's opening monologue – 'Space: The Final Frontier'. This Euro-American dream of a virgin emptiness away from the stagnation of the old world, in which new lives and possibilities could occur, was reinvigorated by the sense of progress in the 1960s. Along with travelling to the moon, this was the era of Jacques Cousteau (who in fact collaborated on a design study for a floating megastructure city off the coast of Monte Carlo),[9] and

---

8   Reyner Banham, *Megastructures*, p. 162.

9   Justus Dahinden, *Urban Structures for the Future*, p. 134.

the USA had a long-running 'SeaLab' project that involved a submersible laboratory spending long periods at great depth. For every study in the architecture press examining the technology of space capsules there was another examining the new world of the high-pressure submersible.

A great many megastructures were designed to be floating habitats, whose partial motivation was the alleviation of housing crises, but also of course because they were attractively futuristic proposals in their own right. Buckminster Fuller designed and marketed 'Triton City', which was a floating ziggurat housing block with plug-in units, a more detailed and believably scaled version of his Tetrahedral City. In addition, Kenzo Tange's Tokyo Bay project, a master plan for a new town of 10 million people, would have expanded Tokyo right out into the sea on a grid of raised roads and railways, interspersed with housing and office blocks perched above the water, reminiscent of the oil settlements the Soviet Union had built off the coast of Baku. More practical still was 'Sea City', a British study commissioned by Pilkington Glass which suggested a floating horseshoe-shaped 'wall' structure with – yet again – ziggurat housing embedded within it, which would create a calm, protected internal harbour where up to 30,000 people could permanently live off the coast of Norfolk.[10]

But one environment which really lent itself to megastructural thinking was the extreme climate of the polar regions. English-Swedish architect Ralph Erskine, who had already worked in the Nordic Arctic, designed a small town for Resolute Bay in Canada, one of the most remote settlements in the world, in which he developed his ideas of 'wall' housing which would later be put to great use in the UK's Byker housing estate. Resolute Bay actually made it into construction, but only one block of the wall he proposed was actually built. On a larger scale, a group of Soviet architects proposed a series of environmentally contained hollow pyramid structures with one side glazed to create a winter garden underneath. These were for the brutally inhospitable former gulag of Norilsk, a nickel-mining town and one of the most polluted places on the entire planet. Larger yet was the proposal for an oil-mining town in Alaska with

10   See *Architectural Design*, March 1968, p. 101.

a completely sealed interior environment. Named 'Seaward's Success', this would have housed more than 20,000 people in what looked in the architect's drawings to be much like an indoor shopping mall. This project was only thwarted due to a legal delay over the construction of the pipeline it depended upon.

But by far the most interesting Arctic proposal came from a collaboration between Frei Otto, Kenzo Tange and the engineer Ove Arup. In 1970, Hoechst AG, the German chemicals manufacturer split off from the de-Nazified IG Farben and one of the prime movers in the German 'economic miracle', commissioned this trio of specialists to work up proposals for a city of 30,000 people, designed to allow them to live comfortably in the most inhospitable environment on the earth. If people could settle easily in such locations, the potential for industrial and mining developments in these areas would be huge, and might rapidly pay back almost any initial investment costs. Otto's team produced a feasibility study, not a finalised design, but compared to almost any other visionary scheme from the period it is one of the most sophisticated and well developed.

Otto, who was in the process of enlarging his Expo 67 roof design to accommodate the forthcoming Munich Olympics of 1972, had, like Fuller, been proposing giant envelope structures that could encompass large areas for a number of years. His suggestion for the Arctic City was a pneumatic domed roof two kilometres across, under which the city could be built. It would be sited at the head of an estuary with a harbour for shipping access, with an airport on the outskirts. A nuclear power station would provide the energy for the construction and running of the city, and its heated cooling water would be used for climate control and keeping the harbour permanently ice-free.

The first step in the construction would be to dig large foundations in a ring around the perimeter of the roof. The roof would then be made by laying a mesh of giant nylon cables across the site, fastening transparent pillows between them before slowly inflating the ensemble to a height of 240 metres. By using a new plastic compound instead of steel, the changing loads over such a large structure would be far easier to cope with as it behaved not as a true dome but more like a skin, breathing in and out depending upon pressure imbalances between the exterior and interior. Once the dome had been inflated and sealed, the city inside could be constructed without exposure to the Arctic climate.

The city that Tange developed for the interior was remarkably similar to that of the Hook New Town proposals. There would be four main air-locked entrances to the dome, which would connect to external facilities and of course the industrial activity that was to be the main employment in the city. Submerged roads would connect the housing to a civic centre containing commercial, entertainment, civic and cultural uses. Like Hook, there would also be segregated pedestrian routes through parkland. In case of emergency, such as a loss of power or a roof collapse, there were secure basements planned beneath the entire city that could function minimally even if the climate failed above. The Arctic air would be warmed by heat exchange from the power plant and then distributed throughout the housing, and while the internal climate was allowed to fluctuate alongside that of the exterior, the interior temperature would never sink below freezing, and the town was depicted as verdant, with parks and forests surrounding the housing. Louvres in the dome would block out the low twenty-four-hour summer sun in order to maintain a semblance of a diurnal rhythm, while in winter a huge 'artificial sun' lamp would run across the roof on tracks for the same purpose.

Arctic City was remarkable for the level of detail in its structural and urban planning. But it's even more remarkable for its juxtaposition of familiar modernist architecture and visionary structural and environmental engineering. One can picture living in a modern flat, walking

Under the roof of the Arctic City

along a landscaped pathway towards the large concrete shopping centre in the middle of the town, but all the while everything is set under a lacy abstract grid high above, with blizzards and snow-covered mountains visible in the distance. Or spending the day working in subzero conditions before boarding a bus, passing through the air lock and returning back into the mild evening climate of the city. Despite its fantasy qualities, the Arctic City is easily one of the most believable and plausible megastructural visions of the age, looking for all the world like Cumbernauld inside the Crystal Palace, and its combination of the space age and the actually existing modernist urbanism of the time is tantalising.

If space was the final frontier, this was definitely borne out by the last, most daring and perhaps most ridiculous megastructure of the era to be taken at all seriously. In the late 1960s a particle physicist at Princeton University, Gerard O'Neill, started investigating the economical, physical and engineering challenges of setting up permanent orbital settlements. Originally conjured up as an engineering problem to keep an undergraduate physics course occupied, the surprisingly promising results of his initial calculations led O'Neill to conduct further investigations. The initial thinking was that the primary benefit of these facilities would be the mitigation of the extreme inefficiencies of lifting heavy loads into earth orbit, which requires massive rockets and a huge amount of fuel just to take a few tons out of the earth's gravitational well. If permanent orbital manufacturing facilities could be established, then the costs of all future space exploration would henceforth become a whole lot cheaper.

O'Neill's original investigations fell on the mostly deaf ears of his professional peers, to the extent that he couldn't get papers on the subject published, but his suggestions awakened something within many of his students and friends. In much the same manner as the story of Buckminster Fuller, the idea that O'Neill was developing, of building permanent settlements in space, managed to reach outside his milieu and stimulate a great yearning for the remarkable way of life and the opportunities that it suggested.

Over the early 1970s, O'Neill's ideas developed further: colonies could be established around Lagrange points, areas of gravitational equilibrium between the pull of the sun, earth and moon. The colonies would take the form of large cylinders, potentially over a kilometre long, which would spin at a constant rate to recreate the effects of gravity within, pressing the inhabitants to the outside, much like how swinging a bag prevents the contents from falling out. The cylinders would be partially glazed to allow for sunlight to reach the interior, while large shades and baffles would protect the inhabitants from glare and cosmic rays. Other variations involved spherical or ring-shaped environments, familiar from science fiction scenarios such as *2001: A Space Odyssey*, surrounded by orbital crop-growing facilities that O'Neill called 'Crystal Palaces'.

O'Neill saw numerous technical possibilities for his concept, and the development of space colonies was suggested as a potential cure for just about every problem that the world was suffering and which appeared to have become more acute over the previous decade. In the context of the increasingly apocalyptic rhetoric depicting the plight of the earth, O'Neill claimed, 'The human race stands now on the threshold of a new frontier, whose richness surpasses a thousand fold that of the new western world of five hundred years ago.' In much the same way that colonialism allowed Europeans to escape the stagnation of their own societies centuries before, space colonies would open up a new chapter in the history of the world:

> If we use our intelligence and our concern for our fellow human beings in this way, we can, without any sacrifice on our own part, make the next decades a time not of despair but of fulfilled hope, of excitement, and of new opportunity.[11]

Space colonies began to get attention from all sorts of places; scientists, ecologists, students, even disgruntled former members of the counterculture began to see in the colonies the promise of a way out of the doldrums of the mid-1970s. Finally, NASA and the US government became interested, as the prospect of unlimited free energy and new sources of raw materials in exchange for an expenditure measured

---

11   Gerard O'Neill, in Stewart Brand (ed.), *Space Colonies*, p. 11.

in just billions of dollars began to seem more plausible with each new study that was completed.

O'Neill gave evidence to the US Senate on the prospect of space manufacturing, and NASA began to publicise the idea from within. NASA's artists Don Davis and Rick Guidice produced a number of famous paintings and visualisations of the potential space colonies, utilising an already-existing language of science fiction art but given a new layer of credibility due to being the result of state-organised research. They show landscapes wrapped around the inside of these artificial worlds, with water features, trees, animals and people all sheltered within this artificial environment, and outside the blank vacuum of space. In these new cylindrical worlds, the ultimate megastructures, NASA's artists showed just how they thought the new space pioneers would live: they depicted the houses within the orbital stations as a series of stacked ziggurats.

The space colony project went no further, however, when in the late '70s the US government decided it had not the spare funds to develop space travel beyond the already completed Skylab project and the forthcoming space shuttle. It's almost too ridiculous to believe that the idea got as far as it did (although the gradual growth of the International Space Station is to a certain extent a testament to O'Neill's vision). Overall it's much too easy to laugh at the trajectory of megastructure, an answer to the crises of modernist architecture – uniformity, inflexibility, lack of choice for the people who used it – that demanded the very acceleration of the modernist processes themselves.

Far too often, megastructure proposals today appear too much like fantasy, like something from the cover of a cheap 1970s sci-fi novel. Giant tents over cities, cities built out over the ocean, underwater cities, space cities – mostly these appear to us now like trite fantasy. Even the rise of 'Google Earth urbanism', such as the giant island reclamations of Dubai from the first decade of the twenty-first century, carried nothing of the promise of new ways of living that these earlier schemes did. In a certain way, we could think of this as the curse of the expo, the instilled assumption, based upon a mixture of experience and propaganda, that rapid technological growth was changing everything, for ever.

NASA's vision of a Space Colony

But it is worth looking further into how these ideas disseminated into the mainstream of building, as they inevitably did. The most obvious individual case, and one that Banham picked up on as the last word in megastructure, was the Centre Pompidou in Paris, designed by Richard Rogers and Renzo Piano and completed in 1977. Frequently seen as the last hurrah of Archigram's 'Zoom' wave of indeterminate, flexible and replaceable architecture, it's both a hugely successful public space and a monument to the failure of that new idea of the city to take proper root, never achieving even a fraction of the potential social uses that it was originally envisioned to accommodate.

Even in its compromised reality, it is one of the most remarkable buildings of the era. Almost completely lacking in the refinement or grace that would later inflect high-tech architecture, its simple yet vast structure, its cheap plastic details and exposed services point to the political reality suggested by megastructure, where the monumentality of the bourgeois city is abandoned in favour of a functional egalitarianism.

After this flawed high point, the trajectory of high-tech architecture led off into the more corporate environment of the 1980s. Rogers's next major building was Lloyd's of London, and with every project afterwards he would gradually abandon his youthful experiments in order to succeed in the world as it was. In 1971, another young architect of the era collaborated with Buckminster Fuller on a speculative project called the 'Climatroffice'. This was a variation on the Expo 67 dome, with the dome squashed to allow for a wider and more practical internal space. Inside, steel platforms were to function as work rather than exhibition space, and the entire interior was shown as being swathed in foliage. This young architect was Norman Foster, perhaps the most influential architect the world has seen in the last forty years.

Foster's influence has been primarily due to his firm's innovations in the design of corporate workplaces and transport buildings, but in his early years he was deeply influenced by Fuller's call for more materially conscious design. Foster's early projects of the 1970s, with their light-weight structures and exquisitely refined details, all seemed utterly remarkable when compared to the heavy concrete that surrounded them, appearing more like product design than what was conventionally thought of as architecture.

In the 1970s Foster would build a remarkable art facility on the grounds of the University of East Anglia, facing Lasdun's complex of ziggurat housing. This new building, donated by the Sainsbury supermarket dynasty as a vessel to display their incredible art collection, was a shed with a space-frame roof enclosing a large flexible internal space, clad to the outside in featureless white panels. It was a rather shocking juxtaposition of a high-culture space with the clean and featureless architectural technology of a computer chip factory, and to this day is a thrillingly odd architectural experience – Bacons and Giacomettis in an airport lounge.

But the imagination of these and other projects by high-tech architects, so clearly indebted to the previous experiments, was not enough to stop their ideas being gradually diluted into the banality of the contemporary office block as we understand it today. A modern office block does satisfy many points of the megastructural ethos. It is typically built with the most blank plans possible, including a raised floor containing electrical connections and a suspended ceiling containing lights and ventilation. This blank, polished interior is then typically completed by designers working for the companies who are renting the space. In go carpets, desks, partitions and all the rest, flexible and replaceable. Within the curtain walls of an office block, and indeed in the robotic arms which run on rails and hold the window-cleaning cradles, some flickering echo of the megastructure dream continues to exist.

On a larger scale, Norman Foster again pioneered the large envelope as the dominant approach for another typology, this time at Stansted Airport, built throughout the 1980s, which became a new model for airport terminals. Today one can still get a hint of the megastructure ideal when passing through an airport, with their massive roof structures, their miles of continuous internal space, the flexible shops and security facilities that can be taken down and moved over time without disturbing the exterior, not to mention the connecting arms which rotate and extend towards the aircraft, the ever-so-futuristic monorails and the intersecting transport facilities.

Elsewhere, Martin Pawley's vision of the space frame at the Osaka Expo in 1970, the blankest of boxes serving an interior of constant change and mediated consumption, gradually mutated over time into the gargantuan sheds that serve as distribution points for goods – vast blank forms connected into transport infrastructure at important nodes of activity and capable of being erected and taken down in a remarkably short space of time. Pawley believed that these buildings, known as 'big sheds', were 'the architecture that will dominate the twenty-first century',[12] and it has been said that in their massive blankness 'they render architecture redundant'.[13] But in their way they really are the technology that Fuller and Otto and all the others were dreaming of, especially now in their roboticised form, with their optimised networks of demand and distribution.

If we move further back in the distribution chain, we come to the container port, these eerie zones celebrated as the utterly blank spaces of

---

12   Martin Pawley, *Terminal Architecture*, p. 181.

13   Film directed by Chris Petit, *Content*.

trade, their giant robot cranes unloading and loading ships in automated, computerised synchronisation. It was in 1968 that the shipping container was standardised, and the effects are well known: the sudden increase in size of ship that the container made possible meant that many of the old ports were rendered useless and had to be moved to deep water locations where they could spread out further, leaving millions of people across the world without jobs. And of course, what is the shipping container if not a plug-in unit par excellence? Mobile, lifted and carried anywhere and everywhere around the world, it is a flexible, universal spatial unit. The piles of containers at ports are the real plug-in cities, endlessly shifting, stacked high, never the same from one moment to the next.

The megastructure future does therefore exist, in a great many places, and affects our lives in innumerable ways. But never has it been implemented in the functional role for which it was originally envisaged: housing. The reason for this is political. One the one hand, megastructure would have required new legal structures, new forms of procurement and new standards for the construction industry, massive undertakings within each individual state and throughout the globe. But they also required a leap of faith in what the individual was prepared to demand from their living space – trends for greater consumer choice and demand were apparent at the time, but these failed to translate into demand for more nomadic housing, and the tendency towards nostalgia was fully reasserted by the 1980s. Furthermore, the idea of the house as an ephemeral product went against the very notion of land and territory.

The dream of megastructure was not simply a formalist explosion in optimistic times. Rather, it was an attempt to allow the state to create spaces in which people could consider themselves individually fulfilled, while never hiding from view the infrastructure and service provided. Unlike in conventional housing, where heating, plumbing and waste infrastructure are all hidden, megastructure was in the last instance an attempt to make clear the functions and systems that are constantly required to live in a city at all. We should understand it not as an indulgent fantasy but as a political aesthetic of togetherness, immune to the deliberate aesthetic atomisation that would so often occur in architecture in the decades to come. It was an attempt to resolve the antagonisms between conformity to society and individual freedom, and in that way it represents many of the important struggles of the time. That it lost out in the end to changing fashion, growing cynicism about institutions and the very notion of progress, should not blind us to the potential of the options that were closed off in the process.

Chapter 4

Systems and Failures

Since the last decades of the twentieth century, the sight of the demolition of public housing has been transformed into spectacle. Time and again, crowds have gathered to witness emptied housing blocks brought to the ground in seconds by explosives. Stripped of all their furniture and windows, draped in demolition contractor's banners and with the public held behind barriers at a safe distance, the crowds wait until small puffs of grey smoke appear in lines across the façade and the gigantic hulk of the building begins to shift. An instant later, the sound of the explosion is heard and the whole thing comes cataclysmically down. The following quiet is broken by cheering from the crowds, the birds fleeing to the sky and huge clouds of dust wafting slowly away.

Most often, the buildings brought down in this way are the relics of the building boom of the post-war years, which ended up having a far shorter lifespan than the slums they so often replaced. Despite the quiet sadness of the people who once lived inside, these spectacles of destruction are often accompanied by the triumphal rhetoric of improvement, the erasure of past mistakes and movement into a brighter social future.

Even before the political battles and aesthetic scrapping that came to dominate the architecture of the late 1970s, there were signs that things were not all going to plan. A number of high-profile disasters and failings, both technological and political, managed to cast doubt upon the narratives of progress and development that were current at the time. In some cases these events have formed a grand narrative or turning-point that historians have utilised to mark the apogee, or perhaps nadir, of the architectural culture of the time.

The most prominent of such events was the demolition of the Pruitt-Igoe housing estate in St Louis, Missouri, in 1972. Less than twenty years old, it was the victim of a precipitous social decline that for many years was blamed upon the architectural style of the project itself. Charles Jencks, seeking to clear a critical path for the postmodern architecture he was then promoting, infamously defined this act of demolition as the very moment at which modernist architecture died.

In the UK, the Ronan Point disaster of May 1968 performed a similar role: when a gas explosion caused the progressive collapse of the corner of a twenty-two-storey tower block, it became in the public imagination the moment that the tide of opinion turned firmly against modernist housing. These hinges in hindsight simplify and render monochrome the difficult situations and debates of the time. They also make political developments and decisions seem inevitable when they are, in certain cases, contested to this day, but they are of course not lacking in basis.

In the years following its initial completion, Cumbernauld town centre won – somewhat infamously in retrospect – an award from the American Institute of Architects for its innovations. People visited from across the globe, travelling to examine the UK's first shopping centre and one of the world's first modernist megastructures. Despite the high praise for the complex, its reception was not universally warm. Many questioned its reliance on large expanses of voguish concrete in such a grey and wet location. Meanwhile others noted that it was rather too out in the open for the local climate and its situation on the crown of a hill, meaning that the wind tended to blow through harshly. One wag, in *Architectural Design*, was able to quip: 'It's not Cumbernauld's fault that it happens to be in Scotland.'[1]

---

1   *Architectural Design*, September 1968, p. 409.

In addition, in a familiar story from the era, the quality of the construction was soon found to be defective. The penthouses that ran along the top level were discovered to have structural problems and were decanted not many years after the building was completed, first turned into offices and then eventually storage. Gradually, various areas that had been open to the elements – the external ramps and staircases, the open atria that connected the different floors to each other – were enclosed, and parts of the building, such as the Golden Eagle Hotel or the Galbraiths supermarket (the first supermarket in the UK) were demolished.

Cumbernauld town centre, as it was originally envisaged, was supposed to have been open-ended and extendable, but in the years since 2000 it was subject to large redevelopments that have demolished large areas of the building. Its new interconnected neighbours – the Antonine Shopping Centre, an utterly nondescript shopping mall named after the Roman defensive wall that ran nearby, and on the other side of the building a gigantic supermarket – both mock the original building by being far larger, far more technologically sophisticated, but far less civically ambitious architectural objects. In fact, they almost completely block off any views of the complex's rugged composition, leaving it hidden, dilapidated and forlorn.

The town centre complex went on to become a favoured target for popular anti-modernist sentiment. It was publicly nominated the 'Worst Building in Britain' by a 2005 television series entitled *Demolition*, and it twice won the 'Carbuncle Award' from the Scottish architecture magazine *Urban Realm*, in 2001 and 2005. It's not really hard to see why – its design was outlandishly experimental, it was built from inappropriate materials, and it had suffered a long decline, with much of the complex either empty or dilapidated, and having suffered all manner of unsympathetic works done to it. Photos taken as it neared completion look for all the world like something directly lifted out of Archigram's Plug-In City, and images of its early years show a grey but nonetheless dramatic and stylish environment. By the time it was almost half a century old, however, with wear and tear and innumerable cheap tweaks to keep it going, it was not really surprising that it would be criticised in such a way. Visiting the building now is a sad affair, although flickers and shadows of what it might have once represented still remain.

Cumbernauld town centre manages to embody the tension between the formal qualities and the underlying organisational principles of the architectural dreams of megastructure. Considering its contemporary supermarket neighbour, this tension becomes abundantly clear: the new building is a steel-framed shed, with little or no decoration whatsoever. Thin columns on a spacious grid create a wide, genuinely flexible interior, with the potential to be rearranged at any point depending upon retail trends. These structures can be built at an extremely quick rate, and they can be deployed in almost any location that there is an opportunity.

The contemporary supermarket building embodies the values that people saw in buildings such as Cumbernauld town centre when they appeared in the 1960s – adaptability, change and high technology, but in doing so the supermarket both loses any architectural and thus civic quality and also ruthlessly excludes any extraneous space and function. The town centre is inefficient and has no doubt required ridiculous sums on maintenance and adaptation over its life. But it is also a loose building, with all manner of quaint and unpredictable spaces, which constitute a kind of publicness that the supermarket could never achieve. Furthermore, even taking into account its obvious decline, the town centre is an attempt at a conglomeration of all the different functions of the city into one single complex, neither denying nor subjecting itself fully to commercial imperatives.

Banham noted that it took the remarkable financial and political arrangement of the New Towns project for a comprehensive urban object such as Cumbernauld town centre to become a reality at all.[2] And it would seem that the failure here, the impasse that seems apparently irresolvable, is that the conditions of flexibility required for an architecture to respond to changing societies militate against the potential to create spaces that express this very public desire for change. The pursuit of flexibility almost paradoxically leads to a very specific form of space, often far

---

2   Banham, *Megastructures*, p. 183.

less public in nature. You can have flexible cities, as long as the functions that they accommodate are the very least flexible in any political sense.

The taste for giant envelopes inspired by the engineering experiments of Buckminster Fuller and Frei Otto didn't only lead to imaginary schemes and visions. Throughout the 1960s and '70s there were many large projects built with the deliberate intention of creating interior environments for social and entertainment purposes. In some cases this involved spanning across the roof of sports stadia, but in more experimental cases, much like the crystal palaces of a century before, these sometimes created dreamlike environments of artificial nature, fantasies of leisure and recreation, using the latest architectural technologies in the service of a reimagined interior world.

In 1966, Kisho Kurokawa, the young lion of Japanese architecture, designed the Yamagata Hawaii Dreamland, a thoroughly Metabolist project based upon a diagram of a cell. It was a curved concrete wall-building that enclosed a large outdoor swimming pool and other entertainment facilities, marking a definite interest amongst the avant-garde for such leisure projects – the new affluent future was one in which fun was something that designers were going to have to take very seriously.

A year later, a far more ambitious project opened on the outskirts of Tokyo. Summerland Water Adventure Park was built as a leisure complex with an indoor beach, complete with wave machines, palm trees and fake rock formations. Remarkably, it was completely indoors, contained within a giant lozenge-shaped steel space frame, 162 by 81 metres, much wider – although far less tall – than the dome at the US pavilion at Expo 67. This space frame was completely glazed, surrounded by a battery of giant-nozzled air-conditioning units tasked with maintaining the appropriate internal environment. The whole structure rose up at one end, culminating in a more solid building containing restaurants and other entertainment uses. The Tokyo Summerland is still extant, famous for its tendency to become exceedingly crowded, with thousands of swimmers crammed tightly into its wave pool. It is still popular despite its apparent age and is now surrounded by rollercoasters, flume rides, a Ferris wheel and other such family entertainments.

Over in the UK, there was also growing demand for similar facilities. One project, also called Summerland, was built on the Isle of Man, a semi-autonomous island sitting roughly half-way between Ireland and the north of England. It was an experimental space of public leisure, whose brief existence ended in disaster.

By the 1960s the Isle of Man, with its unreliable weather and relative lack of entertainment facilities, was in danger of falling into terminal decline from its traditional role as a tourist destination, especially considering the rise in foreign holidays taken by the working classes in the UK. Faced with the worrying prospects for the local economy, the authority on the island decided that they should tackle this problem head-on. They held an architectural competition with a very vague brief, and two architects – James Phillips Lomas, a local man, and Brian Gelling from the mainland UK – proposed a new entertainment complex of remarkably experimental design.

Their proposal for the site, a rugged cliff-side space previously used as a goods yard, was for a giant envelope similar to the Japanese Summerland building, with a geodesic dome containing swimming and leisure facilities. As the design developed, however, the design was divided into two separate phases of development. The first part was to be an Olympic-sized swimming pool and leisure facility, entitled 'Aquadrome'. This was later followed by the giant envelope structure, Summerland itself, which would be designed to maintain a consistently subtropical internal environment, giving the impression of being outside.

Summerland was intended to be available year-round, and it had the potential to revolutionise British leisure architecture. Inside the envelope would be everything that a visitor might find at a Mediterranean resort. In four fully enclosed basement levels were a disco, bars and a play area for children, with slides and other amusements. Spread around the huge main volume of the complex, which rose up stepped terraces for another four floors, were bars, restaurants, amusement arcades, lounging areas, shops, an ultraviolet tanning room, saunas and even a communal television area. In total the complex could hold as many as 10,000 visitors at any one time. The envelope space, or 'solarium' as it was called, was over 100 metres long and 30 metres high, and was embedded into the cliffs at one side. The terraced areas rose up at one end within a concrete box, while the rest of the solarium was contained within a trussed steel structure with a space-frame roof, infilled with pyramid-shaped panels made from the very same Oroglas acrylic material that was used for the USA pavilion at Expo 67.

Summerland was a remarkable project, not only because it was an example of the experimental architecture of expositions being built elsewhere around the world, but because it was a project that catered directly to ordinary working-class people. It was not highbrow – activities inside included slot machines and bingo, variety shows and talent contests. The design was not particularly accomplished, architecturally speaking; it had rather ungainly concrete massing and detailing. Within the futuristic shell, the interior design was the antithesis of 'high' architecture – there were areas dressed like log cabins, marquees, deck chairs and lurid carpets everywhere, a fake waterfall. But there was also an odd 'cybernetic' geodesic structure stretching all the way up to the roof, which held the Tannoy and other communications devices.

Despite the hotchpotch style, Summerland genuinely aimed to be a new form of leisure space, a quotidian adaptation of the futuristic technical advances that were going on at the time. This did not mean that it was necessarily well received: Warren Chalk, one of the Archigram team, visited the building for the *Architects' Journal* in 1971. You might expect him to have been positive, considering that the building seemed to embody many of the things that he and his cohort had been advocating for almost a decade, but his enthusiasm was very much tempered, perhaps even condescending. Not only was the building's collage of styles a little crass for his taste, but as far as Chalk was concerned, there simply wasn't enough change inside:

> To organise any leisure complex, much more attention should be paid to open systems that are not preconceived, adding a new dimension to entertainment. In fact technically the most successful responsive environments are film and TV studios, ready and tuned up to do a complete about-face any moment in time, allowing for variety, chance and change.[3]

---

3   *Architects Journal*, vol. 154, 1971, p. 644.

It was at this time that Archigram were working on their great lost opportunity to build, having won a competition for an entertainment complex in Monte Carlo, with what was essentially a more luxurious version of the Summerland brief. Their idea was not to create a greenhouse but a black box, buried under a park, very highly serviced, with a variety of different configurations that could be changed at a moment's notice. Chalk's dismissive response to Summerland was clearly demarcation, cutting the actually existing building off from his more avant-garde work, but despite years of development, Archigram's Monte Carlo project would never make it onto site.

Outside the world of architectural criticism, Summerland was doing remarkably well. Its initial visitor numbers were high, and they remained so over the first couple of years, with the centre turning over a substantial profit. But on the evening of 2 August 1973, with 3,000 people inside the complex, a small fire started just outside the building, caused by three teenage boys discarding a cigarette. This fire managed to catch on the outside of the solid part of the facade, where it began to grow in a gap between the outer wall and the inner skin. By the time anyone became aware of the fire it had already invisibly spread deep into the building's fabric, and within just a few minutes of being spotted the entire building was ablaze, the fire sweeping through the vast interior space, melting and igniting the acrylic panels.

As in many notable fire disasters, there had been terrible mistakes made: many of the exit doors had been locked by management to prevent people entering without paying, while the location of escape routes was far from clear. The staff failed to set off an alarm or begin evacuating the building until the conflagration was well underway, and it was almost half an hour before the fire brigade arrived. Once there, the fire was of such ferocity that there was little the fire brigade could do but wait for it to burn itself out and then dowse down the embers.

In total, fifty people died in the fire, and almost twice as many suffered severe injuries. Some of the victims were found in small cupboard rooms on the upper levels where they had hidden from the fire, some were trapped in a stairwell, while the majority of the dead were found on or around a large staircase that stood out in the open in the main hall.

This was the most prominent circulation route and thus became completely overwhelmed with people during the escape, but it was also one of the first parts of the building engulfed in flame; besides the dead many people were seriously injured by throwing themselves over its balustrades to escape the flames.

The Summerland disaster was one of the worst fires in the UK in the twentieth century and shocked the entire nation. In the weeks and months following the disaster, a number of architectural flaws became apparent, which hinted at negligence or even corruption during the design and construction of the building. The rear wall of the building where the fire had started was built from a coated steel material called Galbestos, which was not fire-rated. This had been chosen for cost reasons – if the wall had been concrete, as originally planned, the fire would not have spread into the structure. Escape routes were considered both inadequate and not properly signed, and the disorganised behaviour of management through the disaster came under criticism. Attention also focused on the flammability of the Oroglas panels. It was known that these were highly flammable, but the local authority had given permission for their use, on the assertion from the manufacturer that in a fire situation they would soften and simply pop out of the frame long before they caught fire.

Although it was later ascertained that the casualties had occurred long before the Oroglas caught fire, mostly when people were trapped on the open staircase as it was engulfed, the experience of people being injured by melting plastic dripping from the roof as they clambered towards the exit suggested that a high-tech, untested material had put people in danger. The implication was that the architects' eagerness to be innovative had contributed to the death toll. The fact that the building was itself a highly innovative form of leisure facility also added to the sense that novelty had led to great mistakes.

The Summerland catastrophe fed into a story that was growing in popularity at the time – that modernist architects had forced the public into new and untrustworthy experiments – and helped to seed the distrust of modern architecture that would break into outright reaction a decade later.

Surprisingly, Summerland was not demolished immediately after the disaster. The swimming pool, the lower floors with the disco, bars and play areas all escaped relatively undamaged, so it was eventually decided to rebuild on top of the solarium level. This time, however, the construction was unambitious, a closed steel shed with a space-frame roof. It was apparently still used and valued by the local community but suffered a long decline, as various parts were gradually demolished or rotted away. It was in a rather pathetic state when it was finally demolished in 2005, leaving nothing but the rear walls of the swimming pool, still embedded into the cliff face behind.

The inspiration of Fuller's geodesic dome on the Summerland centre is clear, but the resonances go further. After the close of Expo 67 and the demolition of most of the pavilions, the giant dome was retained and donated to the City of Montreal. By the middle of 1968, it had been converted into a 'biosphère', an indoor park and aviary, and images from the time show a set of formal gardens (including fake ruin walls) on the inside, with statuary, fountains and full-size trees, much like an updated nineteenth-century winter garden. But on 20 May 1976, repairs were being made to the exterior of the dome, which after nearly a decade of Canadian summer and winter extremes had begun to leak and required maintenance. Sparks from a welder's blowtorch fell onto the Oroglas panels, and much like what had occurred a few years earlier at Summerland, the whole building's skin caught fire, with the flames sweeping rapidly across the sphere. Despite the fire crews' efforts, within a few hours the entire skin of the biodome had burned, leaving nothing but the skeletal space frame.

Despite the differences between the projects, both Summerland and the Montreal Biosphère were born out of the desire to create massive interior spaces, climate controlled and gently hospitable within, giant hothouses of leisure and comfort for a coming world of machine-assisted leisure. What Summerland shows in particular is just how close to being realised so many of those dreams actually were, but its tragic failure contributed to the fear of taking bold steps that would eventually overwhelm the world of architecture.

*   *   *

The experimental housing of Habitat at Expo 67 was not quite as unique as it might at first have seemed. All over the world, pre-fabricated systems of construction were being utilised to tackle the housing shortages that affected countries after World War II. Although most frequently associated with the Soviet Union and their affiliates, factory-made housing was a strategy enthusiastically investigated across the globe. Cheap and rarely designed by famous or even talented architects, these new dwellings nonetheless provided the context and launching point for the early experiments and proposals of radical architects such as Archigram.

In the UK, a fortuitous alignment of demand, ambition and technology occurred that created some of the most experimental housing in the world. There had been a series of reciprocally escalating promises made by the two main political parties to build greater numbers of houses after the war. It would eventually become known as 'the numbers game'. However, it seemed almost impossible to make good on these promises based upon the construction technologies that were available in the post-war years, especially when what increases in building there had been had already caused a serious materials and labour shortage.

What promised a way out of this predicament was the use of the latest in pre-fabrication technology, using proprietary systems that had been developed in the years after the war. Encouraged by great demand and the prospect of government subsidy, the generally conservative construction industry embarked on a remarkable modernisation drive, the results of which were huge numbers of new dwellings across the country, sometimes concentrated in large areas of entirely new urban fabric. This was a future that came, failed and mostly vanished.

The general thinking behind a systems approach to construction was the elimination of inefficient and messy site labour. If parts of buildings could be manufactured in controlled conditions and then brought onto the site, they could be assembled by a much smaller workforce in a much shorter time. This strategy had been deployed immediately after WWII, where wartime industrial production was quickly put to use creating emergency temporary housing. In peacetime, however, the development of mass pre-fabrication was an early attempt at mimicking the developments in automobile manufacture and other industries that would so preoccupy architects moving into the 1970s.

In the Soviet Union and its affiliates, pre-fabrication had become the norm for the Khrushchevian estates of large blocks of flats with a high degree of uniformity, and in France and Scandinavia, research into pre-fabrication had been ongoing since the 1950s. But in post-war Britain, which had reverted to conventional labour-intensive construction, very little research had been done into large-scale pre-fabrication apart from various isolated examples. Thus, in order to deal with the perceived demand for pre-fabricated building methods, already existing systems were brought in from abroad.

The main logic behind what became known as 'system building' was the factory production of large concrete panels. These included floor, internal and external wall panels, all of which were load-bearing, with various steel junction connections cast into them. These were brought onto site and joined together with much less site labour compared to normal construction. Systems with names such as Larsen-Nielsen, Camus and Bison began to be spoken of as a panacea for the housing crisis, a new solution that would lead to greater efficiency and productivity in housing.

The competing systems were heavily marketed, with grand claims made for their thermal and structural performance when compared to conventional techniques. The systems were frequently used for the construction of tower blocks, assisted greatly by both the development of new construction crane technology and increased government subsidies for housing depending upon the height raised. As a result, many panel-constructed tower blocks rose above the UK throughout the 1960s.

As has been mentioned before, there was already much criticism of the infrastructural simplicity of 'towers in the park', and there were plans to develop housing that remained dense and yet low to the ground. Throughout this era there was great experimentation in variations on terraced housing which utilised system-built panel construction, often in areas subject to comprehensive redevelopment. Long blocks of housing

Pure system building: The Ferrier Estate

were built, accessed from raised decks or 'streets in the sky', connected by walkways stretched out over roads and greenery in the manner of the University of East Anglia, albeit in a more financially straightened, more quotidian manner.

Schemes such as Hulme Crescents in Manchester, completed in 1972 and part of a single estate housing 13,000 people; the Aylesbury and Heygate Estates (1971, 1972) in London; Balloon Woods in Nottingham; Leek Street in Leeds; or the Ferrier Estate in Kidbrooke – to name just a handful of these massive redevelopments – all created a futuristic landscape of three-dimensional urban form where pedestrians moved around on various different levels, separated from vehicles below. Occasionally these estates were given additional design consideration – the Hulme Crescents, for example, were intended to be a logical design development from the world-famous Park Hill flats of 1950s Sheffield, and Hulme's long pre-fabricated blocks were arranged in four sweeping curves deliberately derived from the crescents of Bath. This eighteenth-century innovation had been a previous high point in commercial housebuilding, and its repetition marked the the tendency to abstract previously successful typologies to the modern world.

In the new town of Runcorn, in the northwest of England, James Stirling was brought in to design a panel-constructed estate, Southfields. Here he also attempted to create an abstraction of historic urban qualities, in this case Georgian squares surrounding gardens, but connected to the nearby town centre (of similar conception to Cumbernauld's) through a variety of raised decks and walkways. Southfields was panel constructed but given an odd design language of circular porthole windows, and new high-tech plastic panels were used on certain façades, pointing future-ward, as did the new 'SF1' steel-framed and plastic-clad tower blocks in London built in 1968. But by and large, system-built estates, frequently designed by architects employed by the very contractors who were to construct the schemes, were looked down upon by the architectural press as being too formulaic, and far too commercially restrictive. This attitude of condescension helped fuel the disgruntlement that led to the development of experimental schemes such as Habitat, and also the desire for more exciting technological architecture from the likes of Archigram.

It wasn't long, however, before attitudes towards this modernisation began to harden. Among the problems that hit housing in the UK by the end of the 1970s, social, political and aesthetic, one particular issue also became a crisis that challenged the very prospect of technologically advanced building. As the new system-built estates grew older, it became clear that many of them were not performing as well as they were sup-posed to. One recurring problem was of serious damp – not long after construction, the residents of many panel-built estates began reporting problems with mould, damp and infestations of cockroaches and other vermin. This kind of failure shouldn't have been possible with technolo-gies that were marketed as having a thermal performance far beyond what is demanded from new buildings even now, but the problem was clearly widespread.

Furthermore, in the aftermath of the Ronan Point disaster, investiga-tions on system-built estates, including both tower blocks and deck-access flats, found that there were frequent serious defects in the way that the panels had been put together, including inadequate reinforcement and, in some notorious cases, none at all. Panels began falling off buildings, gaps appeared between walls and floors at high level, concrete was rotting away already. It seemed that in the rush to complete as many houses as possible, all manner of short cuts were taken and mistakes made. There were also accusations of systematic corruption between contractors, local authorities and architects, culminating in the conviction and disgrace of architect John Poulson and politician T. Dan Smith (who had been one of the authors of *Traffic in Towns*) in the early 1970s.

The sheer desperation to build quickly, combined with the gener-ous subsidies for various kinds of building, had led to shocking levels of incompetence and a blasé disregard for good practice. When all this became clear and investigations were undertaken, many of these suppos-edly high-tech new estates were found to be in need of serious repairs. In the context of a political mood that was turning against modern housing in general, it started to be seen as far more feasible and desirable to tear these buildings down.

In certain cases these initially futuristic buildings lasted less than twenty years before they disappeared again. For example, the Hutcheson-town E flats in Glasgow, a series of long concrete deck-access blocks that had been opened by Queen Elizabeth II in 1972, swiftly became unin-habitable due to mould and were emptied and torn down again in 1987. In the passion for demolishing tower blocks and estates in the 1980s and '90s, many thousands of dwellings all over the UK were removed, fre-quently being replaced by more traditional housing in vernacular style, leaving nothing whatsoever remaining to suggest that these areas had been remade in the image of the future just a generation before. Even the estates which remain to this day, the ones that were built properly and without major flaws and defects, are still incredibly vulnerable, as they frequently sit on land which property developers (and local governments) consider too valuable to be wasted on the tenants who currently live there.

This world of system-built estates did not die out altogether, of course. The Eastern Bloc continued building panel-constructed housing, vari-ously known as 'plattenbau', 'Khrushchyovka', 'panelák', right up to the fall of the Berlin Wall, and in South-east Asia they continue to be built. But for various reasons – lack of choice, commitment to state provision, lesser inequality and perhaps a lack of nostalgic aesthetic conservatism – there has been no aggressive public reaction against the method nor large-scale demolitions. Meanwhile in cities such as New York, vast numbers of people still live in the 'towers in the park' that so incensed Jane Jacobs more than fifty years ago.

In the UK, where post-war housing was perhaps more ambitious and certainly more politically contested, there are some areas where the production of a new experimental urban landscape still remains more or less intact, and these can be strange locations, places out of time. Perhaps the most famous is Thamesmead, an area at the very edge of south-east London along the Thames. The estate was conceived in the mid-1960s by the newly created Greater London Council, whose enlarged scope, created by amalgamating the planning powers of various London boroughs, allowed them to propose the creation of a single estate that eventually housed as many as 100,000 people. On land that stretched from a ruined medieval abbey in the south across flat marshland to the banks of the river Thames, planners set to work devising new roads, infrastructure, housing, lakes, marinas and landscaping, and began building the factories that would pre-fabricate the concrete panels making up the estate.

The urban designs for Thamesmead, as displayed to the public by a huge model of the area in 1967, appeared as a summation of experimental ideas for housing strategies and policy. A variety of housing types was apparent – tower blocks, deck-access terrace blocks regularly arranged

Varying the system: Thamesmead

in rows, and long housing spines many kilometres long snaking over the landscape. Road and rail links threaded through the scheme to link it to central London, and a new town centre would be constructed to act as the urban focus for the whole scheme. Although not in itself a new town, Thamesmead's eventual population was comparable in size, but none of the New Towns (apart from, of course, the unbuilt Hook) would propose areas of such consistently designed, experimentally planned urban form.

The first phases of Thamesmead were on-site by the end of the 1960s, gradually being filled by the council in a more tightly controlled manner than usual by giving priority to extended families, thus attempting to avoid the anomie that had already been noted in many new estates. The earlier phases to the south were entirely raised off the ground partly because the land was on a flood-plain, but also due to then-current thinking of traffic segregation. The panel construction was a hybrid design, using irregularly shaped panels as well as rectangular ones, a complication which allowed for the creation of roof terraces in the ziggurat housing form that so enticed that generation.

Large lakes were dug as part of a strong landscaping strategy, and schools and an architecturally ambitious medical centre were part of the mix. Most remarkable, though, were the spines of housing – highly complex single buildings stretching along the edge of the estate, with raised walkways on a number of levels, rising and falling in height. The houses (in a variety of shapes) stacked up in a cellular arrangement which had much in common with the megastructural designs of Safdie, Archigram and many others.

As it went up, Thamesmead appeared to be quite a success, a vindication of the radical ideas for the future of housing that had been brewing over this time. But despite appearances, there were misgivings from within the architectural world. Banham, in *Megastructures*, looked at Thamesmead, still under construction a decade after its beginning, as a warning rather than an encouragement: 'The ultimate tombstone of the institutionalized and run-down concept of megastructure must be the largest and most terminal monster of them all: Thamesmead.'[4]

---

4   Banham, *Megastructures*, p. 190

According to Banham, part of the problem with Thamesmead was letting experimental ideas get into 'the hands of average salaried architects'. He considered Thamesmead a megastructure without the overarching frame, designed not by his friends such as Archigram, but by council architects. Banham worried that the monotony of grey form across the entire estate, with little opportunity for local customisation, would render the area impossible as a viable urban form. Indeed, Thamesmead gave Banham the opportunity to ask one final damning question of megastructure as a whole:

> Is it humanly credible that one man, or one design team, can genuinely conceive a single unified architectural system that can serve all the needs of a growing city for the first half century or so of its life?[5]

It wasn't just Banham, however. Stanley Kubrick's film version of *A Clockwork Orange* has some of the most infamously chosen architectural settings in cinema history. In this dystopian satire of government attempts to meddle in morality, modernist architecture is deployed to devastating effect. The scene of the protagonist Alex's most horrendous crime is a luxury house designed in the 1960s by Team 4, a practice made up of Norman Foster and Wendy Cheeseman, Richard and Su Rogers, while the sinister Ludovico Institute where Alex is experimented upon is played by the brutalist lecture halls at Brunel University.

Most spectacularly, however, the Thamesmead area of Southmere is used as the estate where Alex lives and goes about his terrorising, and a walkway down the side of one of the lakes is the setting for a particularly chilling part. Elsewhere, the obnoxiously groovy Chelsea Drugstore – the interior design, clothes and make-up of the characters, almost the whole production design – caricatures perfectly the mash of grey modernism and garish consumer taste that defined much of the aesthetics of the 1970s. *A Clockwork Orange*, despite being withdrawn by Kubrick after tabloid reports of copy-cat violence, still played its part as a preparation for the generalised depiction of working-class modernist

---

5   Ibid, p. 192.

housing as a world of squalor and danger which would come in later decades.

In the real world, Thamesmead suffered plenty of the problems of other estates. Despite best intentions, facilities constructed were thin on the ground and there was a distinct lack of shops, while the transport infrastructure that was promised never materialised to connect the area to London effectively. There were some issues with the construction, but not enough to warrant demolition, and the majority of the estate still stands. Later phases of construction moved away from the original architectural vision and provide a strange lesson in the history of housing architecture from the 1970s on. The second phase was still mostly system-built but was less bold and thus cheaper, with walls of taller deck-access flats surrounding smaller terraces on streets whose addresses include 'Malthus Path', a peculiar and perturbing name for state-built housing for the working classes. Later developments, moving north towards the Thames, involved an abandonment of high-rise in all its forms and featured creative attempts to enliven vernacular idioms with the modernist innovations of the previous decades. However, by the time Thamesmead Town Centre was constructed in the 1980s, it was built in a thoroughly postmodern, quasi-vernacular idiom, with pitched roofs and arches, a wholesale rejection of the modernist era.

There is a strange irony that becomes apparent upon visiting Thamesmead today. As one of the last large-scale industrialised modern developments, it is an environment of uncompromising consistency. The estates may be mostly low-rise, but the repetition serves to heighten the spatial experience, especially when walking on the many paths with their long vistas and channelled perspectives. But the monotony that so troubled Banham has been subverted in different ways: almost all of the houses have replaced their original timber window frames, meaning that there is a fantastic variety of visual treatments of the windows, including many historicist ones. Furthermore, the external spaces, whether terraces or small gardens, have frequently been augmented and redesigned by the residents to their own idiosyncratic tastes, a sort of Thamesmead vernacular. In all, it means that despite the repetitiveness of the housing forms themselves, there is a great variety of customisation, which in fact goes a

Bucolic modernity: Thamesmead

little way towards embodying Habraken's notion of support structures – a tantalising glimpse of the megastructural dream after all.

Furthermore, despite its greyness, and despite having suffered rather significant poverty and its related troubles, the areas of Thamesmead around the lake are genuinely beautiful, with flats that open almost directly out onto a large body of water, nesting waterfowl and abundant fishing, and roaming horses which belong to local travelling communities. At the time of writing, Thamesmead is due to be finally connected to the centre of London via a new train link, and rumours abound that, thanks to the crippling housing crisis, it will soon be a place to buy relatively cheap property. Whether this entails another round of wholesale redevelopment or the bourgeoisie finally coming to terms with their distaste for the aesthetics of industrialised modernity remains to be seen.

Chapter 5

Cybernetic Dreams

The 1960s was a decade of rejection. A growing proportion of people vociferously and wholeheartedly abandoned the status quo, along with the notion of progress that it entailed. This was not a rejection based upon political conservatism but a widely felt desire for political and personal revolution to sweep away the stagnant world of the bureaucratic military-industrial complex. In the late 1960s, the civil rights movement, the war in Vietnam, the rise of youth culture and new assertions of personal freedom all inspired a great number of experiments in new ways of living. In many cases, these new ways of life involved the creation of completely new spaces in which to live, whether this involved squatting, communes, eco-communities or other models.

These movements were in the hands of an educated youth who felt betrayed by their parents' generation, their conformity and their complicity in the horrors of recent decades. Technological advances seemed to be offering more to the world, but the premises of technological society were increasingly questioned, both by those who called for the outright rejection of this society and by others who felt that a new utopia could be built by redirecting its incredible energies. This was a period in which the world first became aware of the impacts of computer technology, and the germinal intellectual cultures around this new form of machine began to change the way people viewed the world. New forms of knowledge, especially the developing field of cybernetics, inspired the establishment and counterculture, capitalists and socialists, intensifying battles over who held the key to the future. And through it all, in the background at first but growing in intensity throughout the period, was a new knowledge of the limits of the world, a sense that what had seemed abundant was fragile, and that natural systems were delicately balanced and vulnerable to destruction.

Herbert Marcuse was a German political philosopher, born at the end of the ninteenth century, with an intellectual background deriving from Hegel and Marx. One of the primary members of the Frankfurt School, along with Theodor Adorno and Max Horkheimer, he had emigrated to the USA in the 1930s. In 1964, while teaching at Brandeis University, he published a book entitled *One-Dimensional Man*, which touched a nerve far outside of the normal audience for such academic publishing. Almost instantly, Marcuse became a galvanising influence on a new generation of left-wing activists in the late 1960s.

The book itself was a melancholy call to recognise that the modern systems of administration that had arisen in the post-war Fordist society had, despite their ability to tend efficiently to needs, comforts and immediate desires, also begun to close off the very possibility of ever radically changing that society. Opposed to the scientific rationalism that he saw as the dominant intellectual character of Western society, Marcuse's own method was a negative, dialectical analysis, which traced all the different ways in which critical thought was thwarted in the modern world. Marcuse described his own method as 'two-dimensional', providing a pure negativity that was the only way to think beyond the ontological structure of society and thus create an opening for real, genuine change.

One-dimensional society was the complete impossibility of the negative, of change, of a kind of freedom that was not automatically channelled into harmless distraction. Modern 'administered society' transformed the social and economic activities that it required for its perpetuation into the population's own individually perceived needs. This was achieved through a combination of satiating comfort, propaganda and advertising, a process that led to the creation of a soporific, deadened world of cultural unfreedom.

One-Dimensional Man encapsulated many of the feelings of unease that new Western generations were beginning to feel towards the societies they were growing up in. The social conformity; the cheapening of culture; the acceptance of injustice, terror and exploitation; the political quietude; the incessant rationality; the comfort which appeared to mask a greater malaise: Marcuse provided an intellectual framework which could explain all of these problems.

> Scientific management and scientific division of labor vastly increased the productivity of the economic, political, and cultural enterprise. Result: the higher standard of living. At the same time and on the same ground, this rational enterprise produced a pattern of mind and behavior which justified and absolved even the most destructive and oppressive features of the enterprise. Scientific-technical rationality and manipulation are welded together into new forms of social control.[1]

Marcuse argued that scientific rationalism was beginning to make it impossible to even *think* outside of the system. Rational, 'positive' thinking was in itself a block to more critical, creative types of thought. He also criticised the deadening of cultural refusal, the possibility of art's critical power being sapped by its accessibility, its antagonistic potential negated through its very acceptance. This included not only the typical Frankfurt School focus on Germanic modernism in music, literature and art, but also involved discussions of architecture. In an almost perfect rejection of the trends towards amalgamation and functional overlapping, and the infection of all culture by commerce, he wrote:

> The artistic alienation has become as functional as the architecture of the new theatres and concert halls in which it is performed. And here too, the rational and the evil are inseparable. Unquestionably the new architecture is

---

1   Herbert Marcuse, *One-Dimensional Man*, p. 146.

better, i.e., more beautiful and more practical than the monstrosities of the Victorian era. But it is also more 'integrated' – the cultural center is becoming a fitting part of the shopping center, or municipal center, or government center.[2]

In his sophisticated analysis, Marcuse provided ground for what would later become standard tropes of the counterculture: a rejection of conformism, a distrust of bureaucracy, a radical refusal of the status quo. Despite being written in what now appears to be the straightened, almost dowdy dialectics of the post-war Frankfurt School, occasionally inadvertently comic in its bitterness, it connected with a whole new generation of radicals and their gut-felt desire for a less structured, less hierarchical, more immediately free existence. Marcuse suggested that although the technological society had been oriented towards almost completely stifling ends, there was still hope that it could be transcended:

Further progress would mean the *break*, the turn of quantity into quality. It would open the possibility of an essentially new human reality – namely, existence in free time on the basis of fulfilled vital needs. Under such conditions, the scientific project itself would be free for trans-utilitarian ends, and free for the 'art of living' beyond the necessities and luxuries of domination. In other words, the completion of the technological reality would be not only the prerequisite, but also the rationale for transcending the technological reality.[3]

By rescuing dialectical thought from its one-dimensional bounds, there was still a fragment of hope that the technologically administered society could become a technologically fulfilled society of freedom, where art, science, life and nature were all brought together: 'The free play of thought and imagination assumes a rational and directing function of a pacified existence of man and nature.'[4]

---

2   Ibid., p. 65.

3   Ibid., p. 231.

4   Ibid., p. 234.

One-Dimensional Man marks a connection between older Marxist and negative-dialectical theories and the new revolutionary libertarianism that blossomed in the late 1960s and early 1970s under the name of the New Left, of which Marcuse would become seen as a father figure. It, and later works such as *An Essay on Liberation* of 1969, gave intellectual succour to the student revolts and credence to ideas of radical refusal, as well as the prospect that the processes of technology could, in theory, be set free from the real technologically controlled society, leading to authentic freedom for all.

The Technological Society by Jacques Ellul, also published in 1964, was another influential book that positioned itself squarely against technological optimism. In this work Ellul, a leading French sociologist, attempted to provide a comprehensive understanding of 'technique', referring not to machinery or technology per se, but to the logic of rationalism and development that accompanies them. According to Ellul, machinery and technology had to be integrated into society through the development of technique, meaning planned behaviour, evaluation of life on numerical terms, and utilitarianism:

> It might be said that technique is the translation into action of man's concern to master things by means of reason, to account for what is subconscious, make quantitative what is qualitative, make clear and precise the outlines of nature, take hold of chaos and put order into it.[5]

Understood this way, it appeared to Ellul that technique had become the sole master of society, where any new mechanical or industrial development had to be put to use, not for reasons of value but for its own sake. Humans themselves were becoming slaves to their machinery, to the unstoppable logic of technique:

> No technique is possible when men are free. When technique enters into the realm of social life, it collides ceaselessly with the human being to the degree

---

5   Jacques Ellul, *The Technological Society*, p. 44.

that the combination of man and technique is unavoidable, and that technical action necessarily results in a determined result.[6]

In this Fordist world of metrics and measurements, production lines,
atomic bombs, freeways and technocratic conformity, Ellul saw technique as unstoppable. It was a process that could not be diverted to other
ends: each new step, each new efficiency created unintended effects that
made necessary new developments in technique, which in turn had their
own effect of increasing technical demands. Ellul argued that unless
something was done to arrest this process, society would race off into a
socially homogenous, technologically sophisticated fascism, where nature
would cease to exist in any meaningful sense, where human beings were
completely and totally unfree:

> When we reflect on the serious although relatively minor problems that
> were provoked by the industrial exploitation of coal and electricity, when
> we reflect that after a hundred and fifty years these problems are still not sat-
> isfactorily resolved, we are entitled to ask whether there are any solutions to
> the infinitely more complex 'hows' of the next forty years. In fact, there is one
> and only one means to their solution, a world-wide totalitarian dictatorship
> which will allow technique in its full scope and at the same time resolve the
> concomitant difficulties.[7]

Here, then, was another alarm call, but one that held out no hope for a
technological freedom. Instead of Marcuse's assertion that there could be
a technologically developed 'pacified life' of freedom, Ellul saw a logic
to the use of technology that inevitably led to terrible conclusions. Ellul
calmly predicted a science fiction dystopia in the pages of an academi-
cally published book of anthropology, assuring the reader that he was
in no way a pessimist. We might look back now and consider it a little
ironic that Ellul could find Keynesian economics far more threatening
to human dignity than the potential of a return to laissez-faire, but *The*

6   Ibid., p. 138.

7   Ibid., p. 433.

Technological Society also struck a chord with the young, with its implied call to radically abandon technological development.

These and other books – such as Lewis Mumford's *The Myth of the Machine*, published in 1967 – seriously refuted the techno-optimism that underpinned the prevailing Zeitgeist. The interdisciplinary methods of scientists developed during WWII had been cultivated by the US after the war ended, creating a well-funded matrix of intellectuals from military, scientific and social fields, developing new systems for running the government. Money that had been poured into research on weaponry and the space race, necessitated by the competition of the Cold War, also found itself percolating into research on computing, psychology, sociology and many other fields, creating a boom in the humanities as well as the sciences and allowing many social scientists to become powerful figures in government.

American economists and sociologists provided the conceptual framework for these processes, analysing the growth of intellectual labour within the US economy and promoting the idea that the universal wealth created by high-tech and non-manual work would provide America with the edge in the Cold War. Close to power in a way that's almost impossible to imagine sociologists being today, thinkers such as Daniel Bell wrote works for the US government that mixed utopian interpretations of information technology drawn from Marshall McLuhan with more materialist historical analysis drawn from many of the authors' own disavowed Marxist backgrounds. In books such as *The Coming of Post-Industrial Society*, Bell set forth a view of the world where automation and bureaucratic, planned administration reduced the burden of work and raised living standards, leading to a society where everyone could be a creative knowledge worker and where the major driver of the economy was services rather than industrial manufacture.

This premonition of a high-tech, post-industrial society was highly attractive to the US government, then at the very height of its industrial and technical dominance. The Soviets' early lead in the space race was over, and heavy military investment in companies like IBM was paying dividends. The countries around the world that were within the US orbit also felt the influence of this technocratic ideal, and it was undoubtedly attractive to the corporations whose innovativeness and power it flattered. At its most extreme, this vision promised an end to the ideological battle between capitalism and socialism, whose futurological attraction of a society without class struggle and exploitation would be rendered moot by administered capitalism's delivery of a better life for all.

What united both promoters and critics of this technical utopianism was a faith in the promise of a life relieved of drudgery. Thus, the primary hinge around which the opposing arguments were structured was whether or not the new consumer society was in any sense 'free'. For the optimists, working in a bureaucratic capitalism meant that more people were more comfortable, with greater wealth and more time in which to spend it.

But the counterargument was that this leisure was effectively circumscribed by a huge web of subtle propaganda, making it harder to be truly critical of a society which was spending billions of dollars on nuclear weapons and continuing to wage war abroad, not to mention suppressing large numbers of its own population purely on the basis of their race or class. But in many respects the goal was the same – a life of freedom from compulsion, where human faculties could be engaged to their fullest, where creativity flourished. It was a recurrent theme in dreams of the future, whether in the form of a technological communism, an anarchic turn to smaller communities or in the ongoing transition to intellectual work in an ever-wealthier capitalism.

In architecture, this sense that people in the future would have more time away from work, free from the pursuit of base sustenance, was a driving factor in many of the visions of the period. Archigram, among many others, wondered how the city could accommodate all the commercial and leisure activities that it was going to require in the near future. The promise of the so-called 'three-day working week' was a defining factor looming over the development of architectural planning throughout the 1960s, not only in the mainstream of architecture but also in the more abstract and revolutionary proposals of the period.

*   *   *

Yona Friedman was a Hungarian-born French architect who, like the younger Safdie, had spent time around Haifa in the years after WWII. During the 1950s he had operated on the periphery of radical architectural groups such as Team 10, building little but developing a body of conceptual work that was to have great influence over coming generations. Around the turn of the 1960s he developed a project that he called the 'Ville Spatiale', which he described and depicted through essays, drawings and photo-collages. Many of these showed typical street scenes in Paris, over which Friedman scribbled the skeleton of a space frame propped up to a level high above the Haussmann-era roof level. This frame, sketched in black ink, was mostly empty but interspersed with all manner of solid spaces in seemingly random arrangements.

The Ville Spatiale presented the idea that the coming world of leisure time and freedom through technological automation was likely to make traditional architecture redundant. As a result, the architecture of the future should be no more than a frame into which nomadic subjects could build and rebuild their own homes wherever and whenever they needed. This was all fairly standard rhetoric for megastructure, but Friedman's work refrained from depicting anything in detail, consisting instead of sublime sketches of gigantic structures extending in all directions as far as the eye could see. On the one hand this vagueness meant that it lacked a sense of immediacy, but on the other it also meant that the revolutionary aims and potential of the new city could be expressed more clearly.

It is easy to look at the experiments of this time – the grandeur of a Friedman sketch or one of Archigram's sillier ideas like the 'Walking City' – and then conclude that most people were operating in the realms of science fiction fantasy. Friedman may have stirred debate, but the attractiveness of work like his occludes the genuinely experimental architecture that was being attempted at the time. Experimental architects frequently attempted to distance themselves from the everyday architecture that was being built at that point, but what becomes more relevant today is just how close these different streams were at the time. As we saw, many of Archigram's proposals were not as highly differentiated from current practice as they might have appeared, and while Friedman may have operated in a rarefied field, within a decade his ideas were already visible in the giant roof at the Osaka Expo.

A peak for this kind of conceptual treatment of revolutionary spaces of leisure was reached in the mid-1960s by Constant Nieuwenhuys, frequently just known as Constant. A multidisciplinary artist, working at various points in painting, sculpture, architecture, film and writing, he passed through various important moments in twentieth-century artistic history. In the late 1940s he was one of the members of CoBrA, the radical neoprimitive, pan-European painting group, before becoming involved with Guy Debord and the Situationist International in the 1950s, as well as the architects of Team 10. Constant's primary contribution to architecture is New Babylon, an architectural fantasy that he worked on from 1959 into the late 1960s.

Originally developed in conjunction with the situationists (before a falling out and denunciation so typical of Debord), New Babylon was an abstract city depicted through model, collages, film and text, whose nomadic inhabitants would be free from all labour, living in an ever-changing spatial frame with no concept of ownership or employment. New Babylon was a hypothetical proposal based upon situationist notions

Constant's New Babylon

such as psychogeography, where the material of the city itself would be subject to the whims and imaginations of the inhabitants, *Homo ludens*: men at play.

New Babylon had only the barest of visual or technical skeletons, mostly in the space-frame aesthetic, inspired by the engineer Konrad Wachsmann. In its various guises it mostly appeared as a space-frame city raised up off the ground, straddling the landscape wherever it went. The details weren't necessarily the point, however – Constant was basically acting out the role of 'The Architect' throughout this project, and the 'designs' of New Babylon are perhaps better thought of as artworks with architecture as their theme. But what is most remarkable about New Babylon is the way that it manifested the furthest extreme of revolutionary ideas about space, ownership and freedom, the dreams of nomadic societies engaged in creative play.

Inspired by cybernetics and developments in computing, New Babylon was a vision of the technological communism that Marcuse captured ghostly glimpses of – a utopia. But it was a vision of utopia that reflected back the more quotidian ideas of the time: at the far limit of the possibilities of the city, it made clear the dreams of freedom that united them all underneath.

Throughout the 1960s, the internal rejection of American bureaucratic capitalism was growing in pace. Inspired by Marcuse and others, a new kind of leftist activism, less concerned with vanguardism and labour organisations and more interested in free speech and social activism, was growing on the campuses of American universities. Towards the fringes of this New Left were all manner of libertarian groups attempting to enact their own revolutions. What set them apart was a sense that change was going to come not from a process of engaging with the existing structures of society but as the result of inward revolution. In this case, the oppressive order could be cleared away through micro-revolutions – in consciousness, in familial structures, in ways of living.

During this time, as many as one million young Americans moved into communes, attempting to forge new ways of living separate from the murderous and oppressive establishment. Many of these communes were completely new settlements, and a number of these in turn created novel forms of architecture, models of the new world.

The image of the hippie is now so thoroughly entrenched in the public mind that some of the very strangest aspects of the counterculture can easily be forgotten. Those in the rural commune movement were frequently not in any sense running away from technological society. Indeed, the commune builders were often some of the staunchest believers in the transformative power of new technology, making experimental multimedia artworks and installations, pioneering many passive and renewable architectural technologies and construction methods. While some communes attempted to recreate pre-Columbian patterns of life, building pueblos and tepees for their new society, others became in thrall to Buckminster Fuller, creating delirious versions of his ecological technocracy and reinforcing the strange links between the military and the hippies, the government and the counterculture, that so defined those times. And eventually, some of those who fled the city as part of the 'back to the land' movement ended up as powerful members of new elites as the Cold War drew to a close.

Clark Richert, Richard Kallweit, Gene Bernofsky and JoAnn Bernofsky were a group of artists who met while they were studying at the University of Kansas in 1961. They were interested in experimental art practices, and influenced by the cultures of 'happenings' and early performance art, they developed a form of early conceptual art that they called 'droppings'. After a number of years in countercultural and anarchist art circles, they decided to head out of the city and form an experimental community.

While still at art school they had attended one of Buckminster Fuller's long-form lectures and were inspired by his anti-authoritarian futurism and his discussions of cosmic geometry, which immediately began to appear in their own work. Buying a single field in rural Colorado, the group established Drop City in May 1965, and with Fuller's ideas as their guide they set to work building their first domes, conceived as an extension of their art practice. These domes were built out of timber using rough calculations and trial and error to work out the geometry, rather than the highly complicated junction details required for a steel dome,

Trash futurism: Drop City

and they formed the infill panels by cutting sections of scrap metal from the bonnets of wrecked cars.

From such fudged beginnings, Drop City was joined a year later by Steve Baer, an inventor with mathematical training. He assisted the commune in creating a new series of dome structures, utilising the geometry of 'zomes', Baer's invention of an alternative circular domed geometry that eliminated some of the difficulties that geodesic structures themselves posed. Drop City grew in size, until eventually it consisted of a variety of dome structures, clad in many different colours of steel panel, a strange mix of high- and low-tech, a vernacular architecture constructed from industrial waste. Drop City has been described as a 'new shingle style',[8] a quintessentially American architecture, a futuristic version of folk art such as quilts. Buckminster Fuller was sufficiently impressed by the efforts of the founders of Drop City that he awarded them one of his Dymaxion awards for the settlement and its 'poetically economic structural arrangements'.

In this ragged collection of scrap-built domes, it was almost as if every different futuristic architectural tendency was being brought together all at once. The spherical domes, still in development for Expo 67 and already recognisable as military installations, here managed to signify not only ecology but also a primordial oneness, an existential circularity.

---

8   Felicity Scott, *Architecture or Techno-utopia*, p. 163.

But despite their 'back to the land' qualities, they were still products of high technology and development. Built from the detritus of American industrial civilisation, they were a most clear rejection of that world, but at the same time they subscribed to its belief in a form of techno-utopia. It wasn't that technology had to be destroyed, but the consciousness that utilised it had to be transformed in order to achieve its full potential.

Drop City attracted not only new members but streams of journalists, adventurous travellers and even architects, whose curiosity was piqued by this gang of anarchists going ahead and creating the new world. Not only was this the utopia of those who thought that architecture should be personalised and created by and for its users, but it was also an embodiment of the revolutionary dreams of a completely free society:

> Faced with a situation in which all 'survival is provided for' and all 'time is free-time', Drop City cast creative activity as a positive form of desire that filled the void created by exodus from normative social and economic expectations.[9]

Drop City inspired many others to form their own communities as well. As this process developed, communes such as Libre, New Buffalo or Lama sprang up across the plains of the Midwest, creating their own futuristic vernacular architectures. At the same time a whole new network of countercultural information sharing began. As each new group made their way onto the land, they picked up new techniques on how to build their shelters with limited and unskilled labour, and eventually started self-publishing simple books and pamphlets on how to go about it.

Lloyd Kahn was one such American who found himself drawn out towards the counterculture, beginning to experiment with geodesic structures after encountering Buckminster Fuller's work. He was commissioned to create a series of seventeen geodesic domes for Pacific High School, who were practising an alternative educational lifestyle in the mountains above Santa Cruz, California. These domes, which were the school's own utopian version of boarding houses, were small

---

9   Ibid., p. 174.

and hand-built but featured a wide variety of materials, including plastics, vinyls, even concrete. The school itself was fee-paying, but once there the students were free to do almost whatever they wanted, which basically involved sex, drugs, swimming in the lakes and being taught lessons by whatever interesting person might have been passing by at any one time.

Into this milieu of people taking the future into their own hands, building some kind of dream of what might be on their own initiative and at their own risk and expense, entered Stewart Brand. Born just before the start of WWII, he had studied biology under Paul Ehrlich (who would later become world-famous as the author of *The Population Bomb*), later studying photography and then spending time in military service. After floating around the edges of the New York art scene, Brand had made his way to California, visited Native American settlements and become involved with Ken Kesey's Merry Pranksters, the ephemeral group who culturally bridged the 1950s Beat Generation and the 1960s counterculture. He was connected to USCO (the 'company of us'), an experimental art group involved in film, video, happenings and psychedelics. He even took LSD as part of a government research project.

Brand was fascinated by the colliding worlds of experiments in consciousness, new ways of communal living, systems theory and cybernetics, as well as high technologies such as geodesic domes, computers and the space programme. After visiting Drop City and other communes, and inheriting a sum of money, he decided to embark on an endeavour that would bring all of these different worlds, and the people who were working within them, together.

The *Whole Earth Catalog* was born out of Brand and his wife's travels around the Midwest and the world of the communes, where they attempted to sell items that would be useful to the commune builders. But the project also hoped to share information and news about what others were doing. After these trips, they decided that a mail-order publication might provide this service better, and so they set to work. Assisted by the Portola Institute, an organisation dedicated to the development of computing culture, Brand began to publish the *Whole Earth Catalog*, a mail-order magazine with a difference. The subtitle was 'Access to Tools', and from a first cheaply produced pamphlet of 1968, the catalogue began to swell, inviting contributions from builders, scientists, hippies, anyone who had something to bring to the conversation.

Its contents were divided into different categories: Understanding Whole Systems, Shelter and Land Use, Industry and Craft, Communications, Community, Nomadics, Learning. There were adverts for all kinds of survival and building materials, instructions on how to use them, discussions of scientific developments, philosophical essays, questions and calls for assistance. In effect, it was a network of information for the small society of people who were actively creating a new world of interrelations, connectivity, small-scale high technologies, revolution from the ground up. It was a potent mix of high and low, ancient and modern, a cybernetic ecology of new informational worlds.

Within the *Whole Earth Catalog*, Buckminster Fuller's geodesic dome began to play the role of visual motif. There was no better symbol of this new interrelated informational world than the dome, which was both highly sophisticated mathematical object and esoteric cosmological symbol. The chords and connections of a large dome were so sophisticated that it frequently required electronic computers to calculate its structure, but a small dome could be fudged together with the bare minimum of unskilled labour. Metaphorically, the dome could stand for the earth, the cosmos; it could be a primitive, primordial space; its roundness could be seen as an antithesis to the 'squareness' of normal society. But a dome could also, due to its efficiency, be an object lesson for society making better use of resources. With its structure based on the complex interactions of many small and flimsy pieces, a dome was a symbol of the self-regulating cybernetic systems that were so capturing the imagination of these experimental counterculturalists:

> Domes, … like backpacks and calculators and many of the other 'tools' carried by the Catalog, became terms in a contact language of sorts that was evolving for communication between the world of high technology and the tribes of the New Communalist movement. Domes embodied the counter-culture's critique of hierarchical politics and the celebration of distributed 'energy' common to the mythos of LSD and multimedia theater, but also

the celebration of form, system, and homeostasis common to cybernetics, population biology, and information theory.[10]

Steve Baer, who had by then built a solar water heater for Drop City, marking an introduction of 'green' technology to the mix, published *Dome Cookbook* in 1968. Lloyd Kahn, using information that had been acquired and distributed via the *Whole Earth Catalog*, published *Domebook*, a ramshackle mix of instruction and anecdote in 1970, followed the next year by *Domebook 2*. These books provided information on techniques and methods for constructing domes, stories about just how people had gone about making theirs and what they were like to live in. They mixed cartoons with tables of mathematical formulae, anecdotes on drug experiences with essays contributed by Buckminster Fuller.

The domebooks were enthusiastically received by the more progressive architectural press, who watched these disseminations of Buckminster Fuller's innovations with interest,. At the same time, a historical narrative of 'alternative architecture' began to spring up that included the customised California houseboats of Sausalito and visionary builders like Bruce Goff and Paulo Soleri. Like many aspects of the counterculture, the dome-builders frequently found themselves in the mainstream press – *Time*, *Life*, *Popular Science* and many others wrote articles about Drop City and the new dome communities, while Stewart Brand himself was profiled in *Playboy* and *Time*. The USA's latent passion for the pioneer mythology allowed these young rejectionists to be portrayed as the latest in a long line of American free spirits.

Cybernetics provided the intellectual sustenance for all of these developments. Popularised by Norbert Wiener, the new multidisciplinary topic managed to bring together military scientists, anthropologists, mathematicians, sociologists, computer scientists, biologists, ecologists, anti-psychiatrists, revolutionaries and of course hippies, in a feverish stew of interconnected research and collaboration. From arcane mathematical beginnings, it spread to become a catch-all term for interconnected,

10   Fred Turner, *From Counterculture to Cyberculture*, p. 95.

self-regulating systems, inspiring perceptions of ecology and of political organisation, as well as feeding into management and computer studies. The origins of cybernetics were born during WWII, when scientists and researchers working on the war effort were thrown together and encouraged to collaborate in a way that was completely unfamiliar to them. Enthralled by the experience but painfully aware that all these fields lacked a common language allowing them to compare their findings, they entered the peacetime world with a hunger to find a way to communicate properly with each other.

Wiener, a mathematician, had spent part of the war working on anti-aircraft gunning installations, attempting to develop systems that automatically made corrections to the aim of the gunners, anticipating the possible trajectories of the target as its pilot attempted to evade the attack. By mathematically modelling the processes that governed the behaviour of both the gunner and the pilot, Wiener began to consider the concept of feedback, how the information in a system at any point continually affects the future behaviour of that system. As a participant at the Macy Conferences, organised to stimulate conversations between elite thinkers in different fields, Wiener noted that there was growing scientific interest in feedback, from new discoveries in the biology of cells to weather patterns, from electronic circuits to the processes of the brain. In the years after the war, with the increasing performance of computers allowing for advances in the computation of partial differential equations, Wiener saw that there was a convergence of thought occurring.

Wiener's *Cybernetics, or Control and Communication in the Animal and the Machine* was published in 1948. Noting the Greek etymological root of 'cybernetics' as a word meaning 'helmsman', Wiener introduced the theory as the study of systems of control. A common example is the thermostat, which constantly measures the temperature in a room and either switches the heating on or off depending upon whether that is above or below its setting. This is an example of 'negative' feedback, where oscillations in the system are reduced by the structure of the system, thus tending towards a state of equilibrium. The opposite, 'positive' feedback, is the process whereby an oscillation in the system is reinforced, thus sending it further out of equilibrium.

The universal context for cybernetics is entropy, the measure of dis-organisation in a system. Entropy, in accordance with the second law of thermodynamics, always tends towards maximum disorganisation – everything becomes less distinct and things fall apart. But all around us, from the burning of the sun to plate tectonics, from the weather to the existence of life itself, there are islands of negative entropy making possible systems of negative feedback, stable equilibria wherein things become more complex and differentiated. Mathematics was making great strides in being able to model these processes, and Wiener saw, at the end of the 1940s, all manner of possibilities for further research into cybernetics, and the prospect of uniting mathematics and biology, mind and machine.

This first book on the subject caused quite a public stir, despite most of it being made up of mathematical equations and demonstrations. As the field developed and more scientists and mathematicians became involved, Wiener then published *The Human Use of Human Beings* in 1950. It not only attempted to give a description of cybernetics and its uses that would be legible to a less specialist reader, but also widened the scope of the field to include possible social impacts and offered Wiener's own moral and philosophical take on the subject, as he explained:

> The purpose of this book is both to explain the potentialities of the machine in fields which up to now have been taken to be purely human, and to warn against the dangers of a purely selfish exploitation of these possibilities in a world in which human beings, human things are all important.[11]

Wiener was both enthralled and horrified by the potential of cybernet-ics. He spent much of *The Human Use* decrying the short-sightedness of humanity, the myth of progress, the inability for people to think outside of their own immediate self-interest. It cemented, right at the very initia-tion of the field, a moral dimension to cybernetics – the uncovering of the natural processes that maintained equilibrium, but also the terrifying ease by which positive feedback could occur, and thus the disintegration of all stability.

---

11   Norbert Wiener, *The Human Use of Human Beings*, p. 2.

Shot through with an elegiac sense of the *wärmetod*, or the heat death of the universe, Wiener's cybernetics contained within it a call to use this new knowledge for good, in the service of humanity and the world itself. This was done in the knowledge that all life was but an infinitesimal flash in an overall process towards total entropy:

> To those of us who know the extremely limited range of physical conditions under which the chemical reactions necessary to life as we know it can take place, it is a forgone conclusion that the lucky accident which permits the continuation of life in any form on this earth, even without restricting life to something like human life, is bound to come to a complete and disastrous end.[12]
>
> ...
>
> There is a very true sense in which we are shipwrecked passengers on a doomed planet. Yet even in a shipwreck, human decencies and human values do not necessarily all vanish, and we must make the most of them. We shall go down, but let it be in a manner to which we may look forward as worthy of our dignity.[13]

Wiener saw that cybernetics – in biology, in physics, but perhaps most of all in the new field of artificial intelligence – was a potential source of great good but could also become a terrible burden if put directly into the service of industrial capitalism. In this, Wiener's work is remarkably similar to the arguments that were made a decade later by thinkers such as Marcuse as they despaired over the deadened Cold War bureaucracy. From the very beginning, Wiener's cybernetics carried with it a latent critical edge, where its insights promised to both revolutionise human life but also point out just how tenuous the status quo actually was.

Of course, a field of such promise could not remain the ideological property of just one thinker. Within a few years, all manner of research was going on in cybernetics, with the American military funding huge

---

12   Ibid., p. 25.
13   Ibid., p. 26.

amounts of electronics, computing and systems research. Fields such as artificial intelligence and game theory deployed similar mathematical methods, but in the service of developing systems for nuclear strategy in the Cold War, or for improving supply chains and distribution under Fordism.

Mathematicians in the US such as John von Neumann and Claude Shannon (both Macy Conference attendees) worked on systems and information theories which greatly assisted in the development of networks, cryptography and other emerging fields in the world of computing. Meanwhile other scientists such as Herbert Simon or J. C. R. Licklider developed links between economics, sociology and artificial intelligence. This immense and fertile world of theoretical work was being funded by the boom in academic research, where abstract and conceptual developments were applied to new military technology and methods, eventually finding their way into the public sphere. Despite the left-leaning and sensitive attitude of Wiener's introduction of cybernetics to the world, throughout the 1950s its insights were being developed according to the aims of the military-industrial complex.

The power of cybernetics, however, was in its conceptual versatility. For every establishment or militarised use of Wiener's work, there were radical and sometimes revolutionary applications. Intellectuals such as Marshall McLuhan took insights (and metaphors) relating to self-organisation and flows of information, and applied them to their own research in the humanities. McLuhan's *Understanding Media* of 1964 told a highly seductive story of post-Fordist society, where the 'explosions' of individualism caused by the introduction of industrial technology were being surpassed by the socially 'implosive' effects of electronic media. McLuhan coined the term 'global village' to describe the processes whereby physical distance and alienation were being eroded by the interconnectivity of the new electronic world.

The British anthropologist Gregory Bateson was another attendee at the Macy Conferences on cybernetics, and he brought its insights on interconnectedness to many different fields, from studies of indigenous peoples and semiotics to psychology and ecology. Bateson noted that 'cybernetics is the biggest bite out of the fruit of the Tree of Knowledge that mankind has taken in the last 2,000 years'.[14] He consistently deployed this knowledge across his various areas of work, exemplifying the synthetic role that was originally envisaged for the field.

Bateson attached cybernetics to the new thinking on the natural environment occurring throughout the 1960s. He argued from a similar position to Wiener's worried futurology and discussed resource depletion, population increase, positive environmental feedback and other worrying trends. In his pessimistic view, human society was in real trouble, but,

> there is also latent in cybernetics the means of achieving a new and perhaps more human outlook, a means of changing our philosophy of control and a means of seeing our own follies in wider perspective.[15]

Bateson, with his theory of mind, had a strong influence on a new generation of radical critics coming out of the European left, and his warm reception in the work of thinkers such as Deleuze and Guattari provided a quiet link between cybernetics and the postmodern turn in critical thought that was coming by the 1970s.

Elsewhere, cybernetics became, briefly, a flickering dream for the Soviet world and other socialists. After Stalin's death, Khrushchev attempted to modernise architectural production, setting in motion the Soviet Union's adoption of modernism and pre-fabrication. The early Soviet lead in the space race suggested that it might be possible for the Soviet Union to compete and perhaps exceed America on technical achievements; one field in which it seemed as though the Soviet Union might have been able to take the lead was computing, with the Party adopting computerisation across the economy as a goal for the nation at the 22nd Congress in 1961.[16]

The work of Wiener was becoming influential in the Soviet Union, with his left-wing emphasis and warnings against uncontrolled development. As a result, the notion of 'Soviet Cybernetics' was formed, having

---

14   Gregory Bateson, *Steps to an Ecology of Mind*, p. 484.

15   Ibid., p. 485.

16   See Richard Barbrook, *Imaginary Futures*, p. 160.

as its goal the implementation of the 'Unified Information Network', a conceptual forerunner of the Internet. A 'Cybernetics in the Service of Communism' promised to go a long way to solving one of the persistent problems in a planned economy – the setting of prices. Against the Austrian School attitude of thinkers like Friedrich Hayek (whose beliefs were still an eccentric fringe during the 1960s) that any and all attempts to artificially influence commodity prices have unintended negative effects, meaning that the only possible way for an economy to run efficiently is through the unrestricted setting of prices by free and unhindered individuals, socialist cybernetics promised to alleviate the long-standing problems of pricing in a planned economy, all ostensibly in the service of the people themselves.

Famously, in Chile in the early 1970s, the Allende government invested in an experimental electronic system for modelling resources. Entitled 'Cybersyn', it was constructed with the assistance of British mathematician Stafford Beer, who was another eccentric pioneer of cybernetics, working in the field of business management. Although Cybersyn was already active in the new Chilean socialist economy (ironically, its best early demonstration was in co-ordinating the breaking of a strike), it was abandoned after the Pinochet coup in 1973. Interest in Cybersyn has recently been revived, partly as a result of the appeal of the vintage futurist design of the control centre, with its plastic chairs and embedded video screens, but also partly because of the tantalising sense of a lost, high-tech, non-totalitarian socialism. That the Soviet Union abandoned its own dreams of being the leaders of the race for cybernetics and artificial intelligence, after the Prague Spring and the realisation that self-ordering network society was the opposite of bureaucratic control, merely adds to this sense of paths untrodden.

Architecture had its own proponents of cybernetics. From initial metaphorical mentions in the architectural press, the prospects for cybernetic planning and design became more serious as the 1960s moved along. For example, the September 1969 issue of *Architectural Design*[17], edited

---

17 *Architectural Design*, 1969, p. 494.

by Royston Landau, one of the main promoters of megastructural architecture in the UK, began to ask whether more mathematically oriented models of planning, based upon computing and cybernetic theories, might provide a new direction in which design could move as the next decades arrived.

Gordon Pask, a British psychologist and cybernetician, gave his own version of 'The Architectural Relevance of Cybernetics',[18] where he considered the possibilities for a more responsive, more systematic approach to the creation of the built environment. As far as Pask was concerned, a cybernetic theory of architecture would give designers and planners far more predictive power about the effects of what they were creating. He believed that cybernetics would help develop computer-assisted design procedures, draw in concepts from many different disciplines and lead to far more powerful descriptions of how architecture acted as a social control mechanism. Pask stated that the maxim 'a machine for living in' could be cybernetically reformulated as an 'environment with which the inhabitant collaborates', and that the upshot of this could be the creation of more a responsive architecture.

The hopes for cybernetics in architecture resonated heavily with various desires of the time. The idea that computation might play a much more prominent role than before was of course exactly what happened, and today the computer is the primary tool of architectural production. Furthermore, the desire for a more interactive environment is something that we have seen again and again. Interactive architecture was making a strong case to be the next significant field of experimentation, whether it was born out of observing the boredom and lack of ownership in mass housing as noted by Habraken and others, or whether it was the obvious tendency of an architecture industry that was adopting mass production techniques from the car industry, or even if it was just a general fascination with new media technology.

The cybernetic influence can be seen most clearly in the work of Cedric Price, who was a homegrown guru for the British anti-architecture scene. Thick-set, his face surrounded by a black halo of slicked-back

---

18   Gordon Pask in *Architectural Design*, 1969, p. 494.

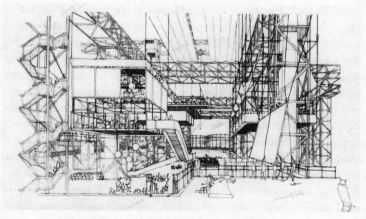

Cybernetic architecture: Cedric Price's Fun Palace

hair, the cigar-chomping Price was a jovial contrarian, fêted by the Archi-gram generation for which he was something of a wise uncle, consistently setting the intellectual pace with very little inclination to get much built. Price had such a lack of aesthetic consideration in his work that it almost constituted an anti-aesthetic, instead relying almost entirely on the mod-elling of the systems that made up the institutions of the clients he was working for. Throughout a project, flow diagrams depicting hierarchies of spaces and human agents would eventually coalesce into architectural propositions that were both utterly rudimental but socially exciting.

Price's most celebrated project, the Fun Palace (1961), was an experi-mental public entertainment centre to be developed in the decrepit industrial Lea Valley that more than fifty years later would be the site for the London Olympics. Designed with the theatre director Joan Lit-tlewood, the brief was to create a sophisticated physical infrastructure that could allow the visitors to adapt and reorganise the space depending upon their whims and desires. Through seemingly endless development with a wide variety of experts, the design for the Fun Palace gradually coalesced into a giant industrial space frame with a wide grid of highly serviced towers.

Inside this space – half factory, half cathedral – stairs and circulation could be reconfigured and internal spaces could be moved around by crane to create the spaces for activity. As part of the process, Price even set up a 'Cybernetic Committee' of experts, including Pask, to help develop the systems that would control the changing structures and activities within, and learn from previous use patterns the sort of arrangements that would be useful in the future. Eventually the project lost its funding and was cancelled in the mid-1960s, but only after it got as far as having its fire strategy submitted to the council, which is remarkable considering just how adventurous it was.

The Fun Palace has become one of the great unbuilt projects in architecture, inspiring generations of architects and in particular artists. Its social implications regarding public freedom and participation have been influential on 'relational aesthetics' and other recent artistic ideas. With its experimental space-frame architecture and the prospect of constantly shifting modes of activity, it was a high-tech space devoted to *Homo ludens*, and the closest any one project came to realising a part of the New Babylon dream. Of course, its failure to materialise means that it will only ever exist as a hypothesis, its actual potential for success rendered moot.

Price was the sort of architect who would claim his favourite town was the Stoneleigh Royal Show, a livestock festival lasting just four days a year, and he delighted in ideas provocative to received opinion, especially regarding conservation and heritage. The anti-aesthetic that Price brought to his projects was one way of defining its technological sophistication, and instead of the fetishised engineering that became the default strategy of those that followed him, Price's work prioritised cheapness, simplicity and by implication adaptation and replaceability. Cybernetics was an ethos for delivering buildings and systems that had the logical qualities of a circuit board, a new electronic functionalism.

One project, entitled Potteries Thinkbelt, was Price's attempt at revolutionising the university. A series of 1960s university buildings by Candillis Josic Woods, including the Free University of Berlin, had taken the radical approach to campus design and moved it in a more generic direction, downplaying the architectural dramatics and accentuating the systematic aspects of their designs. But Price would go a stage further: choosing various sites in abandoned industrial areas (the 'Potteries' of the title) with substantial railway infrastructure, Price suggested they maintain varying degrees of adaptability. Underneath short towers of pre-fabricated student housing, moving cranes would lift and drop teaching and research facilities that would be mounted on the railway sidings. Everything could be adapted based upon changes in the different functions and the needs of the student population.

Potteries Thinkbelt was the cybernetic version of the 'plateglass' megastructures of the University of East Anglia and the University of Essex, a vision of the sophisticated and adaptable, if rudimentary and totally unstylish, architecture of the cybernetic future.

The first edition of the *Whole Earth Catalog* in 1968 had sold only a thousand copies, but by 1971 the last edition was selling well over a million. It came to be seen as a landmark in the development of information technology and the culture of think-tanks and, eventually, as a precursor of the Internet. It gave birth to a new kind of utopian thinking that saw all bureaucracies as restrictive and suffocating, and advocated the free play of interrelated individuals as the source of emergent natural order. What's more, like cybernetics, the publication proposed a pivotal role for the computer in the coming world. At the start of the 1960s, computers had been viewed as oppressive tools of the military and corporate elite. But a decade later, the computer was also a symbol of the end of labour, the restoration of man's balance with nature and a harmonious future for all humanity.

In contrast, the 'back to the land' movement was, on the whole, short-lived. The attempts to create small communities with no hierarchy and experimental familial structures broke down into animosity and fighting, and nearly all of the communes were abandoned by the early 1970s. Drop City, the most emblematic of the dome communities, first shed its original members when they could no longer cope with the influx of stoners and hangers-on and was eventually abandoned completely, becoming an odd, scrappy ruin still visited by drop-outs long afterwards.

This decline was partly due to the age-old problem of the fragility of explicitly horizontalist social orders, all too prone to disruptive feedback.

It was partly to do with the fact that many of the counterculturalists were getting older and wanted to return to bourgeois life away from the struggles of living communally. It was also partly because many of the energies of the early counterculture were being absorbed into the world of pop culture, with music festivals like Woodstock providing a more carnival-like opportunity to drop out, temporarily, without completely revolutionising one's life.

The boom in geodesic domes, which had led to more than 60,000 being built throughout the 1960s, also came to a halt. Some people stuck it out: Steve Baer completed a radical zome house for himself out in Arizona, where a wall of water-filled barrels is used to both cool the house during the day and heat it through the night, thus eliminating the need for air conditioning. Baer's company, Zomeworks, continued to develop and market his geometric and structural innovations, still out on the land but also engaged in the wider economy in a more conventional manner.

Many of the communalists returned to California, where the *Whole Earth Catalog* had been published, and became involved in new countercultures there. Stewart Brand himself became installed in the culture of hacker communities, groups of young computing experts working together and in competition to develop their own systems. At the Portola Institute, academics from Stanford, Xerox and other research establishments had mingled with LSD-taking communalists, and their worlds would combine in the milieu of hackers and early programmers.

In a 1972 article for *Rolling Stone*, 'Spacewar: Fanatic Life and Symbolic Death among the Computer Bums', Brand explicitly made the connection between the development of small personal computers and their potential for liberation, and the dreams of an alternative future that had driven people into the communes in the first place nearly ten years previously:

In 'Spacewar', Brand brought together two visions of personal computing and linked them in terms set by the New Communalist technological vision … Both groups, he suggested, were high-tech versions of the Merry Pranksters, and the computer itself was a new LSD. Drawing on the rhetorical tactics of cybernetics, Brand offered up Xerox PARC, Resource One, and the Merry Pranksters as prototypical elites for the techno-social future.[19]

Brand, who by 1974 was under the influence of Gregory Bateson and his version of cybernetics, began to publish a new magazine entitled *CoEvolution Quarterly*, in which he and his colleagues discussed the notion of the natural world as an embedded set of informational systems. It was less optimistic than the counterculture of the '60s, less concerned with individual revolutions – a change influenced by the failure of the communes, the desultory end of the Vietnam War and the energy and ecological crises. Instead, the new focus was on notions of shared consciousness and the germinal foundations of what would later become the Internet. By the 1980s and the rise of the personal computer and dreams (and nightmares) of cyberspace, the world of the counterculture and its rejection of bureaucratic society had metamorphosed into the digital libertarianism that has come to be one of the dominant ideologies of the twenty-first century. The garage industries that later went on to become Apple and Microsoft emerged from a milieu of ex-hippies and ex-military researchers, radical individualists and drop-outs.

In 1976, the twenty-one-year-old Bill Gates wrote the famous 'Open Letter to Hobbyists', complaining about the fact that people were using the BASIC software he'd developed without paying for it. Since the earliest development of the technology, computer scientists had collaborated with and coexisted with the hackers and hobbyists, but Gates's open letter is seen as a turning-point, when the frontier aspects of computing began to be brought into the corporate fold. By the 1980s, in a changed political landscape where entrepreneurialism was treated as the ultimate virtue, the surface traces of the counterculture had all but vanished. Instead, the stage was set for the digital utopia to metamorphose from a digital communism exemplified by the sharing of information and expertise, to the world of billionaire gurus such as Steve Jobs and Gates himself.

As the enclosure of the digital commons was beginning, Stewart Brand was engaged in one last push towards a genuinely physical cybernetic

19   Turner, *From Counterculture to Cyberculture*, p. 117.

revolution, via the most unexpected of subjects. Through a series of articles, comment pieces and arguments, first in the pages of *CoEvolution
Quarterly* and then in a book published in 1977, Brand became the most
vocal proponent of Gerard O'Neill's space colony proposals. Drawing a
remarkably wide range of scientists, artists, authors, architects, psycholo-
gists and others into the debate, Brand thought that with the prospect of
space colonies, the potential for the technological leap forward that the
'60s had promised and the '70s had spectacularly failed to deliver, was
actually in reach:

> If we're lucky we may enact a parallel with what happened in Europe when
> America was being colonized. Intellectual ferment – new land meant new
> possibilities; new possibilities meant new ideas. If you can try anything you
> think up things to try.[20]

Brand's promotion of space colonies was even-handed, open to wide
debate and most importantly concerned with synthesis and further
development, with positive responses coming from Carl Sagan and Buckminster Fuller, who both saw space colonies as a natural step forward
in the development of human society; cautious but intrigued calls for
further investigation from Paul and Anne Ehrlich, Lynn Margulis and
James Lovelock; and outright rejections from the likes of Steve Baer and
Lewis Mumford. The stakes involved in this project seemed spectacularly high, as Brand commented:

> If built, the fact of Space Colonies will be as momentous as the atomic bomb
> … On the other hand, suppose that the Space Colonies don't work, that we
> do find some fatal flaw. It would be no less of an event. 'We cannot leave
> the Earth' is a thought so foreign to the 20th Century that nothing would be
> unchanged by it.[21]

So in the end, the space colonies didn't just mark the limit of megastructure, of the architecture of the future; it also marked the point where

---

20   Brand (ed.), *Space Colonies*, p. 5.

21   Ibid., p. 72.

the cybernetic dreams of a nature transformed by technology flipped from the largest possible scale to the smallest. From the decline of the space colonies project, the spatial revolutions dreamed up by the counterculture began to exist entirely within the digital realm of the computer. Gone were pretensions towards large-scale physical change; from then on the utopia was within cyberspace, in the frontier lands of the Internet. The geodesic dome had been a symbol of the dreams of high-tech communal societies, but in their failure the dreams retreated into intangibility. Message boards and chat rooms became the 'spaces' in which people could transcend the limits of society, rather than communes and new settlements.

In this severance, something important was lost. Abandoning genuinely spatial terrain in favour of conducting battles in the frontier of cyberspace meant also that the fight over the ideas that had been so vital – over how people should be housed, over what rights they had to the spaces of the city, over notions such as dwelling itself – were completely forfeited. The stage was set for the social relations of the city and living space, which had been undergoing transformation after WWII thanks to changes in technology, wealth and progressive political reforms, to suffer a full-blown reaction.

Today's world bears the traces of this abandonment: while almost every experience of space, from shopping and travelling to the workplace and spaces of trade, has been technologically transformed in the last half a century, the house is the one spatial form where nothing appears to have changed. Radicals such as the Situationist International, Henri Lefebvre and Constant could see that everyday life, including its spatial manifestations, was one of the most important sites in the fight for a better world. Furthermore, the communalists as well as the planners detected that the places and structures of dwelling were ripe for change, and from different sides of society both groups attempted a revolutionary transformation of dwelling. But the transfer of utopia into a purely digital world is reflected in the stubbornness of the house as a physical, political and economic form, and also in the lack of a proper ideological counterattack to the resurgence of historicism and reactionary postmodernism.

The cybernetic future of architecture promised intangibility, the reduction of space to its bare minimum, space frames and systems, everything changing all at once. But this disappearance became total, and the digital future found it didn't need new spaces and new forms to create utopia, merely a plastic box on everybody's desk. But what was lost in that process? What happened when the city of the future became the city of the past?

Chapter 6

Reactions and Defeats

The last American lunar mission, Apollo 17, took place in December 1972, and since then no one has stood on the moon or even left the earth's orbit. At the time, no one would have guessed that this was the end of an era in space exploration, not least those who went on to promote the space colonies project over the next few years. But the end of the most ambitious phase of the space programme was not the only project for the future that saw its scope dwindle over the course of the 1970s. Throughout the decade, the future of architecture and urbanism went through a series of remarkable changes. The different versions of functionalism that had been the 1960s norm across almost the entire world were suddenly challenged. Gone was the passion for novelty, for a form of architecture intended as an appropriate mode of expression for a technologically sophisticated society, and gone was the trust in expert planning. In fact, for many, gone was the very belief that cities could be improved at all.

In the aftermath of the Vietnam War, the student uprisings of 1968 and scandals such as Watergate, cynicism seemed to sweep the political landscape. Radical groups in architecture began to subvert the utopian pretensions of their immediate predecessors and, in many cases, rejected a political role for architecture completely. This was reflected in two ways: on the one hand, there was a growing appreciation for what had been missed and neglected by the bureaucratic plans and designs of the previous decade – for what actually made cities worth living in, but on the other hand, there was also a visceral rejection of the modernist project that frequently swung into the realms of absurdity and that, despite its mostly good intentions, often played directly into the hands of the most cynical of political actors.

In many ways, the aftermath of the reactions of the 1970s still dominates architectural debate to this day and continues to hold back any real discussion of change in urban life.

On 6 October 1973, the Egyptian and Syrian armies mounted a joint surprise attack on Israel, attempting to recapture the Suez Canal and the Golan Heights, which they had lost in the previous war of 1967. Like so many conflicts during the Cold War, it became a proxy battle between the USA and USSR – the Russians supplied the Arab countries with weaponry, the Americans did the same for Israel. The war lasted less than a month, during which time Israel rapidly took back its early territorial losses and defeated the Arab armies. But as this was unfolding, OAPEC, a coalition of oil-producing Arab countries, initiated an embargo upon the US and its allies, rapidly decreasing oil production, increasing prices and instigating an economic and energy crisis.

In the 1970s, the post-war economies began to crack. The oil crisis exacerbated the economic turmoil already unleashed by the US ending the Bretton Woods agreement and floating their currency earlier in the decade. In the US and its allies – the UK and other industrialised nations such as Japan – petrol had to be rationed, causing sharp declines across the economy. In the UK, a 'three-day week' was imposed, in a mocking irony of the post-industrial predictions of the leisured society of the '60s, instead meaning that electricity for business was rationed on a day-on, day-off basis. As a result of the chaos, 'stagflation' occurred all over the Western world, and high unemployment coincided with high inflation, which challenged the very foundations of the Keynesian mixed economies. The rest of the decade was characterised by long, grinding industrial battles and economic precariousness, and was bookended by a second energy crisis after the Iranian Revolution in 1979.

While the US and Western Europe were going through their recessions, in the Soviet Union the Brezhnev administration experienced its own stagnation as the political, technical and social reforms of the Khrushchev era were rolled back or simply allowed to dissipate. South America was dragged into an era of military dictatorships. South Asia was still being torn apart by the aftershocks of the Vietnam War, while China spent much of the decade enduring the chaos and political power struggles unleashed by the Cultural Revolution. In this context, it was intensely difficult to sustain anything like the techno-optimism of the previous decade. The bruised and deflated world was virtually pummelled into submission, set for the rise of neo-liberal economics in the West, the final decline of the Soviet Union and Deng Xiaoping's capitalist reforms in China.

One of the many effects of the oil crisis was to shift focus away from the hydrocarbon economy and onto potentially renewable technologies. The abrupt end to the cheap oil that the advanced economies depended on meant that interest in solar, wind and hydroelectric power surged, while energy efficiency became an important area of official research. In November 1973 President Nixon initiated Project Independence, a strategy to achieve energy independence for the US by the end of the decade through investments in alternative energy and efficiency. Environmentalism became mainstream: this was the era of *The Ecologist* magazine, *The Limits to Growth*, and other spectacular interventions that built on ideas that had been developing throughout the 1960s.

In 1970, Alvin Toffler published his bestselling book *Future Shock*, a worried look at the speed of social and technological transformation in the 1960s. Concerned about the ordinary person's ability to withstand the rapidity of change and the rise of obsolescence, transience and the throw-away society, in the context of a world that had only been experiencing industrialisation for ten generations, he argued that 'unless man quickly learns to control the rate of change in his personal affairs as well as in society at large, we are doomed to a massive adaptational breakdown'.[1]

Among his anxieties about the rise of rejectionist politics amongst the youth, Toffler gave particular attention to the radical fringe of architecture of the time, mentioning Cedric Price and Buckminster Fuller, and hinting at Archigram when he noted that 'proponents of what has become known as "plug-in" or "clip-on" architecture have designed whole cities based on the idea of "transient architecture"'. For Toffler, these developments represented deeply worrying trends. He considered the changes inevitable unless something was done about them, and that they were incredibly dangerous for human culture: 'they all conspire towards the same psychological end: the ephemeralization of man's links with the things that surround him'.[2]

Toffler had hit a nerve: the rapid social change of the 1960s was beginning to seem as threatening to some people as it was exhilarating to others, and the calls for applying the brakes were getting louder.

Of course, the seeds of these rejections had been sown much earlier, and no figure embodies this rejection better than Jane Jacobs. An ordinary New Yorker, an outsider to the fields of architecture and planning, Jacobs was one of the principle organisers of a campaign to prevent the construction of the Lower Manhattan Expressway, creating a grass-roots movement which managed to halt the plans by 1964.

Jacobs was also the author of a number of books, most famously *The Death and Life of Great American Cities*, published in 1961, a bestseller that has gone on to become an almost biblical text for some architects and planners. What Jacobs achieved in this remarkably original work was to create a radical, ground-up theory of urbanism that went entirely against the planning consensus. From its description of the intricacies of social life on her neighbourhood streets, the layering of sight and gentle surveillance, the concern for others that was apparently fostered by certain aspects of these street relationships, to the economic uses and benefits of

---

1 Alvin Toffler, *Future Shock*, p. 11.

2 Ibid., p. 64.

dilapidated old buildings and loose space, it was a remarkably powerful counter to the top-down, statistics and modelling approach to planning.

Jacobs's nemesis was New York's arch-planner Robert Moses, who, in a strange and perfect harmony with Jacobs and her saint-like status, is now seen as something like a cartoon villain of the intersecting worlds of planning, politics, and power. He created the Flushing Meadows Park for the 1939 World's Fair and was the primary organising force behind the 1964 World's Fair, held at the same location. But he was also one of the most powerful political influences in New York, a planner who, from his rise in the 1930s, constructed massive highways, numerous bridges, set out a number of parks and public amenities, and cleared huge areas of slum housing.

Moses's incredible power, despite never once being elected to office, was fuelled by the political opportunities presented by the New Deal, where large infrastructure projects were being used to provide employment and encourage economic activity. And although his projects were all ostensibly for the public good, with many of them acknowledged to have been of great benefit to the city over the generations, there is a sense that they began to take on a life of their own, a self-reinforcing process of development, with the classic images of Moses gesticulating over models of his proposals a perfectly incriminating, quasi-religious image.

One of Moses's projects, the Trans-Manhattan Expressway, was the only one of his many attempts to plough highways through the city that came to fruition. It cuts across Upper Manhattan, linking two bridges at either side of the island in an almost straight line, taking only a slight bend to match the street layout that it blasts through. The expressway is sunk into a cutting as it crosses the island, is the width of a city block and includes a variety of other programmes as part of the overall development.

Pier Luigi Nervi, the Italian pioneer of the expressive use of reinforced concrete in bridges and other engineering structures, designed a bus terminal that sits on a structure over the expressway. It has a roof made of concrete trusses, slightly reminiscent of a space frame, and contains commercial spaces on one floor, the bus terminal itself and a series of on- and off-ramps connecting down to the snaking intersections below. Further along the expressway, built on decks over the road, are four 32-storey residential towers housing nearly 4,000 people, famous for both their large size (notable at this less highly developed end of the island) and also for their close proximity to the transport infrastructure.

Less architecturally accomplished than Paul Rudolph's LOMEX studies, or the autobahn housing in Berlin, the Trans-Manhattan Expressway blocks are known for the noise, fumes and vibrations of the vehicles incessantly passing below. Nevertheless, this giant unified complex was singled out for attention by Reyner Banham in *Megastructures*, who noted the low quality of the architecture overall but also remarked upon its resemblance to the Futurist visions of Sant'Elia. Banham also noted that it was by far the largest built megastructure in his whole study.[3]

But this kind of radical restructuring of urban form was, to Jacobs, a recipe for disaster. Top-down redevelopment crushed the 'ballet of the sidewalk', the intense interrelated networks of activity that occurred in traditional neighbourhoods. Thus, no real city life could be expected to thrive in these new environments. The greatest targets for her ire were the 'towers in the park' of the New York City Housing Authority (NYCHA), which after the war had built hundreds of high-rise apartment blocks, frequently with typically New York brown brick façades, set in green space. These were architecturally unremarkable in comparison with much of what was going on in Europe at the time, but as part of the Moses-era slum clearances and redevelopments, eventually more than 400,000 people across New York City would be accommodated within these public housing projects. For Jacobs, though, they were everything that was wrong about cities, and *Death and Life* is filled with tirades against Ebenezer Howard, Le Corbusier, their 'garden' and 'radiant' cities, and their gullible followers who were inflicting these monstrous environments on the people.

Nonetheless, Jacobs was not an architectural conservationist. She did not have an axe to grind over any particular style and did not reject modern housing on the basis of its being modern. Her complaints were related to the life of cities, which could only ever thrive thanks to the emergent properties of simple street relationships, rather than

3   Reyner Banham, *Megastructures*, p. 30.

the emptiness and lack of contact of vertical cities and Corbusian planning.

Death and Life did not change things overnight, but it gradually became a powerful motivating force for opponents of the strictly planned environment and defenders of heritage, awakening forces in architecture and the built environment. Perhaps the most powerful theme in Jacobs's work is the idea that cities have a complexity that emerges from the interactions between citizens and spaces but cannot be controlled or designated by any one authority. This is comparable to both cybernetic ideas of interacting systems, but also the increasingly prominent Austrian School ideas that planned intervention in economies will always have unintended negative effects. As a result, it's possible for Jacobs to be interpreted in very different ways, politically.

But for every brave rejection of urban orthodoxy in *Death and Life*, every challenge to received wisdom, there are frequent bald assertions of opinion presented as facts, which sometimes do not bear up to great scrutiny. Half a century later, we can also see that what is now known as gentrification was something that Jacobs did not anticipate. Where orthodoxy had it that substandard housing had to be destroyed to remake a neighbourhood, Jacobs argued that given the opportunity, and protected from massive gestures of destruction and construction, neighbourhoods would go through a process of 'unslumming' of their own accord.

While this can be seen to have occurred in many parts of American and European cities over the last few generations, Jacobs had believed that this would improve the lives of the residents of an area rather than driving them out through economic pressure. And for all her emphasis on the economics of cities, there is little acknowledgement in Jacobs of the fact that state provision of housing could provide protection from the failures of market housing, or that people could be vulnerable to gentrification and other urban processes that do not themselves originate from the tainted hands of the planners.

In 1968, the Greater London Council, who were then planning the Thamesmead Estate out to the south-east of the city, published a proposal to redevelop the area around Covent Garden in central London.

The fruit and vegetable market that occupied the centre of the area, set under a series of nineteenth-century iron and glass structures, was by that point considered unfit for purpose, and the traffic surrounding the area was under ridiculous strain. It seemed to be exactly the sort of issue that *Traffic in Towns* had predicted, where the city became clogged and unusable due to the inability to deal with the massive growth in vehicle use.

In a report entitled *Covent Garden Is Moving*, the GLC proposed that the fruit market be relocated to the outskirts of London where it could be more conveniently located for distribution, that new sunken roads be laid out across the neighbourhood to ease the traffic problems, that pedestrian decks be built to separate different kinds of traffic, and that much of the area be redeveloped for new housing and offices.

This was fairly typical of the plans for cities that were being made at that time, and redevelopments of this sort had been happening all over Britain, but the Covent Garden redevelopment became one of the first major conservation battles of the era. The ambitious scheme was already proving more controversial than usual when local residents, aghast at the lack of consultation and the prospect of losing not just their homes but a vital and irreplaceable part of the city, began to actively oppose the plans.

The Covent Garden Community Association was created in 1971, and the group campaigned tirelessly against the redevelopment, in much the same way that Jacobs had done in Greenwich Village a number of years previously. They managed to bring many outsiders on board with their campaign, from disgruntled planners who switched sides, to conservative politicians dismayed by what their colleagues were doing to the historic city. Even architecture students, who would have been expected to be on the side of development, joined in the campaign. Eventually, after an inquiry, the conservative government settled on a poisoned compromise: the scheme was given permission to proceed, but at the same time hundreds of local buildings were added to a conservation area, meaning that the project was all but cancelled. Eventually the market left for a more suburban location nonetheless, but the locals had won their battle, for the time being.

Voices such as Jacobs and the CGCA, arguing for the relevance and vitality of the existing city, were joined by waves of conservationists. For example, in the UK, the Victorian Society was set up in the late 1950s by a group including the architectural historians Nikolaus Pevsner and Henry-Russell Hitchcock in order to raise awareness of nineteenth-century heritage. Throughout the 1960s, it was just one of a number of new organisations and activist groups that attempted to shift establishment behaviour towards a greater concern for the historical built environment. Writers such as Ian Nairn or John Betjeman in the UK spoke up in the mainstream media for the merits of existing buildings that planners and councils were unable to understand. But what is often overstated is the level of iconoclasm that actually existed at the time.

There were indeed famous cases, such as Penn Station in New York or the old Euston Station in London, both of which were demolished, where large nineteenth-century buildings of great significance were treated with total disdain. But the idea that all historical architecture was considered beyond the pale was not altogether true, and it is important to differentiate between two separate situations. On the one hand, architects and planners studied architectural history, appreciated it on its own terms, but then designed according to what were seen as contemporary methods for an industrialised world. On the other hand, at times whole neighbourhoods were consigned to demolition due to broad-strokes plans, a belief that renovation was an expensive and inefficient approach, a generally blasé attitude to development, and in certain cases a culture of corruption in local government and the construction industry.

Overall, what really broke down in the 1970s was the belief that modernism was the most appropriate way to design for contemporary society. The pressure that had accumulated around the hope for architecture to move in a futuristic direction began to dissipate as the attacks on the modernist housing that already existed began to mount up. Instead, a new, backward-facing attitude towards the future was adopted.

What Jacobs in the US and the CGCA in the UK managed to achieve was to allow the voices of ordinary people to be heard in discussions on the future of cities in a way that they never had before. This was a genuinely empowering development that shows the level to which planning, which had been seen after the war as a vital task to avoid the chaos of the Great Depression, had become a symbol of the inhumanity of bureaucratic capitalism, with more than a hint of Soviet totalitarianism thrown in.

These struggles marked victories for ordinary people making their voices heard in a faceless system, but on the other hand they indicated a rising individualism in society, where wide goals that encompassed whole groups of the populace were becoming more suspect. And in later years, both Greenwich Village and Covent Garden had their communities hollowed out by unregulated commercial forces, leaving the historic buildings intact but the original communities dissipated, thriving local networks replaced by expensive restaurants and boutiques. This was a Pyrrhic victory, in many ways just as bad as losing the buildings would have been in the first place.

In the 1970s, the revulsion felt towards modern housing reached a crescendo. The economic crises of the decade put great strain on the social structures around housing – not only in the lives of the public who were living in these estates, but also for the authorities who were entrusted with organising and maintaining them. The optimistic reach in provision throughout the 1950s and '60s now found itself strained, with estates (or 'projects' in the US, the *banlieue* in France) becoming labelled as new slums.

In the UK, a still-unexplained rise in crime began from the late 1950s onwards, which tended to affect people in poorer areas of council housing, and this, combined with rises in unemployment and economic problems, compounded the troubles of the 1970s working class. These were exacerbated by well-meaning but short-sighted legislation such as the 1977 Housing (Homeless Persons) act, which had the unintended consequence of forcing councils to abandon their strict housing policies, in many cases leading to further decline in the social environment around housing. These factors, along with the faults and mistakes in the construction of system building, meant that by the 1980s the public perception of modern housing had reached a nadir and was vulnerable to all kinds of political attack.

Into these complicated situations with their intertwined problems arrived sociologists and academics who claimed to be able to explain the decline in mass housing through the very form of the buildings themselves. Like Jane Jacobs before, they argued that the urban structure of people living in flats accessed by lift and stairs, or the provision of large open spaces around buildings, created physical conditions that contributed to the deterioration of social order and civilised behaviour. In a bleak mirror image of the ambitions to create modern housing for ordinary people seen in previous decades, architecture was given a vital starring role in the social strains of the 1970s – indeed, the naive notion that a well-designed environment was conducive to social improvement was turned on its head: modern housing actually encouraged people to become delinquent.

Books such as Oscar Newman's *Defensible Space*, published in 1972, argued that a person's sense of ownership and responsibility for a space was a vital part of the process of keeping that space safe. But unlike Jacobs, whose research was mostly the result of her own observations and experiences gained while campaigning, Newman attempted to make the transition from anecdote to numerical and thus quasi-scientific analysis. He argued that in modernist housing, where large areas were of unclear (i.e., the state's) responsibility, residents were unable to assert their own authority and identity. Thus criminals could act with greater impunity, especially in areas of dense and interconnected housing.

Later, in notorious works such as Alice Coleman's *Utopia on Trial*, published in 1985 in an utterly changed political context, everything about mass housing, from multi-storey design to the number of doors, from overhead walkways to blocks raised off the ground plane – the whole gamut of modernist planning – were all accused of having causal effects upon social breakdown. Unable to analyse figures for unemployment and crime rates between individual blocks of traditional and modern housing, Coleman and her researchers had to make do with walking around and noting instances of graffiti, vandalism and, infamously, public excrement. Then from this data, Coleman claimed to prove that all blocks of flats caused delinquency, dismissing other factors such as unemployment and inequality, in an unpleasant display of social Darwinism:

> Living in a high-rise block does not force all its inhabitants to become crimi-
> nals, but by creating anonymity, lack of surveillance and escape routes, it
> puts temptation in their way and makes it probable that some of the weaker
> brethren will succumb.[4]

Debates raged within the worlds of architecture and urbanism about the methods and conclusions of these studies, especially when there were obvious contradictions – both the existence of luxury apartment blocks in their own countries, and also other countries without such stigmas against high-rise living. But the overall effect of these works was a huge gift to the conservative forces who were on the rise, and in whose eyes the attempts at modern housing of the previous decades had been dangerous socialist experiments. By blaming buildings for social problems, it was possible to obfuscate the complex and difficult forces that caused break-down in communities, and thus negate the state's responsibility to assist and provide support for these communities.

By blaming modernist housing, the free-market right could demol-ish state assets, sell the land to property developers, and simultaneously claim that they were performing a vital role in improving living condi-tions for the poor!

The result of this turning tide against mass housing was the rejection of high-rise, and in many cases new housing began to return to a ver-nacular and suburban familiarity. Gone was the excitement at the very modernness of the housing environment, which had been so clear in previous decades. Into this milieu, ideas regarding 'community' archi-tecture emerged, sometimes drawn from the failure of debates around adding choice to mass housing such as megastructure and Habraken's 'supports' concept. A new interest in informal settlements such as barrios and favelas in the global south, or famous books such as *Architecture Without Architects*, first published in 1964, led to a greater interest in vernacular architecture and the unplanned urban environment.

The commitment to the new did not just vanish, of course. The London Borough of Camden changed its housing policy to abandon

---

4   Alice Coleman, *Utopia on Trial*, p. 22.

high-rise construction but throughout the 1970s built a remarkable series of housing estates designed by modernist architects, which took as their models the traditional London streets that they replaced, while incorporating many of the functional benefits of modern design. Some of these buildings, such as the massive terraces of the extraordinary Alexandra Road estate, were prototypical megastructures. These estates were sometimes built in the face of serious political opposition, and eventually only a handful of these remarkable works of social architecture were constructed before social housing was taken clearly off the agenda.

Elsewhere, Ralph Erskine, the architect of the small arctic settlement seen in Chapter 4, embarked upon the design of a large estate in the industrial city of Newcastle in 1968. The Byker estate was a strange hybrid of high-modernist city planning with community consultation: as the thousands of new homes were built, Erskine set up office in a shop in the neighbourhood and consulted the residents as the scheme was developed. The result was a massive wall-building, a few kilometres long, which shielded most of the estate from the noise of a nearby motorway. This wall was filled with deck-access housing, and at a number of locations rose up to become high-rise blocks of flats. The scheme was as

Housing megastructure: Alexandra Road

programmatically experimental as any system-built estate, but had an abstract yet folkish style of detailing, with brick patterns on some walls and timber balconies in a variety of different colours. The Byker estate showed that it was possible to achieve both high-density modern housing and design that the residents felt that they had a stake in. Unfortunately, it was just one island of opportunity during these years of decline.

As the '60s moved into the '70s, the more radical architectural press began to feature experimental work coming out of northern Italy. At first it appeared to be more of the same stuff that had been covered before – giant space frames, structures stretching out over the existing city, endlessly flexible interiors and many of the other megastructure and cybernetic architectural concepts – but on closer inspection there was a darkness to this work, a bitter edge to it that came more from the left-critiques of technological society than establishment optimism.

For example, a project entitled No-Stop City, developed from 1968 to 1972, was the work of a group calling themselves 'Archizoom', a collective founded at the University of Florence in the late 1960s. No-Stop City, at first appearing as just another development in its field, is actually more like a cynical parody of the dreams of flexibility and choice in the architectural landscape.

No-Stop City depicts, in various drawings and models, an unbounded internal space, air-conditioned, artificially lit, divided only by a grid of columns stretching off in all directions and enclosed above and below by a large space-frame structure. Inside this space, humanity would live as nomads, moving around, setting up tents, plugging in at any location. In this sense it resembled the utopia in ideas such as New Babylon. But No-Stop City was based upon the premise that modern architecture was nothing more than a strategically deployed reforming strategy, attempting to ameliorate the struggle between the workers and bourgeoisie through spatial means, reconciling them both to industrialised capitalism.

Instead of allowing this compromise, No-Stop City depicted the intensification of the processes of industrialisation, technological development and capitalism in general, to an absolute limit of architecture and the urban, or 'a city without architecture'. It had no character, no details,

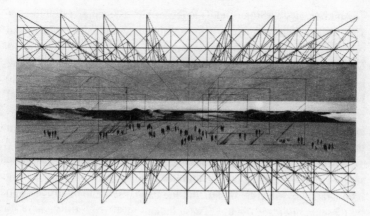

Architecture's limit: No-Stop City, Archizoom

nothing but an infinite space rendered comfortable through technology. In this way it was conceived both as the consummation of these processes and also the point at which their contradictions collapsed – it was designed as a revolutionary space, a utopia of quantity, not quality:

> A metropolis corresponding directly to the market, where any distinction of places and different functions no longer existed.[5] … A city without architecture, therefore, where the urban landscape (cityscape) was formed by large anonymous containers, merchandise, industrial products, the plankton of data, and the market.[6]

The success and failure of No-Stop City, viewed from almost half a century later, is that it cannot help but resemble the world of hyper-efficient office space, airports and shopping centres that was actually being developed at the time. Its predictive power was strong, but the acceleration that it foresaw has not taken us beyond the limits of capital, at least not by this point.

5   Andrea Branzi, *No-Stop City*, p. 151.

6   Ibid., p. 153.

Another group, Superstudio, took part in a seminal exhibition of 1966 called *Superarchitettura* with Archizoom, and had their own take on the critique of technological architecture. Their project Continuous Monument also parodied the space-frame future, with an utterly blank gridded volume shown stretched out across the world, interrupted only by mountains, draped across existing cities, appearing both blank and monumental. In this and other works, Superstudio mocked the counter-culture, depicting naked families of hippies cavorting sarcastically in their simplistic nomadic heaven.

Where Archizoom demonstrated 'cities without architecture', Super-studio's proposals were 'architecture without cities', critiques of the iconography of futuristic design and the capitalist society that conjured up those technocratic dreams. These Italians, unlike the Brits emerging from state architecture or the Americans from the fringes of the New Left, were creating work born out of the radical Marxist cultures of north-ern Italy, of Operaismo and Autonomia, accordingly their work had a far sharper critical sensibility than anything coming from elsewhere.

This ironic inhabitation of a design language, proposals which were simultaneously critiques, were to be a strong influence on the tradition represented by the work of OMA and Rem Koolhaas from the late 1970s to the present day. Thus it has had its own strong influence on modes of what is called 'critical practice', a way of designing that is not unaware of the contradictions of the modern city but reconciles itself to their con-straints through ironic detachment. Koolhaas's early conceptual projects such as 'Exodus, or the Voluntary Prisoners of Architecture' of 1972, bear strong graphic similarities to the work of the Italians, and trade in a similar critical distance from their often dark subject matter. But OMA ended up becoming massively successful, and debate continues as to the sincerity or not of Koolhaas's continued critical intent.

In addition to their conceptual architecture, both Archizoom and Superstudio and other north Italian designers such as Ettore Sottsass and Alchimia initially worked on interior design in a critically vulgar style, mocking the taste of the middle classes by taking 'pop' aesthetics to garish and unpleasant excess, utilising cheap materials like laminates and sub-verting classicism and historical taste. Ironically, in later years bourgeois taste moved so far out in that direction that it would become difficult to tell what was coming out of a ruthless Marxist critique and what was just enthusiastic kitsch.

If modernism was falling from favour, what was to replace it as the architecture of the future?

In January 1971, *Architectural Design* ran a short article written by Peter C. Papademetriou, discussing some recent appearances in advertising of a private residence by the young American architect Richard Meier. The house in question, the Smith House, was designed in a mode highly reminiscent of the 1920s international style of Le Corbusier – white surfaces, the manipulation of solids and voids, a building set in green space, with almost completely abstract details. The adverts depicted the building as a seductive space of leisure and wealth, with beautiful couples and even a personal helicopter. For Papademetriou, this was too much:

> Through a softening of the revolutionary overtones of its sources, it must appear inevitably as another form of packaging; one either currently available to a corporate capitalist elite or one to be aspired to. The dialectical tensions of Le Corbusier are gone, and the International Style stands before us finally to be recognized as a *décor de la vie*.[7]

Never mind that this recuperation was nothing new, with the celebrated 1932 MOMA exhibition on the international style just one in a long line of attempts to depoliticise European avant-garde movements. What was seen to be problematic here were two things: one, that avant-garde modernist architecture was now a fashionable lifestyle choice within mass culture, and secondly, that a young architect seemed to be creating pastiche modernism – designing according to a method which had been surpassed nearly fifty years previously.

A few months later, the magazine published a response from Peter Eisenman, a friend and colleague of Meier's, defending the appearance of the Smith House in advertising and also defending the house in general, with the rhetorical angle of pointing out the failure of modernism's claims

---

7 *Architectural Design*, 1971, p. 24.

for universality: 'In the end, what your correspondent may be objecting to, is that while he aspires to a populism, the Smith House aspires to high art and in the process it may also eventually become popular.'[8]

Eisenman and Meier, along with architects Charles Gwathmey, John Hejduk and Michael Graves, were the subjects of a small exhibition at MOMA that year, in which their private housing work was collected and exhibited. *Five Architects* showed that all of these young architects were working on different variations of the white functionalism of the early international style, mostly for rich, cultured clients from the university towns of the eastern US. The exhibition and the book that was published afterwards gave a worldwide boost to their careers, all of which would be globally significant through the rest of the century, but it also shows remarkable insight into the intellectual culture that would come to dominate architecture in the coming decades.

In the introduction to the exhibition, the head curator of architecture at MOMA, Arthur Drexler, provided what is almost an apology for the architects and their apparent turn away from the social and political aspects of architecture and on to questions of form and style. He expressed a fatigue with political architecture, or with architecture's claims for its own social function, and suggested that it was time to rediscover the art within architecture:

> An alternative to political romance is to be an architect, for those who actually have the necessary talent for architecture. The young men represented here have that talent (along with a social conscience and a considerable awareness of what is going on in the world around them) and their work makes a modest claim: it is <u>only</u> architecture, not the salvation of man and the redemption of the earth. For those who like architecture that is no mean thing.[9]

The breakdown of the consensus on modernism was creating a fractious and difficult environment in architecture. One way out of the situation was to simply give up on politics and move into questions of form

---

8   Ibid., p. 524.

9   Drexler in *Five Architects*, p. 1.

and meaning. An essay by the historian and theorist Colin Rowe which accompanied the exhibition extended these ideas further and made a case for abandoning what was by now a naive understanding of architecture's role in progress. Rowe picked over the narrative of functionalism, the idea that modernist architecture was somehow an 'objective' reaction to the demands of the brief and the constraints of each project.

Admitting that European modernism in architecture had definite socialist roots, and that these were elided or ignored when the style became globalised, Rowe took issue with the idea that modernism had a special claim on the twentieth century, on industrialised society, on the spirit of the age:

> The theoretical presumptions of modern architecture, located as they once were in a matrix of eschatological and utopian fantasy, began to mean very little when the technological and social revolution whose imminence the modern movement had assumed failed to take place.[10]

Instead, Rowe argued on behalf of the five architects, and thus architects in general, that notions of the Zeitgeist ought to be abandoned. Instead architects should find their own free will instead of attempting to follow a spirit of the age. Architecture was not as tied to technology or function as it was once thought to be. It need not provide a vision of a new or a better world, and the repetition of historical precedent was not anathema. Without mentioning the term, and long before it became common currency, the intellectual positions that would come to define postmodernism in architecture were thus set out.

The decline in the belief of architecture's social mission was accompanied by a blossoming of architecture's critical mission. A self-reflexivity entered the field, and at the cutting edge there was a decrease in focus on technology, social issues and the future, and a new focus on architecture as a language, a mode of cultural communication. In the journal *Oppositions*, centred around Eisenman and his milieu, many internal debates on the subject of architectural cultures went on through the 1970s. One

---

10   Rowe in *Five Architects*, p. 6.

of the early conflicts was between two different treatments of architecture as a language. In this debate, the five architects mentioned previously became known as 'the Whites', due to their source material, and in opposition to another group of architects engaged in reintroducing historical reference into design, 'the Greys'.

The primary 'grey' architects were Robert Venturi and Denise Scott Brown, the authors of the celebrated *Learning from Las Vegas*, which looked at the low-brow architecture of the strip with a seriousness that modernists had been previously unable to bring themselves to attempt. Their approach sought to develop various methods of bridging the gap between architecture and the public that had become so apparently wide in the reactions against abstract modernism. By utilising historical reference, symbol and decoration, Venturi and Scott Brown attempted to make an architecture that was more humane, more connected with its audience and generally more satisfying than the debased modernism that had become so exhausted.

While there were many high-minded beginnings to postmodernism in architecture, as the 1970s progressed the political implications of the ongoing rejection of modernism began to become more apparent. The interest in architecture as a communicative medium led to a resurgence of interest in Beaux-Arts architecture, the dominant civic style in the late nineteenth century, originating from Paris but widespread in Europe, the US and their colonies at the time, before being swept away by modernism in the mid-twentieth century. In many ways Beaux-Arts architecture was postmodernism before the fact, with its eclectic use of different historical styles and methods, and its focus on *architecture parlante*, which communicates its function and cultural meaning through formal and decorative motifs. Derided for much of the twentieth century as decadent and confused, even complicit in the imperialisms that led up to the World Wars, it had been generally considered beyond the pale.

But when Drexler wrote an essay to accompany a show at MOMA in 1975 on the architecture of the École des Beaux-Arts, it was now clear that it was time for this history to come in from the cold. Modern architecture, from its origins in the nineteenth century, had posited itself as a technical act, tied to engineering, technology and development. The eclectic culture that it had fought against saw architecture as something completely different – an art form that gave cultural meaning to the utilitarian structures that it sheathed. But now, in a period of dismay, Drexler argued that it was time to rediscover that distinction:

> What we may now see as the common ground of all historic styles is not structure, as radical thought in the nineteenth and twentieth centuries concluded, but rather the built metaphorical image by which value is declared.[11]

For generations architecture had presented itself in falsely refined terms, and as a result it would seem to have led to a number of failures and great mistakes. Perhaps the Bauhaus-ian swing had simply gone too far, and the built environment had suffered as a result of too slavishly believing all problems were technical: 'Our fantasy now is to escape from dematerialization, which we associate not with the world to come but with the disorienting technological world of the here and now.'[12]

And then, in a remarkably clear explanation of the flight from commitment in architecture, the exhaustion of deceleration, Drexler advocated a full-scale retreat:

> Most of us now understand that architecture is the least suitable instrument with which to achieve social justice. Without abandoning other responsibilities, we might yet wish to concentrate on what architecture and architecture alone can provide, leaving reform or revolution to those better equipped.[13]

The revival of Beaux-Arts thinking in architecture duly came about and provided the US and Europe with an architecture ready to embellish the era of Reagan and Thatcher. As technology continued to develop within buildings, such as new forms of air conditioning and mechanical services, the rise of personal computers both at home and within the

---

11   Arthur Drexler (ed.), *The Architecture of the Ecole des Beaux-Arts*, p. 49.

12   Ibid, p. 50.

13   Ibid, p. 59.

workplace, so buildings themselves became historically literate again, covered in decoration, luxury materials and joking reference.

The great giving-up of architecture as a vector for change that occurred across the 1970s allowed architecture to be gently swept along by the political forces that were remaking the Western city in the 1980s. Postmodernism was the visual language of the decline of industry and working-class life, the expansion in the construction of new spaces for accommodating the post-Fordist service economy, as well as its attendant leisure facilities such as out-of-town shopping centres and business parks.

If there is one figure with whom postmodernism in architecture is most strongly associated, it's Charles Jencks, active within architectural design and publishing since the end of the 1960s. His 1977 book *The Language of Post-Modern Architecture* truly cemented the concept in the public consciousness and provided the intellectual framework within which architectural postmodernity is still discussed. A lifelong proselytiser for variety, Jencks's career has displayed a remarkable desire over the years to create taxonomies and genealogies of architectural history, such as his famous diagram of a 'theory of architectural evolution', showing clouds of different movements and approaches to design spread out across a timeline covering the twentieth century, and the various connections between.

First appearing in 1968 and revised a number of times afterwards, in its early incarnations the future areas of the diagram were given names such as 'cybernetic', 'megaform', 'space colonial', along with others such as 'bureaucratic', 'pop' and 'revolutionist'. But when it came to a remake of Jencks's map in 2000, many of the futuristic terms of course vanished – there were no cybernetics, megastructures, certainly no space colonies, replaced instead with 'post modern', 'deconstruction' and 'high tech', the established narrative of what had actually came to pass.

The inconsistencies in Jencks's story of architectural history over the years are an excellent place to watch the ways in which a narrative that by the 1980s felt more or less fixed, was all the way through the 1970s still being contested, questioned and worked out. In 1972 Jencks, along with an architect called Nathan Silver, published a book called

Adhocism, which presented an altogether different way out of the problems of modern architecture to those that would later be widely adopted. Influenced by Jane Jacobs but also by cybernetics, in thrall to the space age but also neoprimitivist art, *Adhocism* proposed an approach to design based upon collage, juxtaposition and alteration, an ethos of all-encompassing improvisation that was an attempt to make it through the crisis of modernism through synthesis rather than negation: '*Adhocism* celebrates the impossible problem, the question for which there is no final answer. From these recurrent enigmas it drags an accentuated conflict which dramatizes the imperfection of things.'[14]

This attitude, aware of the problems of a vulgar universalism in design, concerned about the cul-de-sac that orthodox modernism had pushed itself into, but still excited by new technologies and the worlds that they promised to create, is one of the only attempts to broaden the scope of modern architecture and design. It included everything from the counterculture to megastructure (Silver wondered earnestly whether the raised space frames of Friedman et al. wouldn't perhaps drip too much onto the citizens below when it rained), computerised supply chains and material catalogues, the Parisian barricades of 1968, do-it-yourself and lunar probes. To a certain extent Adhocism betrays the influence of the *Whole Earth Catalog*, in its scattershot approach to subjects and its highly illustrated, matey rhetoric, but what it appears to be trying to achieve in architecture and design is a modernism with more in common with Joyce or Eliot, a modernism of everyday collage rather than the stern abstraction that seemed to have settled upon architecture.

Even after Jencks had elucidated his understanding of postmodernism in architecture, the recent history of architecture was still malleable. In 1982 Jencks, this time collaborating with William Chaitkin, published a glossy guide to the state of architecture at that point. *Current Architecture* (*Architecture Today* in the US) is partially interesting because of what now seems to be an odd shuffling of different methods and styles. The corporate design that evolved from the British high-tech architects had yet to

14   Charles Jencks and Nathan Silver, *Adhocism*, p. 77.

make its full impact, and the architecture of deconstruction was still a long way from being properly conceived. In addition, so many architects and designers were placed in what now appears completely the wrong place. Jencks gave more prominence than is usually now done to the cybernetic architecture of Cedric Price, believing that it would evolve into a more prominent strand of design. Also, alongside Jencks's advocacy for postmodern design, he attempted to understand various corporate developments as a form of 'late-modernism', a term that did not stand the test of time.

For others, the modern was decidedly dead, late or not. In 1980, the Australian art critic Robert Hughes created *The Shock of the New*, a televised history of modern art from the impressionists onwards. This was one of the last in the series of epic art-historical television documentaries that began with Kenneth Clark's *Civilisation* in 1968 and included John Berger's groundbreaking and politically radical *Ways of Seeing* in 1972. But compared to Clark's patrician air, and Berger's marxism and feminism, Hughes spoke from within the world of postmodernism, and his episode on architecture, 'Trouble in Utopia', is an example of just how deeply attitudes had changed by that point:

> This century has been an age of utopian propositions. They've been drawn, designed, argued about, sometimes even built, and in the process, it has shown that ideal cities don't work. To the extent that planners have tried to convert living towns into utopia, they've destroyed them. It seems that like plants, we do need the shit of others for nutriments.[15]

The entire one-hour episode tells the history of modernist architecture from the viewpoint of a culture which was triumphantly declaring its failure and uselessness. His guide, in fact, the only other voice who appears in the programme, was Philip Johnson, the upper-class American dilettante and erstwhile fascist, who in 1932 had co-organised the International Style exhibition at MOMA that had wiped the political commitment from European modernism, before he headed off to report approvingly from the German invasion of Poland. After the war (and

---

15   Hughes, 'Trouble in Utopia', in *The Shock of the New*.

much chastened after his misadventure), Johnson had spent a period working with and learning from Mies van der Rohe, before at the end of the 1970s he became one of the most enthusiastic promoters of neo-beaux-arts corporate postmodernism in the USA. Johnson's appearance speaks volumes about the tone of the episode, which has the denunciatory anger of the apostate.

Hughes utilised absolutist language for his denunciation of modern architecture. Standing before the admittedly rather preposterous 'clouds' housing development outside of Paris, a series of vertically extruded blobs with blob-shaped windows and coloured camouflage cladding, Hughes asserts that

> without respect for the body as it is and the social memory as it stands, there is no such thing as a workable or humane architecture. And that's why a place like this, La Défense outside Paris, is experienced by everybody, including those who live in it, as a piece of social scar tissue.

Without bothering to ask the children playing behind him whether they find their home to be a form of scarring, he continues:

> That is why so many of the classics of utopian planning have turned out to look inhuman or absurd, and why they don't work, and why the social pretensions behind them seem to be so much hot air. After this, who believes in progress and perfectibility any more?

At the end of the episode, Hughes visits the new Brazilian capital of Brasilia, designed by Costa and Niemeyer and completed in 1960. Sneering his way around, Hughes puts Brasilia forward as the clearest, most deliberate example of the modernist dream of the future city, before drawing his knife: 'The reality is worse than anything that has been said about the place. Brasilia is a façade, run up under political pressure, finished in 1960, and already falling to bits. Cracking stonework, flaking concrete, rusting metal. A ceremonial slum.'

This is accompanied, of course, by shots of various points on the vast main plaza where the paving stones have indeed started flaking away. But it's a total non sequitur to suggest that the whole city was therefore a slum. Had Hughes considered one of the many other Brazilian cities by the coast, he would have found plenty of examples of flaking paint and stained concrete, along with a whole lot more social deprivation.

> So what Brasilia became in less than twenty years, wasn't the city of tomorrow at all. It was yesterday's science fiction. Nothing dates faster than people's fantasies about the future. This is what you get when perfectly decent, intelligent and talented men start thinking in terms of space rather than place, and about single rather than multiple meanings. It's what you get when you design for political aspirations and not real human needs. You get miles of jerry-built platonic nowhere infested with Volkswagens. This, one may fervently hope, is the last experiment of its kind. The utopian buck stops here.

Not quite, but almost. The contribution from Chaitkin in *Current Architecture* was entitled 'alternatives'. Here, a whole taxonomy of countercultural architecture was given, from the Sausalito houseboats to mobile camper vans, from Drop City to 'outsider' architecture such as the Watts Towers, the boom in inflatables to low-energy housing. The juxtaposition of the two sections gives weight and credence to the alternative architectures, as contributions of comparable significance to the houses, offices and airports of the mainstream, of movements requiring their own explanation and critical context:

> Although the architecture discussed within these chapters is current inasmuch as its incidence is still influential, some years have distanced us from the events or spirit circumscribing its origins. Present detachment may even help put them into perspective. To my knowledge, the architectural history and, to a lesser degree, the language of alternatives have not been compiled before in this form.[16]

These alternative architectural cultures documented in the book were among the last examples of new forms of space, of optimistic attempts at changing the spatial and political form of the world and lives within it. They may not have changed the world as they had hoped, but

---

16   Charles Jencks and William Chaitkin, *Current Architecture*, p. 220.

Chaitkin expressed a hope that they were still having their effect upon the discourse:

> The naive and audacious Drop Cities of alternative America would never have been begun if their builders had been intimidated by poor prospects for accomplishment or deficiencies in skill, experience, and systematic direction; the whole movement was an amateur affair. Funkily unafraid, they went ahead regardless, and if the millennium did not arrive, well, that had not been their goal. What did result, tangibly, was new architecture. The uninhibited effort is doubtless still being made, in ways as yet undocumented.[17]

But even this would be closed off. When it came around to reprinting *Current Architecture* in 1988, it appeared without the section on alternative architecture, under the sole authorship of Jencks. Elsewhere, none of the main architectural histories of modernism make any substantial space for this period and its experiments, and they have ended up as a dried stream with little or no antecedents.

The only vaguely forward-looking architecture that actually survived into the 1980s was a gradual dissemination of the high-tech style. This may have had its roots in the 1960s architecture of Archigram and other techno-elites, science fiction comics and Buckminster Fuller, but it owed its success to its ability to tone itself down and become amenable to the values of globalised capitalism. We already saw a premonition of this particular future for architecture in No-Stop City, and in 1971 Archizoom could argue:

> The factory and the supermarket become the specimen models of the future city: optimal urban structures, potentially limitless, where human functions are arranged spontaneously in a free field, made uniform by a system of micro-acclimatisation and optimal circulation of information.[18]

---

17   Ibid., p. 222.
18   Branzi, *No-Stop City*, p. 178.

Also, in 1966, Constant argued with regard to the new Schiphol Airport in Amsterdam:

> [An airport] reflects better than any other building the atmosphere of the age that is dawning, of automation and of non-working man, and hence of the new nomad, *homo ludens*, playing man … The airport of today can be seen as the anticipatory image of the city of tomorrow, the city of man passing through.[19]

The architecture that carried the flame of technological optimism through the 1980s does indeed appear, at first glance, to be prefigured by the dreams of the 1960s. The sleek modernity of the work of Richard Rogers or Norman Foster, for example the factory buildings that they designed in the early 1980s, with cleverly emphasised structures, exposed services and almost featureless expanses of plate glass, was like a breath of fresh air when it appeared in the gaps between an out-of-date, discredited concrete modernity, and the new conservative polychromatic postmodernism.

But delivering an architectural aesthetic derived from the technocratic visions of the 1960s was only made possible by the removal of the political and social change that they were originally conceived to be part of, and understood this way, the fetishised glass and steel of corporate modernism is just another flavour of skin, which still subscribes fully to the logic of the postmodern world.

In coming to terms with this new world of a resurgent economic liberalism, of a new conservatism, this light, sophisticated, shimmering architecture had to be accompanied by the gradual disappearance of the very dreams that were invested in the anticipation of these spaces in the first place.

In the future's arrival, it turned out that this wasn't the future after all. But was this the end of history?

---

19 Constant, *On Travelling*, quoted in Wigley, *Constant's New Babylon*, p.66

Chapter 7

Apocalypse Then

On Christmas Eve, 1968, the three-man crew of Apollo 8 were in orbit around the moon. It had been a year of turmoil for the American public – the North Vietnamese had shocked the US Army and the public with their Tet Offensive, militarily unsuccessful but a massive turning-point in public attitudes to the war. Martin Luther King Jr. had been assassinated, as had Robert F. Kennedy, events that had stoked unrest across the country.

It would be another year before Apollo 11 landed on the lunar surface, but this earlier mission was about to give the world an object of great symbolic power, which for many would become a symbol of hope for the healing of social wounds. As the crew, Frank Borman, James A. Lovell Jr., and William A. Anders, came out from behind the far side of the moon, they saw the earth gradually appearing from behind the lunar horizon. Capturing the sight with a colour camera, the resulting image, depicting the earth half in shadow above the grey desert of the moon's surface, became known as *Earthrise*.

A few years previously, in 1966, Stewart Brand had been handing out badges in San Francisco with the slogan 'Why Haven't We Seen a Photograph of the Whole Earth Yet?' a question which fed directly into

Planetary consciousness: Earthrise

the production of the *Whole Earth Catalog*, which would eventually feature the *Earthrise* photo on its 1969 cover.

Even the concept of an image of the world taken from space was thrilling for counterculturalists, a powerful icon of raised planetary consciousness. By 1968 there were already existing photographs which pulled together an image of the full globe, such as that taken by the ATS-3 satellite in 1967, and there would be later famous images such as the 1972 *Blue Marble* taken by the crew of Apollo 17 or the 1990 *Pale Blue Dot* taken by the probe Voyager 1 as it left the solar system, but *Earthrise* struck a particularly resonant chord. Across almost every part of society, the publication of *Earthrise* touched a sense of the sublime, depicting our home planet as a small, distant, fragile object hanging weightless in the darkness of space. It fed into the countercultural narrative of the oneness of things, it reminded the Cold War world of the proximity of all humanity, it was a sop to Fullerian and McLuhanian notions of global consciousness, and it provided a 'quantum leap' forward for the ecological movement:

> No longer could nature be understood as merely a landscape to be viewed, cultivated or preserved. Once the whole Earth could be grasped in a single image, it made little sense to think of nature as an area that could be set aside from the rest of the world.[1]

Various groups in post-war society had tried to use optimism and hope in the future as ways of achieving their goals. Cold War development studies saw the increases in knowledge and technology, productivity and living standards of bureaucratic capitalism as proof that the world was destined not for communism, but for an affluent society. Planners and architects used this same sense of forward motion to push their own dreams of better and more harmonious lives in cities, while the more radical fringes looked forward to a veritable technological utopia. Even Marxist revolutionaries across the world were mostly still expected to acknowledge the achievements of capitalism and see their task as the chance to take over the productive forces and move to the next stage of human development. But growing throughout the 1960s was a different, more pessimistic attitude, which felt that all the industrial progress already made had inadvertently doomed the earth, the natural world and thus humanity, and that despite best efforts it may well already have been too late.

The primary paranoia of the time was of course nuclear annihilation. The two attacks on Hiroshima and Nagasaki in 1945 were followed by the proliferation of huge numbers of more powerful nuclear weapons by both the USA and USSR but also the UK and France in smaller numbers, and by the 1960s, especially after the Cuban Missile Crisis, the major public fear was that of 'The Bomb', of 'mutually assured destruction'.

At the start of the 1960s, ecology was by no means a new field, but over the decade a new kind of ecological thinking grew, fuelled by such

---

1   Christine Macy and Sarah Bonnemaison, *Architecture and Nature*, p. 293.

developments in science as cybernetics, the growing awareness of pollution and its effects, Malthusian fears regarding population, atomic paranoia and the general mistrust of authority, and of course the radical sense of finitude brought on by these new images of the world seen from space. The result was an increasingly apocalyptic thread in public life, which although rarely specifically partisan, called into question the very aims and assumptions of industrial modernity.

This public dread reached its peak in the early 1970s, when it was obvious in governmental language from around the world, and the sense of doom fed into a great number of the attempts to remake society over this period. As well as adding a sense of impending collapse into daily life, the germinal and frequently inaccurate predictions that were made by ecologists throughout this period, as the initial findings of new scientific fields were translated into vocal and breathlessly overblown predictions, helped to discredit and remove environmentalism from the establishment agenda for a whole generation afterwards.

In June 1962, the *New Yorker* magazine serialised a book by the marine biologist turned popular science writer Rachel Carson. *Silent Spring* was an analysis and warning of the dangers of the unrestrained use of chemical pesticides in the agriculture industry. In the decades after World War II, the American chemicals manufacturers, engorged by wartime investment, had been enthusiastically promoting pesticides such as DDT for widespread use in farming. Encouraged by the general enthusiasm for new technology in government, and employing large numbers of their own entomologists and biologists, the chemical manufacturers behaved as though they had created a miracle weapon in the battle against insects.

In a perfect example of the thinking that technical progress was making repeated and linear developments in the quality of life, it was believed that crop yields would go up, food prices and shortages would be alleviated, and the chemical corporations' profits would increase. It was a win–win situation for everyone but the insects. Indeed, it was even claimed that the use of pesticides, through reducing the chance of famine and disease, could be a valuable tool in the global fight against communism.

But not everyone was convinced. The practice of crop-spraying, where pesticides were dropped over large areas of land from aeroplanes, had already caused tensions and legal action when those who lived under the flight paths objected to their land being sprayed without permission. Elsewhere, studies on crops and animals showed evidence that pesticides were accumulating in a strange way, becoming more concentrated the further up the food chain one observed, an effect most prominent in birds, whose numbers had been in sharp decline. Also, in laboratory tests, it was found that some of the pesticides had carcinogenic effects on certain mammals. Carson, alerted to people's general reticence about pesticides and chemicals in their daily lives, studied the evidence of pesticide build-up and toxicity, and came to the conclusion that terrible risks were being taken, not only with human health, but with the health of ecosystems all over the world.

The title *Silent Spring* refers to the prospect of a world without birds. Carson opened the book with a fable about this world, where the harmony of the bucolic American landscape was destroyed by unconsidered human action. The main argument of the book was that these chemicals were being introduced into ecosystems whose mechanisms and processes were barely understood, and there was very little thought or concern about the consequences. Without careful study, the delicately interconnected nature of these systems, evolved to a point of equilibrium, was such that by the time the damage became apparent, it would already be too far gone to remedy easily, or at all.

Elsewhere, Carson made a strong case that humans themselves were putting themselves in danger through exposure to fruit, vegetables and meat with high concentrations of pesticide residues. Behind the specific dangers that Carson elucidated, there was a secondary message about humanity's ignorance in its rush to intervene in natural processes which had evolved over millions of years and whose subtle workings were almost totally mysterious. Indeed, *Silent Spring* was a warning that faith in technology was bringing humanity to the very edge of destroying nature altogether:

We stand now where two roads diverge. But unlike the roads in Robert Frost's familiar poem, they are not equally fair. The road we have long been travelling is deceptively easy, a smooth super-highway on which we progress with great speed, but at its end lies disaster. The other fork of the road – the one 'less travelled by' – offers our last, our only chance to reach a destination that assures the preservation of our earth.[2]

The chemical companies did not react well to Carson's arguments. In the run-up to the serialisation and publication of the book, they prepared many attacks on her work, character and gender. It is not without merit to compare Carson's work with that of Jane Jacobs – both were relative outsiders to their field, both were women writers who went up against a massive and powerful wall of received opinion, suffering aggressive and misogynistic attacks as a result, but both managed to win much of the public around to their arguments in the process. Carson, who published Silent Spring as she was already undergoing treatment for the breast cancer which killed her in 1964, came across in public as far more believable than the scientists for the chemical industry, and a public distrust of authority claiming to know what was best worked in her favour.

Silent Spring, like Jacobs's Death and Life, had a galvanising effect. One direct consequence was the campaign that led to the ban of DDT in the United States, but perhaps the greatest impact was on grass-roots environmentalism. Silent Spring was a huge influence on the formation of the groups that eventually became organisations like the Green Party. It encouraged people to take a stand against collusions between industry and government that had potentially deleterious effects on the natural world.

But Silent Spring could also be criticised for its easy deployment of a rhetoric of 'harmony' when discussing nature. Throughout the book, the natural environment is eulogised as something at one with itself, which was in the long run a vulnerable point where ecological concerns could be criticised for being far too concerned with aesthetic or sentimental judgements. At the time, however, it also provided a massive public jolt, where concern about the consequences of the rapid change that

---

2   Rachel Carson, Silent Spring, p. 255.

industrialisation had brought to the world was brought into mainstream consciousness.

The reactions against *Silent Spring* tended to portray the book as containing far more extreme arguments than it actually did, but over the course of the 1960s the enemies of environmental action got the opponents they were looking for. For every enthusiastic work on ecology that promoted a more enlightened view of humanity's relationship to their natural world, there was an apocalyptic pronouncement that things had already gone too far.

One of the most successful and controversial of these portents of doom was *The Population Bomb*, a 1968 book by the biologist Paul Ehrlich (and his wife, Anne, who co-wrote the book but was not listed as an author). Ehrlich had taught Stewart Brand at university and was a creator of the concept of co-evolution that provided Brand with the influence for one of his later magazine projects. The Ehrlichs had encountered various strains of neo-Malthusian thinking over the post-war decades, which subscribed to the belief that there was a natural tendency for human populations to grow too fast and thus exhaust their food supply, inevitably causing famines. But what the Ehrlichs did in *The Population Bomb* was tie this centuries-old thinking together with the new world of global consciousness and ecological sensitivity and write their book in a gripping, enthusiastic style far removed from academic writing. In a long tradition of doom-saying, the Ehrlichs announced in the prologue:

> The battle to feed all of humanity is over. The famines of the 1970s are upon us – and hundreds of millions more people are going to starve to death before this decade is out.[3]

Throughout the rest of the book, grandstanding pronouncements on the imminence of the collapse of the food supply and the resulting rise in the death rate were mixed with passages on pollution clearly influenced by *Silent Spring*, as well as strong advocacy for a politically administered

---

3   Paul Ehrlich, *The Population Bomb*, prologue.

'population control', enforced militarily by the US, if necessary. The metaphor that kept reappearing was the notion that humanity is like a cancer – a mutation away from the natural order that cannot help but reproduce uncontrollably until it invariably kills the host organism. Faced with the realisation of humanity's natural malignancy, enforced population control was the aggressive and painful treatment that had to be undergone to save the patient.

The Ehrlichs' book is a mixture of honest concern for humanity's welfare and jaw-dropping insensitivity. It is filled with passages of American exceptionalism, whereby 'undeveloped countries' such as India were to be subjected to enforced population control by the powerful and wealthy US, or advocations of US support for regimes prepared to enforce population control regardless of how undemocratic or brutal they might be. On the other hand, the world that the Ehrlichs were fighting for was clearly influenced by the yearnings for peace and harmony of the countercultures, and their proposed solutions indeed chimed with the ongoing rejection of the industrial bureaucracy of American life:

> It is going to cost industry money. It is going to cost municipalities money. It is going to hit a lot of Americans where it hurts – perhaps doing without two petrol-gulping monster cars per family, perhaps learning to get along with some insect damage in their foods. They may have to get along with much less fancy packaging of the goods they purchase. They may have to use cleaners that get their clothes something less than 'whiter than white'. They may have to be satisfied with slower coast-to-coast transportation. Such may be the cost of survival. Of course, they may also have to get along with less emphysema, less cancer, less heart disease, less noise, less filth, less crowding, less need to work long hours or 'moonlight', less robbery, less assault, less murder, and less threat of war. The pace of life may slow down. There may be more fishing, more relaxing, more time to watch TV, more time to drink beer (served in bottles that must be returned).[4]

---

4   Ibid., p. 95.

The Population Bomb was a bestseller, but in its very nature it was vulnerable to criticism. By making such bold assertions and pronouncements, each failed prediction undermined the message in the eyes of critics. In the decades since 1968, the global population continued to increase, and improvements in agriculture meant that mass die-offs did not occur; indeed, in many parts of the world, hunger was drastically reduced. The discrepancy between the Ehrlichs' apocalyptic predictions and what actually transpired could be seen to have done damage to the environmental cause, especially due to the anti-establishment rhetoric of the book, which did little to bridge the gulf between concerned citizens and corporate and industrial interests.

One particular objection was that campaigning against the forces which brought prosperity and technological development was essentially campaigning *for* the famines and misery that plagued most of humanity – environmentalists were for turning the clock back to an altogether darker age. On the other hand, a more significant objection was that in its reluctance to pay attention to the political and distributive issues of hunger, *The Population Bomb* was wide open to charges of ignorance of what actually causes famines in the first place. Indeed, the book brings the political naivety of much of the American counterculture into sharp focus – a movement made up of mostly wealthy, young white Americans professing global harmony but frequently oblivious to actual struggles that were going on around them.

To focus on poor families breeding too much was to spectacularly miss the point of why there are shortages under capitalism in the first place. But *The Population Bomb* is prescient in its awareness of the potential of human consumption to change the climate (a concern which at that point was still near the bottom of the list of environmental horrors), and in recent years Paul Ehrlich has been frequently asked to discuss the work again, in the context of the new sense of disaster's imminence.

Books such as *Silent Spring* and *The Population Bomb*, among many others, may have made a strong display of speaking truth to power, of going up against the ignorance of the establishment, but it was not necessarily subversive to take a strong position on ecological issues. The year

1970 saw two different Earth Day events, one organised by the UN, and another within the US itself when millions of Americans took to the streets to demand action on pollution and environmental issues. At the end of that year, Nixon set up the Environmental Protection Agency as part of this swell of public concern. The United Nations at this time was also largely concerned with environmental issues, with Secretary General U Thant making apocalyptic speeches about the threats to the planet and setting up the United Nations Conference on the Human Environment that was held in 1972. As well as governmental organisations, there were plenty of people within the capitalist establishment – captains of industry, academics, economists – who were just as concerned by the problems facing the world.

In 1968, Aurelio Peccei and Alexander King formed an organisation that they called the Club of Rome. Both these men were high up in the world of post-war economic power: Peccei was an Italian industrialist who had worked for Fiat and Olivetti developing manufacturing operations in Latin America and China, while King, a Scot, was a high-ranking civil servant at the Organisation for Economic Co-operation and Development (OECD) in Paris. Their intention was to exert influence on governments to take longer-term views on decision making and policy, based upon their shared conviction that the global economy was excessively focused upon short-term goals. To achieve this they brought together a group of economists and scientists to research these matters. They also became involved with Jay Forrester of MIT, a scientist who had been developing cybernetic modelling techniques in the field of industry, an area of research that he called 'system dynamics'. Together, they set out to construct what they called the 'world model' – a cybernetic diagram that attempted, within the technological constraints of the time, to create a computer simulation that could describe and predict the interactions of various key factors in the global economic system – industrial production, natural resources, levels of pollution, the food supply and, binding them all together, the human birth and death rates.

The results of the first years of research were published in 1972 as *The Limits to Growth*, 'a report for the Club of Rome's project on the predicament of mankind'. Inside, the group wished to lay out their

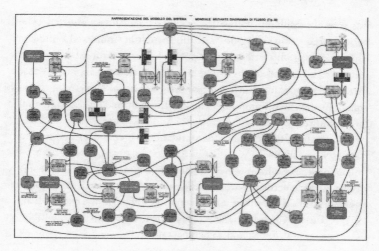

Limits to Growth: The World Model

overriding conviction that the major problems facing mankind are of such complexity and are so interrelated that traditional institutions and policies are no longer able to cope with them, nor even to come to grips with their full content.[5]

The defining problem, as the group saw it, was that growth was exponential within a finite system. Even something that grows as little as 1 per cent per year is still growing exponentially and subject to laws of acceleration and doubling. The growing population and industrial production had to contend with a variety of finite limits – how much arable land there is, the amount of natural resources buried within the surface of the planet, the capacity of natural systems like the ocean and the atmosphere to absorb pollutants.

The purpose of the 'world model' was to try to give an explanation of what was likely to occur in the near to mid-future if trends in industrial society were to continue, and then, to test whether changes in policy might have an effect on these trends. The structure of the 'world model'

---

5   *The Limits to Growth*, p. 9.

was proudly displayed within the book, a huge interconnected cybernetic diagram of small nodes with titles such as 'industrial output per capita', 'average lifetime of soil', 'pollution generation rate', 'mortality age 0–15', all connected by arrows which depicted the various feedback mechanisms in play. This was a graphical depiction of a complex set of equations that their computers ran iteratively to make their predictions for the future.

The results of the first test, 'the standard run', were not encouraging:

> If the present growth trends in world population, industrialization, pollution, food production, and resource depletion continue unchanged, the limits to growth on this planet will be reached sometime within the next one hundred years. The most probable result will be a rather sudden and uncontrollable decline in both population and industrial capacity.[6]

The cybernetic computer model predicted that growing population and industrial demand would cause a severe shortage in non-renewable resources, raising prices to the point of severely curtailing capital investment, which would then lead to a tipping point where industry collapsed, taking services and agriculture with it. Eventually this would cause a sharp drop in the global population due to starvation and disease. All of this, according to the model, would occur before the year 2100.

Limits to Growth also described a number of different scenarios after the standard run, assuming different kinds of action – population and pollution controls, raised estimates of future resource availability. Again and again, however, the model predicted imminent collapse. Some of the adjustments put off the collapse by fifty years or so, while some proposed ameliorations actually led to sharper collapses compared to the standard model. Sometimes the collapse left enough resources and latent capacity for some form of civilisation to be resumed after the collapse, while others suggested that the earth would be left as nothing but a polluted husk.

---

6   Ibid., p. 23.

Each of the scenarios was presented with a charmingly devastating little graph produced by the world model, showing every factor in the model (except resources) rising up until 1970, and then gradually going wild before each time they dropped directly downwards to a tiny fraction of their former level. There is definitely something blackly comic about the various diagrams all predicting more or less the same global civilisational collapse, leading to a simple but devastating conclusion: 'The basic behavior mode of the world system is exponential growth of population and capital, followed by collapse.'[7]

One thing that particularly perturbed the authors of *Limits to Growth* was the impact, or lack of impact, that technological change appeared to make in their model. Against the technocratic optimism they saw all around them, the world model appeared to show that no amount of efficiencies or technological advance could solve the essential predicament of humanity:

> We have found that technological optimism is the most common and the most dangerous reaction to our findings from the world model. Technology can relieve the symptoms of a problem without affecting the underlying causes. Faith in technology as the ultimate solution to all problems can thus divert our attention from the most fundamental problem – the problem of growth in a finite system – and prevent us from taking effective action to solve it.[8]

The Club of Rome decided to turn their attention to seeing if it was at all possible to achieve an equilibrium state in their model of the world. Through a process of trial and error, they managed to stabilise the experiment in order to achieve an indefinitely sustainable civilisation. With a combination of actions including immediately halting population growth, curtailing resource consumption, switching capital investment from industry to education, tackling pollution, improving agriculture and extending the productive life of capital, they found that their model

7   Ibid., p. 141.

8   Ibid., p. 153.

stabilised. In avoiding exponential growth followed by collapse, they had tamed their own collection of cybernetic feedback loops and had achieved what appeared to be homeostasis, just as it was observed in the natural world. In order to understand this condition, they allowed themselves some imaginative political description of their own, an attempt to describe a civilisation not predicated upon growth, but on a social condition of 'dynamic equilibrium':

> Population and capital are the only quantities that need be constant in the equilibrium state. Any human activity that does not require a large flow of irreplaceable resources or produce severe environmental degradation might continue to grow indefinitely. In particular, those pursuits that many people would list as the most desirable and satisfying activities of man – education, art, music, religion, basic scientific research, athletics, and social interactions – could flourish.[9]

So in the end, the Club of Rome's solution to the crisis facing humanity was very similar to that of the communalists and many others – a dynamic, high-tech society based upon renewable energy, concern for the natural environment, intellectually stimulating labour and plenty of leisure time.

But in order to get to these recommendations, they had completed a study using the most advanced means they had at their disposal, and despite frequently stressing the germinal and underdeveloped systems of modelling that they were using, their conclusion was powerful and dark: 'We are unanimously convinced that rapid, radical redressment of the present unbalanced and dangerously deteriorating world situation is the primary task facing humanity.'[10]

Again, predictably, *Limits to Growth* came in for a lot of criticism. The primary objection related to the sophistication of the 'world model'. Although it may have been the most complex that was possible at the time, the authors admitted that not only was it rudimentary, but there

---

9   Ibid., p. 175.

10   Ibid., p. 193.

was also no way of including social and political factors, and anyway, large-scale modelling was by its nature a reductive enterprise. Indeed, in today's eyes, the modelling and calculation methods look terribly primitive compared to even the simplest computing as we experience it now.

Beyond that, the conclusions of the book were challenged vociferously – from accusations that it was nothing more than fashionable doom-mongering, yet another apocalyptic bestseller, to assertions that capitalist market forces would surmount the challenges of dwindling resources and lead industry into alternative, more productive directions. This particular objection had the irony of setting off the computerised simulation of the break-down of interrelated systems against a faith in the self-directing power of the interrelated systems themselves. Furthermore, despite the warnings about technology, a general objection was that *Limits to Growth* singularly failed to take into account such things as human ingenuity and inventiveness, whether technological or social.

Limits to Growth sold 12 million copies worldwide, a massive success. With this kind of exposure, it was no surprise that by the mid-1970s environmental dread was firmly in the mainstream. The new secretary-general of the UN, Kurt Waldheim, spoke in his annual report of 1973:

There is an almost universal sense of apprehension about where the tumultuous developments of our time may take us, a sense of deep anxiety at phenomena which we do not fully understand, let alone control. In all the speculation, much of it depressing, about the shape of the future, there recurs a note of helplessness and fatalism which I find deeply disturbing.[11]

President Giscard d'Estaing of France was also said to have remarked:

The world is unhappy. It is unhappy because it does not know where it is going and because it seems that if it knew it would discover that it was heading for disaster.[12]

11 As quoted in *Creating the Future: Agendas for Tomorrow*, p. 42.
12 Ibid.

The 1974 Spokane Expo, the first world expo after Osaka in 1970, was entitled 'Towards a Fresh New Environment', and drastically scaled back the architectural ambitions of previous years, marking the end of the age of prominent expositions. Despite this massive emotional and political investment in moving the world away from its destructive course and onto more sustainable paths, none of the great many harbingers of doom from the period managed to shift capitalism off its growth-led and industrially intensive direction. There may be no need to defend the primitive systems of *Limits to Growth* and its 'world model' of 1972, but in recent years it has become a common sight to see the graph of the 'standard model' catastrophe with actual data from the subsequent forty years superimposed upon it. When this is done the graphs match almost perfectly, right up to around the present day, which is the point where the collapse is due to begin.

The International Design Conference at Aspen was a yearly event held in Colorado throughout the late twentieth century, bringing together designers, academics and business figures to discuss the issues of the day. In 1970, the IDCA had as its theme 'Environment by Design'. The conference was rocked by disputes and demonstrations from student groups, by no means an uncommon occurrence during that period, but the delegations and meetings were also fractious. The French delegation brought with them a statement prepared by Jean Baudrillard, entitled 'The Environmental Witch-Hunt', which set out hard-left objections to state environmentalism. Arguing that the environmental crisis was part of the fall-out of the failure of the May '68 revolts to change the systems of power, Baudrillard stated that 'ultimately the real issue is not the survival of the human species but the survival of political power'.[13]

To Baudrillard, it was clear that the ruling class were rallying together and 'shouting apocalypse', deploying a fear of break-down in the natural environment in order to render cohesive an obviously fracturing social environment. But further than that – the sense of guilt attached to the

---

13   Reyner Banham (ed.), *The Aspen Papers*, p. 208.

environmental crisis was itself a strategy by the elites to deflect challenges to their power:

> The theory of environment pretends to be based on actual and evident problems. But pollution, nuisances and dysfunctions are technical problems related to a social type of production. Environment is quite another problem, crystallizing the conscience on a Utopian model, on a collective enemy and, moreover, giving a guilty feeling to the collective consciousness. (We have met the enemy and he is us.) The crusade of environment goes from technical problems and technical solutions to simple and pure social manipulation. War and natural catastrophes have always been used to unify a disintegrating society. Today, it is 'la mise-en-scène' of a natural catastrophe or of a permanent apocalypse which plays the same role.[14]

So as opposed to countercultural environmentalism, which attempted to set out diagrammatic and autonomous 'free' communities that could be a model for the freedom of all society, Baudrillard's argument was that the conception of a single environmental crisis was flawed, and that the problem was with precisely the social organisation of global capitalism that was attempting to cement itself through public fear of its own deleterious consequences. Buckminster Fuller's argument that all politicians were intrinsically unqualified to deal with the environmental crisis was being transformed by these politicians from questions of social antagonisms into questions of technique: 'Problems of design and environment only look like objective ones. In fact, they are ideological problems.'[15]

As far as architecture was concerned, a break occurred between visions of the high-tech future and the project of ecology. Architectural technology continued to be developed, but for much of the later 1970s into the 1980s the cutting edge of architecture was still concerned with 'meaning', and postmodern historicism or neo-vernacular was the order of the day. Those carrying the torch for technologically sophisticated architecture

---

14 Ibid., p. 209.
15 Ibid.

that expressed itself as such went forward with airports and transport, office blocks and skyscrapers, with an architectural language drawn from nineteenth-century engineering, Buckminster Fuller and Archigram, mixed in with the glassy corporate style derived from Mies van der Rohe. Eventually, by the end of the century this approach to architecture would become spectacularly successful, but in the process, the delirious naturalism that went alongside many of Fuller's synergetic experiments was dropped, leaving behind an architecture of capitalist refinement, a technocratic expression of shimmering, air-conditioned efficiency.

However at the same time, a genuine ecologically conscious architecture began to form. Against the arguments from the far left that the environmental crisis was as much a political as it was a natural crisis, an attitude became apparent that was less universal, more like 'tending one's own garden'. The rudimentary but effective systems developed by the likes of Steve Baer, with passive heating and cooling strategies, continued to be developed but had become severed from both the drop-out communities' ideas of revolution as well as the space race and the world of Fulleresque high technology.

Projects such as Sim Van der Ryn's 'Energy Pavilion', a 1972 experimental structure at University of California, Berkeley, was a simple timber-framed structure with different technologies plugged in and tested upon it, while his 'Integral Urban House' had no style at all and was rather an experimental project to investigate systems that might make an ordinary conventional house become completely self-sufficient. These were inspired by various technologies that had been developed as part of the space race, such as solar panels, waste recycling systems, and life support systems, and which were often directly marketed back on earth for domestic use by military contractors who had finished their contracts with the end of the Apollo programme. Overall, ecological architecture became widely synonymous with small-scale buildings, materials like timber or even mud-brick and a generalised anti-industrialism – to a large extent, it was giving up on the political terrain of large-scale change and waiting for the collapse.

At the same time as the space-colony movement was entering its last phase, a corresponding argument was made that the impending ecological disaster would require the construction of small capsules, nay, *arks*, which would allow for small groups to survive, alongside mini-ecosystems they would keep with them. As they moved away from the mainstream, 'many environmentally concerned designers became like astronauts, living intellectually within their own ecological capsules'.[16]

One group making this argument was the New Alchemy Institute, founded in 1969, an anti-industrial, anti-urban, apocalyptic anarchist group, who attempted to build their own sealed ecological capsules, or bioshelters. They were an example of the determination of ecological groups to remove themselves from the mainstream of society, claiming in their 1970 bulletin that:

> The New Alchemists work at the lowest functional level of society on the premise that society, like the planet itself, can be no healthier than the components of which it is constructed. The urgency of our efforts is based on our belief that the industrial societies which now dominate the world are in the process of destroying it.[17]

John Todd, co-founder of NAI, built a 1976 'Ark' building on Prince Edward Island in Canada, a pioneering structure for developing 'sustainable' technologies, but its design was somewhat rustic. A long series of greenhouses were connected to a timber building that stretched alongside, somewhere between a traditional log cabin and the later work of Alison and Peter Smithson, with its forcefully expressed roof angles. Inside were all manner of innovations, such as fish ponds that acted as solar heat sinks, assisting in the reduction of energy demands in such a cold location.

One of the key terms that had developed around these kinds of developments was 'Appropriate Technology'. This term originated in a book called *Small Is Beautiful* by E. F. Schumacher, published in 1973. The book, as well as expressing concerns about exponential growth, resource depletion and pollution, argued that development in the Third World

---

16   Peder Anker, *From Bauhaus to Ecohouse*, p. 129.

17   From thegreencentre.net/newalchemy.html.

should not necessarily follow the path that had been set out by industrial capitalist societies in the nineteenth century. Instead, small-scale and sustainable technology should be introduced to allow for developing societies to achieve an advanced modernity without the sense of rupture that had historically accompanied it.

Arguments like Schumacher's resonated in the rich countries, and similar ideas began to take off throughout the '70s. Appropriate Technology could be seen to be emerging out of the *Whole Earth Catalog* and their fixation with tools to lead more autonomous lives. The term focused on systems like solar panels, water collectors and, most prominently, personal windmill generators. For many, the decentralisation of industrial systems was a way that society could be changed for the better, with the self-sufficient ideals of commune life permeating the mainstream of American culture, which could then be drawn away from the harmful bureaucratic industrial path it had taken.

Over time, despite much scientific work and attempts at political applications, Appropriate Technology began to be seen as part of the New Age movement. Energy efficiency, living 'off-grid' and other practices like these became associated with healing stones, alternative therapies, transcendental meditation, not to mention do-it-yourself and a down-to-earth craftiness. In this kind of company, it was distinctly unlikely that questions of large-scale social change were going to become relevant, and commentators discerned that people were retreating within themselves:

> Rather than attempt to change the structures that vexed them, young Americans growing older were settling for exquisite palliatives. If the 1960s proclaimed, 'Let's see if we can change this society', the 1970s answered, 'Let's get out of this skyscraper and go jogging!'[18]

It's not hard to see why – the violent political defeats of the New Left in the US were near total, and the suffusion of environmentalist ideas into the mainstream was perhaps bound to lead to the disintegration of its radical message. Indeed, by the end of the 1970s, apocalypse fatigue

---

18   Langdon Winner, *The Whale and the Reactor*, p. 76.

was setting in all over. The counterculture had all but evaporated, with the 'back to the land' movement over and all but the most hard core of communes disbanded and back in ordinary life. Some of the libertarian fringes were heading off into the germinal, digital world of cyberculture, hacker communities and so on, whose cybernetic utopianism would reappear in a transmuted form two decades later.

Perhaps most importantly though, industry had to a large extent managed to fight off the attacks coming from the environmental movement. Statesmen may have made gestures and moves towards more sustainable cultures, but altering the course of the industrial juggernaut was far more easily said than done. As postmodern design ruled the world of urban space, and as the visionary libertarians gave up on space in favour of cyberspace, sustainable architecture began to have a reputation for being a little bit too wholesome, a little bit too New Age for its own good.

And when, as the 1980s began, the new Reagan and Thatcher regimes took over in their respective countries, and the price of oil suddenly dropped, creating an oil boom that would last for almost twenty years, the urgency of changing the systems of the planet suddenly went out of the window. Appropriate Technology, by that time tied in with federal funding structures in the US, was an easy target, and investment vanished.

Despite all the defeats, there was still one last countercultural blast in architecture yet to come. On the morning of 26 September 1991, a group of eight people, dressed in bright red jumpsuits that appeared to have come straight from the costume box of *Star Trek*, waved to a crowd of thousands of people and climbed into an airlock. This was not a shuttle launch or a mission to Mars – the 'crew' were going to spend the next two years within a gigantic space-frame greenhouse called Biosphere 2, the world's largest 'closed system' experiment, entirely sealed off from the outside world, with no transfer of food, waste, air or water into their temporary home. This event was an odd mix of space-age nostalgia, environmental utopianism and mass entertainment: the scene of their entry was reminiscent of space shuttle launches, the uniformed crew – called 'biospherians' – smiling as they embarked on their uncertain mission, but

Inside Biosphere 2

it also looked forward to the later rise of reality television, the sealed and displayed lives of the inhabitants providing a model for entertainment such as *Big Brother* more than a decade later. In fact, this odd juxtaposition of the scientific and the sensational was the defining characteristic of this most remarkable architectural experiment.

Ostensibly, the Biosphere 2 'mission' was intended to investigate a number of different problems. One was to see if humans could exist within a closed system for an extended period, growing all of their own food, recycling all of their waste and maintaining favourable living conditions all of this time. This would have implications for the possibilities of deep space travel, in particular missions to Mars, and would go some way to resolving some of the primary objections that were made during the space-colony discussions a generation previously.

The other main reason given for the mission was to study various different ecosystems within the abnormal environmental conditions of a closed system, to gain knowledge of the workings of the carbon cycle, the effects of changes in climate and atmosphere on various plants and animals in test conditions. But these were not even the primary aims of the project. In fact, the entire endeavour was an attempt to show by example that humans were capable of existing in a new relationship to nature – a relationship which was not completely a-technological, submissive to the whims of chaos, but which also did not treat nature as material to be put to work, as a resource to be used up. Biosphere 2 was intended to show that humans could have a technologically sophisticated relationship to the natural world that did not involve the destruction of the planet.

Of course, the US government was not the instigator of the project – instead, it was created by a private company, Space Biospheres Ventures, which was the brainchild of John Allen, a counterculture figure par excellence. Allen, born in 1929, had trained as a metallurgist and had an MBA from Harvard, but he also had a restless and inquisitive mind that was out of step with the bureaucracy of his times. Giving up on the office existence, he went off travelling, at one point sitting rapt through the entirety of a six-hour Buckminster Fuller lecture. He eventually found himself in San Francisco in the 1960s, where he became involved in the counterculture, founding a theatre group and meeting like minds.

After a few years the theatre group moved to Manhattan, before in 1969 Allen took himself and a number of young acquaintances off to the hills of New Mexico, where they founded a community called Synergia Ranch. This was very typical of the time, but what happened next would set Allen and his cohort apart. Rather than falling into chaos and disbanding, Allen created a strong if eccentric business structure for Synergia Ranch. Anyone who turned up to stay had to pay a monthly rent, and anyone who stayed was expected to have projects of their own. They worked half the day for the ranch and half the day for themselves, there were communal meals and everyone took part in the theatre group.

Allen's dream was of a science of total systems, opposed to bureaucracy and specialisation, which would be an attempt to synthesise science and art, to draw on the best of all belief systems and begin creating a new world with that knowledge. Influenced by Buckminster Fuller, the Russian-born mystic George Gurdjieff, Western and Eastern philosophies and the growing science of ecology, Allen created a properly structured existence and provided a charismatic, older leader figure, both of which allowed the Synergia Ranch to survive long after the other drop-out communities had faded away back into the cities. The ranch, which was mainly built of adobe but unsurprisingly had its own geodesic dome at the centre of the community, gave Allen his first experience of altering ecological systems as he and the community slowly made fertile the barren soil of their land.

Gradually, the reach of Synergia Ranch began to spread. In the early '70s, afflicted by wanderlust, they managed to build – from scratch – their own ship, the Heraclitus, which they put to sea, enabling members of the ranch to travel across the world. But their fortunes were completely changed by the arrival of a Yale architecture drop-out, Ed Bass. In his late twenties, Bass was the heir to a multibillion-dollar oil fortune but was swept up in the growth of ecological consciousness and wanted to use his money in more productive ways. He joined the ranch, taking part in their activities, and went into business with Allen, who had by now created the Institute of Ecotechnics, a company to govern the activities of the ranch. With Bass's money, the IoE went about purchasing large amounts of land across the world, from savannahs to rainforests, from galleries in London to jazz clubs in Fort Worth, Texas. All their projects were driven by the 'synergetic' ideals of Allen – the land was bought for eco-management projects while their urban endeavours were part of attempts to spread the word about the synthesis of world cultures for the new world. In all, the IoE was a remarkable mix of New Age rhetoric and well-funded corporate activity, and it had a habit of getting things done, a far cry from the ineptitude of the world of communes.

The IoE began to hold conferences to promote their world-view. They hosted a range of scientists and artists, from James Lovelock and Lynn Margulis to Richard Dawkins and Buckminster Fuller, even Ornette Coleman and William S. Burroughs. Eventually, in their desire for humanity to transcend its current deleterious stage, Allen and company began to think seriously about the lost path of the space-colony projects of the 1970s and became involved in researching closed-system technology. At the Ecotechnics conference of 1984, Allen announced that they were going to start work on a large, completely sealed system in which they would recreate various examples of world biomes, and in which a number of human beings would live completely self-sustaining lives. Half a decade later, in 1987, Biosphere 2 (the '2' referring to earth's designation as Biosphere '1') began to rise out of a site the IoE had purchased up in the hills of Arizona above Tuscon.

One of Synergia Ranch's early inhabitants was an architect called
Phil Hawes, who had trained at Frank Lloyd Wright's quasi-commune
Taliesin II and who would be the primary designer of Biosphere 2. Hawes
attempted to create what he described as 'organic architecture', which
followed the synergetic practice of trying to draw the very best from
each world culture to make something entirely new. The design as it
was developed for construction primarily consisted of a series of interconnected space frames, which would be developed by Peter Pearce,
an engineer who had worked with Buckminster Fuller on the book
Synergetics back in the 1960s.

The two main volumes of the building were stepped pyramids, as if
made by some civilisation of futuristic Aztecs, and were connected by
a longer, lower space frame leading down the sloping terrain. Inside
these large spaces were recreated biomes – a rainforest area, a savannah,
a desert, a mangrove swamp, even a miniature ocean with an artificial
coral reef, while each of these was separated by small, relatively sterile
zones. Connected to the biome area by another space frame were arched
space frames that contained the 'intensive agriculture biome', which is
where all the food for the biospherians was to be grown. Leading off the
agricultural spaces were the working and living quarters for the residents,
geodesic domes with a tower containing a library space. To either side of
the building were two large geodesic domes that contained the building's
'lungs' – large membranes which could expand and contract in order to
deal with the daily changes in air pressure within such a closed system.
In total, Biosphere 2 enclosed three acres of space, around 12,000 square
meters, and 180,000 cubic meters, the largest fully sealed volume ever
created.

Aesthetically, Biosphere 2 was like a recapitulation of nearly all the
themes of futuristic architecture that we have encountered, with an extra
dose of New Age symbolism. The agriculture biome, with its semicir-
cular vaults, couldn't help but bring to mind the Crystal Palace, the
original large envelope, but also were highly reminiscent of the 'crystal
palace' agriculture units envisaged by Gerard O'Neill for his space-
colony project. The larger volumes of the structure bring to mind artefacts from the space-frame craze, and Biosphere 2's internal spaces, with

cliffs and bodies of water set off against the space frames above, could hardly help but evoke the two Summerland projects, as well as NASA's own seductive paintings of the space colonies. Although it was mostly rectilinear, the space frames of Biosphere 2 are obviously within the lineage of Buckminster Fuller, with a massive debt owed to the Montreal dome of 1967, and of course the megastructure boom cannot be far from one's mind. Finally, the location for the project, out in the mountains of the South-west, also make the lineage with Drop City and the other countercultural settlements more than apparent.

Closed-system research was a by-product of the space race – all the capsules and rockets that carried humans out of the atmosphere were closed systems, meaning that no material whatsoever could enter or leave their boundaries. All the oxygen and food had to be provided for the astronauts, and all of their waste had to be stored before returning to earth. The Soviets had conducted more research into closed systems back on earth than the Americans, the largest being the BIOS-3 system built in 1972, but Biosphere 2 was the largest experiment of its kind by a long margin. Ironically, however, it was probably closest in spirit to a small toy aquarium called an 'ecosphere', a sealed bowl of water containing algae and a small shrimp which can sustain itself for years, each organism feeding off the waste of the other.

Biosphere 2 was a 'materially closed' but 'energetically open' system, meaning that although it was completely sealed, it was still externally powered. A huge amount of mechanical equipment was stored in the basement, from water pumps and air-handling units to heat exchangers, desalination plants, composting machines and chemical recyclers. The whole space was filled with instruments and tools to measure levels of carbon dioxide, oxygen and trace gases, and various projects of serious research were to be done during the experiment. These included studies on global modelling, biochemical cycles, human physiology and nutrition, with the data generated hopefully going a long way in terms of contributions to ecological and climate research, especially the finer mechanisms involved in the carbon cycle.

The construction of Biosphere 2 was swift, and chaotic. The members of the Synergia community were given major roles to play in

Biosphere 2

the construction process, but many of them had absolutely no experience – they were assigned job titles and simply expected to learn on the go. Meanwhile, the process of designing and creating the interior, the biospheres, involved contributions from hundreds of scientists trying to decide which species to include, how to create a potentially functioning miniature ecosystem and how to create something that would be able to run itself indefinitely. Success was by no means a given, and many expected the entire experiment to descend quickly into 'green slime', where one or two species of algae would overwhelm everything else. The biospherians, all of whom had been picked from the Synergia community and were young adventurers, biologists and other scientists, were expected to fulfil the role of 'apex predators', actively intervening in the environment to maintain its equilibrium throughout the experiment. Eventually, after an expenditure of \$150 million, mostly Ed Bass's money, the biosphere was populated with plants and animals and, with crew inside, sealed.

Once inside, a day in the life of Biosphere 2 crew was a strange mix of hard manual labour and rarefied scientific research. A morning meeting would divide out the tasks, with contact with Allen and others outside at 'mission control', and then most of the day would be spent labouring in the agricultural biome, harvesting crops, sewing and tending to others, composting and other tasks. The diet that was chosen for the project was low in calories but high in nutrients and had been developed by one of the participants – Dr. Roy Walford, who outside the greenhouse was an expert in life-prolongation experiments on rodents. The primary crops grown were such things as yams, sweet potatoes and other root vegetables, leaves, wheat, and so on. Alcohol was almost non-existent and meat was rarely consumed – they had only a small collection of pygmy livestock – while a few coffee plants were only occasionally able to provide enough beans for a pot.

Those not at work on agriculture would tend to the remaining biospheres, conducting research, taking readings from sensors, cleaning algae from the 'ocean' or clearing long grass from the savannah, each working their own specialties. In addition to the agricultural, maintenance and scientific tasks, there was constant media attention, with frequent television interviews or school visits, where groups of children would press themselves to the glass in the hope of catching a glimpse of one of the biospherians at work. The team would eat together each day, a habit that they continued from their time at the Synergia Ranch, and then retire to be ready for the next day's graft. This was essentially to be the pattern for their lives for the entire two years, and to a large extent their search for a synthesis of modernity and nature had turned them into 'high-tech peasants'.[19]

Famously, the Biosphere 2 project encountered serious difficulties. Soon after entering, the crew were in a constant state of hunger, with the rations that they were capable of producing only just managing to provide subsistence. All of the team lost a great deal of weight, although this loss stabilised after a few months, suggesting that the adjustment to their new diet was reasonably successful. More serious however, was a gradual but sustained loss of oxygen in the facility. Due to the tiny relative size of the system, the carbon dioxide levels fluctuated massively throughout the day, as the plants respired, creating massive changes in the internal atmosphere. But over the course of the first year of the experiment, the oxygen levels in the facility slowly began to drop from the 20 per cent, typical of the outside air, down to 14 per cent. This drop in oxygen began to bring on the effects of altitude sickness in the crew, leading to a decision to inject oxygen into the facility over the course of a few weeks to stabilise the levels. It was eventually discovered that the oxygen loss had been caused by chemical reactions with the exposed concrete within the facility –which had not had enough time to cure sufficiently before the experiment began – locking away the oxygen as calcium carbonate.

19   Rebecca Reider, *Dreaming the Biosphere*, p. 144.

Furthermore, over the course of the experiment the crew also had to forcibly sequester carbon dioxide by allowing it to react with chemicals to create a solid residue that they then stored in the basement.

There were also infestations of ants and cockroaches that had made their way into the facility before it was sealed off, which were extremely difficult to control without chemical treatments, while some plants in the biomes threatened to take over everything else and required near constant control from the crew. But even so, the 'green slime' event never took place, and the drop in species diversity that occurred over the two years was far less drastic than had been expected.

Perhaps more significantly, relations within the crew deteriorated soon after the beginning of the experiment. All eight of the biospherians had worked together for many years at the Institute of Ecotechnics and had long taken part in the lifestyle of the Synergia Ranch. But now, as they found themselves in a state of isolation comparable to the crews of Antarctic or orbital missions, they broke off into two factions. The fault-line across which the group split manifested as a disagreement over the confused nature of the project.

Was Biosphere 2 a genuine scientific experiment? Or was it an environmentally themed endurance test? Allen and his team had spent years speaking the language of science and business while also trying to make their visions of the future a reality. All manner of fringe and mainstream scientists had been involved, and even NASA were interested in collaborating on the project, with a view to applying the findings to any future long-term space missions. But as the project progressed, the management became more controlling and less inclined to allow establishment scientists access to the work. Increasingly they cut off the crew from sharing information with external researchers. One group remained loyal to Allen and others, maintaining that the spirit of the endeavour – the live demonstration that humans could live in harmony with nature – was the most important part of the project, while the others felt that the genuine scientific opportunities of the experiment were being squandered due to personal politics and power struggles. The team put on a brave face for media appearances and on their very rare feast days, but away from scrutiny they barely spoke to each other.

Despite these problems, the first crew successfully made it to the end of their experiment and left Biosphere 2 exhausted, gaunt and with skin that had yellowed due to the levels of beta-carotene in their restricted diet. But overall the project was considered a success, and another team prepared to enter. Over the next three months, the system was opened slightly to prepare it for the next experiment, with movement in and out of the sphere for checks and preparations for the next entry.

Less than six months into the second containment, however, in 1994, the business side of the experiment collapsed. Bass, whose inherited money had effectively made the entire project possible, had finally had enough of Allen and the management team. Bass took control of the scientific advisory board, who then decided that the project needed to be more scientifically valid and less about grand gestures. Allen responded by trying to take greater control in order to prevent 'the establishment' from taking over, but eventually Bass commanded the entire project, leaving Allen locked out of the site. He brought in financial managers and bankers to try to stop the project haemorrhaging money, all the while with the second crew of biospherians inside.

Eventually, after two of the original crew who were loyal to Allen attempted to sabotage the project one night by opening the airlock, and after levels of nitrous oxide spiked, the second crew asked to leave, ending the mission. What had originally been conceived as a century-long experiment in containment had lasted only three years. Desperate to get rid of this expensive embarrassment, Bass sought outside offers. The facility was passed on first to Columbia University, who used it as a research centre on climate change and the effects of varying carbon dioxide concentrations. After Columbia withdrew, there was a period of time where it looked like as if Biosphere 2 was going to be sold for a luxury housing development, perhaps an ironic metaphor for the ecological premise of the project in the first place, but it was then taken on by the University of Arizona, who now run it as a research and visitor centre.

Biosphere 2 is widely considered a failure. While in the years running up to the project there was much enthusiasm, with it being called 'the most exciting venture to be undertaken in the U.S. since President

Kennedy launched us toward the moon',[20] by the time the experiment had begun it was also viewed with tremendous skepticism. The Institute of Ecotechnics and the Synergia Ranch were described as a cult, and John Allen as a Jim Jones–type Messiah figure. The association with hippie communes and countercultural drop-outs tainted the view of the project in many quarters, leading to the general perception that it was 'bad science', especially considering the grandiose claims that were made about the project and its potential effects on the future of humanity.

Although Biosphere 2 was the most remarkable example of controlled conditions for the study of natural processes, it was still considered far too vague and unspecialised for the academic science community and the normal experimental method. The popular press found the whole thing somewhat ridiculous, and after the high-profile problems of hunger and oxygen depletion and the breakdown of the second containment, it resembled something of a farce. *Time* magazine would later call it 'one of the fifty worst ideas of the twentieth century', and it would even be ridiculed by a film, *Biodome*, itself thought to be one of the worst films ever made, in which two slackers accidentally find themselves locked into a similar biosphere run by a despot, with 'hilarious' consequences.

Perhaps a more appropriate cinematic comparison to be made is with the film *Silent Running* of 1972, directed by Douglas Trumbull, who had been the special effects supervisor on *2001: A Space Odyssey*. *Silent Running* is a veritable cornucopia of early environmental tropes – telling the story of an earth without vegetation, where the last remaining plants are kept in outer space in a series of geodesic domes attached to giant space frames. Compared to the overwhelming cosmic optimism of Kubrick's film of 1968, which despite its warnings regarding artificial intelligence has been described as 'the ultimate manifesto of technofuturism',[21] *Silent Running* is remorselessly negative, filled with ecological apocalypse and nuclear dread, and even has a theme song performed by Joan Baez. The very last scene, after all of the human characters have died, shows

---

20   *Discover* magazine, quoted in Reider, *Dreaming the Biosphere*, p. 3.

21   Robert Poole, *Earthrise*, p. 5.

a geodesic dome filled with plants tended by a single robot, drifting off into outer space. This has not unintended biblical overtones of arks and purging floods, and the rather blatant insinuation is that everything is all our fault and that we get what we deserve.

The prospect of living in a dome to avoid a collapsing environment was taken up by a great many fictional scenarios at the time, such as the 1976 film *Logan's Run*, which depicts a future society that has managed to achieve the equilibrium state described by *Limits to Growth*. In the twenty-third century, humanity lives in a sealed, domed environment, protected from the decay and destruction wreaked upon the environment outside. Life is easy and hedonistic but comes with a price to pay: in order to keep the population in a manageable state, all humans are ceremonially killed when they reach the age of thirty. *Logan's Run* recounts one man's encounter with rebels who reject the system, and his subsequent attempt to escape from this dystopia into the world beyond where there might be sanctuary. The city shares many of the characteristics of the time: a series of interconnected large domes, like those proposed by Buckminster Fuller or Frei Otto, under which lurks a city with more than a passing resemblance to the Montreal Expo site of flamboyant pavilions in a park. The world that the escapees encounter outside, however, is a fecund landscape of romantic ruination, with Washington, DC, landmarks covered in centuries' worth of ivy, a strange juxtaposition of the apocalyptic aesthetics of the late eighteenth and late twentieth centuries.

Biosphere 2 was itself born from this 1970s apocalyptic wave, and in spirit it was very much the same as these science fiction dreams, and yet it had managed to make some kind of reality from them. The public would have already been familiar with the aesthetics of the project from a generation previously, which perhaps accounts for some of the sceptical response. Rather than being understood as an utterly vital contribution to the attempt to facilitate the survival of the human species off into the future, its arrival at the beginning of the 1990s – after the death of its ultimate inspiration, Buckminster Fuller, in 1983 – probably couldn't help but seem like some sparkle-clad throwback to a kitsch world of yester-year.

Furthermore, the Biosphere 2 project highlights just how fragile the social promises associated with all these visions of the near future could be. The dreams of uniting the arts and sciences, not to mention the digital and organic, the mind and machine, which had all been so very prominent in the development of cybernetics and ecology, only looked ridiculous when they reappeared a generation later in a changed world. Techniques of recursive modelling and system dynamics had all made their way into wider society, to the point of ubiquity in some fields, but the political change that was implied by their development had disintegrated and become part of the past. Biosphere 2 was easily the most advanced countercultural experiment in communal living, but it was anachronistic and dated, an idea adrift from its proper time, a source of amusement in a world that had since lived through the 1980s.

In fact, Biosphere 2 marks perhaps the very last attempt at achieving the synthesis implied in the positive spirit of the counterculture, a vision of the natural world and the world of technology engaged in a mutually beneficial dialectic, where experiments from outside the establishment could connect directly with figures right at the top. In the end, it's tempting to see Biosphere 2 as a metaphor, a dream project of humans in harmony with nature which was let down by the inability of humans to achieve harmony with each other, and one with particular relevance for the world as we experience it today:

> Perhaps the Biospherians were also living out a new creation/destruction myth for the rest of us – a myth appropriate to a time caught between nostalgia for wilderness and lust for technology, and caught between cosmic hopes and apocalyptic fears for the future.[22]

---

22   Reider, *Dreaming the Biosphere*, p. 276.

Chapter 8

Biospheres and the End

We see a delicate network of lines without any clue by means of which we might judge their distance from the eye or the real size. The side walls are too far apart to be embraced in a single glance. Instead of moving from the wall at one end to that at the other, the eye sweeps along an unending perspective which fades into the horizon. We cannot tell if the structure towers a hundred or a thousand feet above us, or whether the roof is a flat platform or is made from a succession of ridges, for there is no play of shadows to enable our optic nerves to gauge the measurements ... it is sober economy of language if I call the spectacle incomparable and fairylike. It is a midsummer night's dream seen in the clear light of midday.[1]

These words were written after a German visitor's first experience of a new futuristic form of architecture. But this was not an encounter with one of Fuller's geodesic structures, nor one of Frei Otto's giant envelopes, nor was it a space-frame biosphere in some inhospitable environment. Instead, these oddly familiar words were written after a visit to the Great

---

1 Lothar Bucher, *Kulturhistorische Skizzen aus der Industrieaustrelling aller Völker*, 1851, quoted in Philip Drew, *Frei Otto: Form and Structure*, p. 58.

Exhibition of 1851 and describe the remarkable experience of entering the original Crystal Palace.

The late 1960s may have seen a blossoming of architectural dreams, but in many respects those dreams had been born at least a century before. At that time, with the coming of the Industrial Revolution and the introduction of new materials and mass production methods into architecture, the ways in which buildings and spaces could be created were completely transformed. And as nineteenth-century industrial cities stretched to breaking point, and the plight of the exploited and diseased workers became more desperate, dreams emerged of new forms of social organisation that could take control of the technological forces that had been unleashed.

In the mid-nineteenth century, this sense of urban crisis was clear, and revolution was in the air across Europe. Around this time, remarkable new buildings that pushed the limits of technology offered a glimpse of a different world, one that had thrown off the yoke of history, of elites and their exploitation. This was a new technically sophisticated world in which people might be free.

Later, at the beginning of the twentieth century, the earliest modernists and functionalists looked back to the structural innovations of the mid-nineteenth century and saw in the huge factories, train stations, covered markets and exhibition halls the potential for a completely new social and spatial organisation. Formally rational and structurally efficient, these new forms of space owed their existence to new capitalist and industrial forces, but also appeared to offer the setting for a new kind of society. These structures promised an alternative to monumental architecture, whose qualities so often represented the weight and power of the human institutions who built it. And while the dreams of the future city later followed various paths, by the 1960s they were returning to the mainstream once more.

The potentially infinite space frames of the last futures of the 1960s and '70s drew their provenance from the giant iron and glass halls of the nineteenth century. Furthermore, the attempts to reconcile technological society with the natural world – the artificial landscapes, arks and biospheres of the era – were descendants of the same nineteenth-century architectural explosion. Like the crystal palaces, the nineteenth-century iron and glass winter garden was a form of architecture never before seen, a product of technological progress, scientific advancement and global trade.

The first winter garden was built in 1789, near Stuttgart, and formed part of an ensemble with a fake ruin in the grounds of the large gardens at Hohenheim. This new type of building spanned two very different worlds: on the one hand, the greenhouse only became possible with advances in technology – of iron and glass production and developments in mechanical heating and ventilation systems. On the other hand, the greenhouse's appearance in the world was a part of a very particular form of the picturesque, of nature artificially rearranged in order to appear more 'natural'. The greenhouse, like the geodesic domes of a century later, simultaneously embodied the most futuristic technology of the time, *and* an aesthetic reaction against this very same modernity.

As the industrial economies rapidly urbanised in the nineteenth century, many large greenhouses were built as facilities for the study of

Technological nature: The winter garden

botany and biology, part of a new spirit of interest in natural history. Yet the same form was also used to provide leisure facilities for the new mass of urban workers. These winter gardens were conceived not purely as a public benefit but as part of attempts to ameliorate the tensions and potential for revolt created by the new social conditions of the Industrial Revolution. Buildings such as the Palm House at Kew Gardens in the UK, or the Jardin d'Hivers in Paris, both of 1848, were masterpieces of the new world of structural engineering, and their iron details offer a prescient foreshadowing of the biomimicry of designers like Fuller and Otto.

To visit a nineteenth-century glass-house now is to experience a space that is torn in two different directions at once. On the one hand, there is the drama of the new structural technologies, with the architecture seemingly dematerialised; while as it rusts, moistens and disintegrates, it almost seems as though it is melting into plant-like form. Yet this ethereal, dreamlike architecture is surrounded by heavy pipes, steam and the rumble of boilers, the diffuse light of the external world rendered unfamiliar.

The great greenhouses allowed various flora and fauna to be transported across the world and displayed in locations in which they would never normally be able to survive. Thus, they became nodes in the intensified world of global trade. Displays of plants from far-off colonies testified to technological ingenuity and economic power, and the ability of humanity to reconfigure their environment to their liking. But at the same time, the greenhouses played their role in the fantasy world of the later nineteenth century, and in some cases seem to be a delirious intrusion of high technology into the decidedly anti-industrial world of high romanticism.

The greenhouse, and by extension the dome and the artificial biosphere, allow us to see the natural world in different ways. The ability to hold living plants in a brightly lit yet environmentally sealed enclosure, with vast networks of pipes humidifying, warming and cooling the building, asserted humanity's seemingly effortless dominance over the material world. But on the other hand, the winter garden provided a dreamlike glance into a romantically aestheticised world of nature worship, where taxonomic and scientific concerns were of little importance to the business of communing with exotically reimagined natural environments.

Inside the artificial world of the winter garden, nature became something so fragile it had to be protected from itself.

In recent years, a sophisticated attempt to understand the spatial qualities of the modern world has been undertaken by the conservative German philosopher Peter Sloterdijk, whose magnum opus *Sphären* (*Spheres*), systematically analyses the figure of the sphere as it occurs in the deep structure of human experience. Sloterdijk's work is remarkable because it provides clues to how we might connect the questions of scale, technology and nature raised by the architecture of the last futures, and their wider philosophical and historical context.

Sloterdijk's argument is that 'life is a matter of form', and that the sphere is not simply a metaphor but describes how we, as humans, experience reality and the world around us:

> The sphere is the interior, disclosed, shared realm inhabited by humans …
> Because living always means building spheres, both on a small and on a large
> scale, humans are the beings that establish globes and look out into horizons.
> Living in spheres means creating the dimension in which humans can be
> contained.[2]

Sphären creates a large and powerful intellectual argument for understanding human history in the long term through analysing the bubbles of protection that human beings create and perceive for themselves. By definition each sphere has an inside and an outside, with all the implications of comfort and rejection that these terms entail. In human life, spheres both material and social can be created, sustained and shattered:

> The theory of spheres is a morphological tool that allows us to grasp the exodus
> of the human being, from the primitive symbiosis to world-historical action
> in empires and global systems, as an almost coherent history of extraversion.[3]

---

2   Peter Sloterdijk, *Bubbles*, volume one of *Spheres*, p. 28.

3   Ibid., p. 67.

The theoretical methodology of 'sphereology' clearly demonstrates a spatial or architectural dimension. We might even say that architecture is one of the clearest examples of the sphere-building characteristics of human culture, from the earliest attempts to create shelter from the harshness of the elements, to the walled settlements of early history, through to the unbelievably sophisticated cities of the present day. What is most useful in this method is the way that architecture here is understood as just one of a number of spheres, both physical and conceptual.

The innovation of the geodesic dome, made possible only in the industrialised world, presents the most naked evidence for the architectural relevance of *Sphären*. The 'deliberate and systemic ambiguity' of the dome meant that:

> The dome is a critique of society, a giant retina and a tympanic membrane attuned to natural rhythms. It occupies an ecological niche, it is the cellular exoskeleton of humanity, and it is modeled after the most fundamental patterns of the universe.[4] ... It could be read as a pop art bubble, a globe of the earth, a breathing skin, or a garden of Eden. Ultimately it was an open container into which both Fuller and others could invest ideas of global interdependency and ecological responsibility.[5]

All of these resonances can be seen through the theoretical lens of *Sphären*, which universalises this symbolism, describing it as an integral part of being human.

Sloterdijk's *Im Weltinnenraum des Kapitals* (*In the World Interior of Capitalism*), published in 2005, outlines a new theory of globalisation, or the gradual becoming-spherical of the world. This work directs the theory of spheres into its most modern, political direction and helps frame the motivations and forces behind the architecture of the future.

Sloterdijk's argument is that globalisation is not a recent phenomenon, the consequence of industrialisation and the huge rise in world trade of

---

4   Christine Macy and Sarah Bonnemaison, *Architecture and Nature*, p. 319.

5   Ibid., p. 300.

The world interior: The Crystal Palace

the nineteenth century, but begins at the very point that the scientific knowledge that the world itself was round began to become a practical, lived experience. The history of globalisation thus opens with the voyage of Columbus in 1492, marking the beginning of the political enclosure of the entire globe, and then comes to a conclusion in the late 1960s with the completion of the global satellite communications network.

Throughout *Im Weltinnenraum*. Sloterdijk presents his view of the problems of modern capitalism after the end of globalisation in terms of his concept of the 'world interior'. This describes what he sees as the creation of a protective environmental system around the communities for whom globalisation has been beneficial, in particular the citizens of the advanced Western economies.

To describe the conditions of modern alienation according to the internal logic of his own system, Sloterdijk turns back to the Crystal Palace of the Great Exhibition in 1851, the world's first globally themed event. For Sloterdijk, the Crystal Palace becomes a metaphor for life within capitalism itself, the 'immunological' sphere that draws in all that is external, domesticates it and thus creates a comfortable 'interior' for the rich of the world: 'Wherever one happens to be, one now has to imagine the glass roof above the scene.' However, this contemporary Crystal Palace is not specifically an architectural structure:

> It does not resemble a residential building, but rather a comfort installation with the character of a hothouse, or a rhizome of pretentious enclaves and cushioned capsules that form a single artificial continent.[6]

The similarities between Sloterdijk's description of the Crystal Palace and conceptual projects like New Babylon are striking. In Constant's imaginary city, its inhabitants were to be maintained in perpetual hedonistic comfort. This is almost exactly akin to Sloterdijk's conception of the Crystal Palace of capitalism as a limitlessly expanded domestic interior, protecting its inhabitants as they engage in their lives of consumption. These hypotheses of the urban future are in a way attempts to make tangible the process of modern alienation. Instead of trying to reunite with nature and a historical, premodern form of life, these nomadic cities of the future attempted to depict a perfected form of the processes that were then shaping modern life.

Sloterdijk's is a conservative project, drawing upon negative reactions from the time, where the Crystal Palace was understood to signify the lack of mystery and the oppressive rationality of the modern scientific capitalist world of the nineteenth century. Sloterdijk sees this negative version of the Crystal Palace as what inevitably occurred when satellites encircled the globe, astronauts brought back the *Earthrise* photograph in 1968, when the whole planet had been explored and there were no frontiers left for capitalist expansion.

> This is where the motif of the 'end of history' began its triumph. The visionaries of the nineteenth century, like the communists of the twentieth, already understood that after the expiry of combatant history, social life could only take place in an expanded interior.[7]

---

6 Sloterdijk, *In the World Interior of Capital*, p. 193.

7 Ibid., p. 170.

This Crystal Palace is what happens when the energies of the system are turned inward, leading to the strange world of mass consumption, and Sloterdijk argues that this process was already foreshadowed in the original palace: 'The psychedelic capitalism of today was already a *fait accompli* in the almost immaterialized, artificially climatized building.'[8]

The argument is that this situation is a negative and dangerous one. Sloterdijk describes a world in which the citizens of wealthy countries are pampered, assisted by the unmatched wealth brought on by petroleum extraction, their populations protected from having to perform, struggle, fight or necessarily achieve anything to deserve the security they enjoy. As far as Sloterdijk is concerned, the pampered state of those inside the Crystal Palace itself is dangerous, because the existential boredom it instills can lead to entirely negative forms of yearning for more intense forms of social life, i.e., fascism.

The 'end of history' that Sloterdijk describes was clearly on the minds of those who campaigned at the time for a greater consciousness of the earth's limits. Expansion had to either stop – as in the 'steady state' of *Limits to Growth*; find a new environment, as in the space colonies; or become introverted, developing the frontiers of individual consumption. This inward turn was also the force behind the desire for developing more responsive environments. The freedom in Archigram's dreams of the city was the freedom of the new individualist subject, whose insatiable desires for consumption were the fuel that capitalism needed to keep moving.

This conservative analysis finds its radical counterpart in conceptual architectural projects such as the No-Stop City of Archizoom. Its infinite interior, part office floor, part shopping mall, is a similar metaphor for the stultifying comfort of lives under advanced capitalism, its apparently unbounded hedonistic freedoms actually intensely proscribed, constrained to what the limited structure itself will accommodate. This is also the argument found in *One-Dimensional Man* and taken up by the counterculturalists, that the apparent freedoms of the modern world masked a far more restrictive unfreedom. But unlike Sloterdijk, who

---

8   Ibid.

considers this moral danger an effect of pampering, for the radicals this unfreedom was an inherent contradiction of capitalism that potentially led to revolution.

If *Im Weltinnenraum* offers a particularly pessimistic view, it is as a counter-argument to a more emancipatory understanding of future architecture. Throughout, Sloterdijk's use of the Crystal Palace metaphor is a deliberate engagement with the earlier work of Walter Benjamin, one thinker who most readily recognised the significance of new spatial forms in the culture of global capitalism. Both writers use early industrial architecture as a metaphor for the contradictions of capitalism, but where Sloterdijk denies the utopian potential in such forms, Benjamin believed they offered visions of how life might be changed.

Benjamin's unfinished *Passagenwerk* (*Arcades Project*), written throughout the 1920s and '30s, told the story of the birth of capitalist modernity through the figure of the Parisian arcades, early iron and glass structures that created interior spaces in the city through which the new social world of modern capitalism took shape. The Crystal Palace and other world exhibitions were significant for Benjamin in that they were physically unprecedented structures enclosing similarly unprecedented uses of space, in which the materials and products of industrialisation were arranged together as an educational display of world capitalism. In a period of such rapid change as the mid-nineteenth century, the world exhibitions became training facilities for the consumer capitalism that was to come in the following century:

> World Exhibitions glorify the exchange value of the commodity. They create a framework in which its use value becomes secondary. They are a school in which the masses, forcibly excluded from consumption, are imbued with the exchange value of commodities to the point of identifying with it ... World exhibitions thus provide access to a phantasmagoria which a person enters in order to be distracted.[9]

---

9   Walter Benjamin, *Arcades Project*, p. 18.

In using the Marxian term 'phantasmagoria' to describe the crystal palaces and arcades, Benjamin intended not only to signify the ideological fantasies created by the world of capitalism but also the dreams of their transcendence, and in this he affiliated himself with the world of radical functionalism, of an architecture based upon materialist technology and socialism. He also prefigured Sloterdijk's understanding of the interiority of capitalism, stating that: 'Arcades are houses or passages having no outside – like the dream.'[10]

Despite his obvious debt, Sloterdijk argues that a proper understanding of the global world interior created by capitalism could never actually be uncovered through Benjamin's methods, rejecting outright his Marxism, his archival methodology and his fixation on architectural anachronisms:

> The gigantic Crystal Palace – the valid prophetic building form of the nineteenth century … – already anticipated an integral, experience-oriented, popular capitalism in which no less than the comprehensive absorption of the outside world in a fully calculated interior was at stake. The arcades formed a canopied intermezzo between streets or squares; the crystal palace, on the other hand, invoked the idea of an enclosure so spacious that one might never have to leave it … This larger and more abstract interior cannot be brought to light with Benjamin's methods of digging for treasure in libraries.[11]

Sloterdijk argues that the original Crystal Palace points towards the forms of architecture that truly embody the capitalist world: indeterminate spaces for shopping, entertainment, travel and transit, buildings that do not obey the normal rules of urban space traditionally established throughout history. Sloterdijk even remarks that to repeat a study of a contemporary architectural form appropriate for today's capitalism, these quintessential non-places of transition would have to be examined, declaring that:

---

10   Ibid., p. 406.

11   Sloterdijk, *In the World Interior of Capital*, p. 174.

If one were to attempt a continuation of Benjamin's important suggestions for the later twentieth and twenty-first centuries, … [they] could then bear titles closer to The Crystal Palaces Project or The Hothouses Project, or ultimately even The Space Stations Project.[12]

When Sloterdijk understands these spaces to be purely symptomatic of capitalist culture, he rejects Benjamin's argument that they also contain glimpses of a better world. This is precisely what was at stake in the radical architecture of the '60s and '70s, and in the end, these forms of generic architecture were where many of the architectural dreams of the post-war world found their only fertile grounds for development. The space frames and megastructures of global airports, warehouses and entertainment centres were in many cases the last fragments of the possibility of a spatial revolution in all of life.

The emergence of the geodesic dome was a new incarnation of the hothouse, but with a transformed understanding of nature and the human place in it. Cybernetics and ecology had influenced an attitude that saw the natural world as one poised in homeostasis, a delicate, balanced harmony that had been put out of joint by the activities of humankind. Instead of the hothouse being 'a museum in which the masterpieces of nature were gathered together, listed in a catalogue, and preserved for the future',[13] domes were part of a holistic project to restore an underlying balance to the world, where humanity might respect the processes of nature, might interfere with them as little as possible and even, with the assistance of the new powers of the computer, actively work towards maintaining their ultimate balance.

But in the transformation of the greenhouse into the dome and beyond, the cybernetic dream of a delicately balanced natural world neglected the romantic sense of nature's vastness and the sublime. Today, however, the notion that there is a basic overwhelming tendency towards stable states or 'harmony' has become untenable. We are now more

---

12   Ibid., p. 175.

13   Kohlmaier and von Sartory, *House of Glass*, p.1

familiar with a world of tipping points, of runaway positive feedback, of a system that is only ever barely stable even at the most apparently calm of moments. In our current time, it seems now that there is no 'rest' state, no home condition from which we came and to which we can return.

The evolution of the greenhouse into the dome, and then eventually into proposals for space colonies and new biospheres, follows an oscillation between the ambition to bring the overwhelmingly powerful, indifferent force of nature within the realm of human competency, and the sense that nature itself is so delicate and fragile as to be in desperate need of technological protection for the sake of our own survival. The greenhouse went from being a system of small-scale control over nature, to being a form of ark where nature could be maintained when in the wider world it had been destroyed by human folly.

All of these spheres of artificial nature, from the nineteenth-century winter gardens to the hippie's own solar domes, from the Biosphere 2 experiment to the plans to put entire cities within controlled envelopes, were not just models of the natural world created in order to dominate it, to taxonomise it, nor were they simply models of nature created in order to help save the world. Underneath it all, they also attempted to come to terms with the chaos of the natural world, by defining it as something apart from human reality, something completely 'outside'.

On 8 February 1996, a document entitled *A Declaration of the Independence of Cyberspace* was published online. The declaration demanded, in stirring prose worthy of its namesake, that the 'Governments of the Industrial World' were to 'leave us alone'. 'Us' in this instance meant the denizens of cyberspace, the online communities forged in the early days of the Internet, who were increasingly being brought under government and corporate control. The declaration claimed, in true libertarian fashion, that:

> We are creating a world that all may enter without privilege or prejudice accorded by race, economic power, military force, or station of birth.
> We are creating a world where anyone, anywhere may express his or her

beliefs, no matter how singular, without fear of being coerced into silence or conformity.

Your legal concepts of property, expression, identity, movement, and context do not apply to us. They are all based on matter, and there is no matter here.[14]

The declaration was written by John Perry Barlow, an erstwhile lyricist for the Grateful Dead and a founding member of the Electronic Frontier Foundation, an activist organisation that had been set up in 1990 to defend civil liberties online. The EFF grew out of an early online community called the WELL, or the Whole Earth 'Lectronic Link, which itself had been started in 1985 by Stewart Brand. The declaration was both a statement of intent about the future of the online world, but it was also a blast from the countercultural past.

A great number of the communalists who fled back to the cities from the Midwest in the 1970s moved to California. This migration was part of a larger shift in power in the United States, one that was to have a profound effect on the shape and scale of the future. Where traditionally the source of economic power in the US had been the manufacturing heartlands of the North, in Michigan and surrounding states, centred on industries such as steel and motoring, there was now a drift towards the Southwest, the oil economy and California. Many at the vanguard of this movement were exhausted hippies who made their home in what would later be known as Silicon Valley. What they found offered a beguiling mix of post-Fordist mode of capitalism, alongside the utopian hopes of a world rebuilt with computers.

The counterculture had been obsessed with computing from the outset. The pages of the World Earth Catalog and subsequent publications regularly juxtaposed mathematics, advanced structural engineering, electronics and programming with drugs, free love and 'back to the land' sentimentality. When, in the 1980s, the environmentalist movement lost the ear of the establishment and was pursuing what appeared to be a

14   John Perry Barlow, *Declaration of Independence of Cyberspace*, from projects. eff.org/~Barlow/Declaration-Final.html.

rejectionist course, the banner of the future was picked up by the apostles of cyberspace, the hackers and the new entrepreneurial class of the digital world. Thus many of the political dreams of freedom from bureaucracy and oppression that had defined the counterculture became defining characteristics of this new world. But these outsiders were mixing and working with the powerful worlds of scientific research and industry; they were returning to the establishment.

As this new arrangement became ever more comfortable, the sense of dread that had imbued this culture began to vanish. Apocalypse fatigue set in by the end of the 1970s. Stewart Brand (who in more recent years has written extensively about climate change) later recounted the sense of futility and exhaustion that he and others had experienced:

> We were completely apocalyptic. The sky was falling, the population was exploding, people were starving, yet we went on. When the energy crisis finally happened in '73, we said, 'Aha, it's here, the end of the world.' It turned out we were wrong again.[15]

The sense of imminent doom was largely dissipated by the rise of the new conservatism, of the drop in oil prices and the '80s financial boom. Environmentalism was, at least in political discourse, largely taken off the agenda. The new future that evolved out of this process was focused on the development of and access to information. The hacker attitude, a strange form of libertarian communism, held that all information should be completely available to all at any point, creating a new communality within the realm of the digital, one that found its ideal medium with the growth of the Internet in the 1990s.

Here was an optimistic, possibly even utopian world forming, which saw the prospect of a genuine kind of freedom, perhaps embodied in the legendary Apple '1984' advertisement, where the personal computer itself was portrayed as a tool against tyranny. For a while, the breathless optimism of the technologically enhanced future was dominant.

With this transition towards a positive politics of cyberspace, space

---

15 Quoted in Fred Turner, *From Counterculture to Cyberculture*, p. 128.

itself no longer seemed to be the terrain upon which new political ideas were to be played out. The digital world brought into being a utopian dream of the potential for anyone in the world to communicate and interact with anyone else in the world, regardless of where or who they might be. In cyberspace, there was no reason to be fixed to one's gender, race, wealth or any other identity.

This tendency held within it the promise of a dramatic flattening of human hierarchies and structures of dominance. The earlier retreat back into the cities from the communes was also a retreat away from the spatial sphere into the 'smooth' space of the digital world. The communes may have failed as models for new kinds of life and new kinds of spatial organisation, but embedded back into the city some of their innovations could still flourish.

While the earlier counterculture had its metaphor of Fuller's dome, symbolising the fragility of the world's natural environment and humanity's attempt to find a proper place within it, the new cyberculture reduced the scale of that shell down to the level of the individual and their device. This alone connected them to the long-desired universal freedom and fraternity.

Where did this leave architecture as a place of spatial speculation and social interaction? The megastructural developments showed that, as the scope for architecture became larger, in the eyes of designers the actual architecture itself began to recede to become an infrastructural network designed to service the whims and needs of the leisured populace. Architecture was becoming larger but less dense, less detailed and, significantly, less permanent. As a result, indeterminacy became an ever more significant concern.

It's almost as though the ultimate building of the era would have been a perfect bubble, of almost infinitesimal thinness, but which nonetheless defined a boundary forming an internal space. The high-tech city promised to banish the shadows, to allow people to encounter their world without the fog of history that had led to so much suffering and exploitation before. And the dream that, within this glass bubble, the house itself would become an industrially produced dwelling unit was not just a reflection of the disposable objects of consumer capitalism, but a dream that humans would not be tied to their own contingent situation, their own history.

While this was occurring, the development of digital and media technologies were apparently eroding the need for an architectural frame at all. At its furthest limit, architecture attempted to vanish, the electronic infrastructure becoming invisible at any scale above that of the individual and their connection into the network.

We are surrounded by a network of satellites creating an information shell around the world, and all around us, mostly out of sight, are the power stations and distribution points that actually service the lives around us. Meanwhile we still live in spaces whose forms and arrangements, both spatial and political, were established long before the world of electronics began to change daily life.

This invisible network is clearly not the consummation of that architectural promise of indeterminacy and freedom. Indeed, the way that the digital world seems to have bypassed the limits of architecture makes it appear almost impossible to imagine significant change in the world as it is. There seems to be a fundamental political boundary that has opened up between the hard world which continues to exist, seemingly unchanged, and the networked computer world that we can only ever peer into and never truly inhabit.

From megastructures to *Small Is Beautiful*, from space colonies to cyberspace, what is the appropriate scale for change to occur in architecture? Time and again, small experiments in new forms of architecture or social arrangements completely failed to make the difference necessary to have large social effects. Meanwhile at the other scale, the attempts of the establishment to encourage deliberate action to keep up with technological and social change frequently failed to achieve their goals – indeed, they sometimes appeared to exacerbate the very problems they intended to ameliorate.

The exposition as a model for the future of urbanism had mixed fortunes. We saw how certain predictions made in expo culture were remarkably prescient, especially those that foresaw the car-dominated Cold War city, or the city of high-rise living. But even when supported by the political weight of nation states with a point to prove, the future worlds predicted by the post-war expositions were frequently wiped out themselves by the crises of the 1970s.

The dome from Expo 67 remains as a ghostly shell in its island park, while the world depicted in the Osaka expo almost completely failed to arrive. Expo culture suffered from the same problems of dematerialisation as the architecture of the counterculture – indeed it was apparent all along, as the spectacle of screens and media began to overshadow the brute weight of the buildings that held them. And the gradual reduction in size of new technology, the shrinking from displays of moon rockets to mobile telephones, also helped to render redundant the expos and their spectacular and expensive spatial display of new technology.

Other model-forms of the future city, however, are still tantalisingly with us. The university campuses of the post-war boom, especially in the UK, remain archetypes of a new form of urbanism, three-dimensional, collegiate, reminiscent of geological formations across the landscape. In almost no other place was it possible to try out the new architecture and planning ideas which were percolating at the time with such favourable conditions: fresh communities of students, a new experimental culture of education, rural landscapes without existing urban formations. They still appear to us as the model for a new way of living in cities, more technologically sophisticated, more integrated with the natural environment, one possible urban resolution of the questions posed by industrial modernity.

Indeed, during that era the universities served as some of the primary incubators of political innovation, the massive growth of higher education creating an environment of anguished optimism and demand for further change. But of course, a university, no matter how much it might model itself on one, is not a city, not even a town. For that reason they can stand only as metaphors for what the city could have been, dreams of a certain form and character of world modernity.

At the larger scale, where entire communities and cities were indeed built along new principles, the picture is mixed. In some parts of the world, such as the Soviet Union or Southeast Asia, millions of people were housed in settlements of what were at that point innovative, high-tech buildings. Reaction against such methods largely occurred in countries whose political ideologies were predisposed towards corporate rather than state power. In such places the house has become the physical form that embodies the great conservative traditions – the family unit, the individual's ownership of property, rather than a method of social organisation.

Indeed, despite the obvious failures of much of the new technology, and the rapid obsolescence of much of the housing produced at the time, it was the convergence of practice between the West and the East, the very internationalism of the methods of building that served to turn the tide of opinion against such innovation. From the very early appearance of the cliché that Western housing projects and estates resembled something from Eastern Europe, it is clear that anti-communism was nourishing soil that fed anti-modernism. That a city such as Brasilia could be rejected in such vague anti-utopian language as that of Robert Hughes, and that specious nonsense such as *Utopia on Trial* could find such a willing ear in the early years of Thatcherism, shows just how much the ideological battles of the Cold War influenced the public reception of the architecture of the future.

There is a certain irony that the most recent global building booms – the brand new cities of the oil-rich Arab countries and the vast Chinese urbanisation of the early twenty-first century, despite their often outlandish formal innovations and unprecedented scale, have taken as their ultimate model the dissipated, car-dominated suburbia already established in the US and across the world. Dubai may have built islands on the sea, but they are covered in low-rise villas, sold to investors, part of an ongoing global transformation of the home into an asset class, a bubble of an entirely different kind.

In all of its defeats, the architecture of the future failed to see any of the changes in day-to-day life that it was supposed to assist. The city maintained its old forms in the end. High technology vanished and became invisible, either in the sky, hidden behind historical masks or kept well away from the city that it serves.

In the end it seems that the fundamental object of change all along was the home, and that the crucial factor was the social relationships embodied in it. The architecture of the last futures raised or gave form to fundamental challenges to these relationships, beginning with the project of mass housing challenging traditional property relations all over the world. But then the drive towards the indeterminate, mobile dwelling unit – and its implied limit of the air-conditioned nomadic subject in an infinite interior – promised to completely redefine not only the social relationships of the city, but also the technological relationship between the people, the city and the natural environment.

Very few changes in ways of dwelling ended up taking place, and the consensus seems to be now that the ambitions themselves were suspect, and that much of what was realised was inherently doomed. But the failure of previous generations to follow through with these changes appears with great clarity in the problems the world now faces today, and humanity might not be in quite such a predicament if they had been more successful.

In 2005, Frei Otto, by then seventy-nine years old, was awarded the gold medal for a lifetime's achievements by the Royal Institute of British Architects. In an interview conducted at the time, he was dismissive of his earlier extravagances. Asked about the world of mass-produced social housing, he explained that 'my generation had a big task after the war and of course we thought we could do it better. Today, 60 years [later], we can't be proud of what we have done. But we tried; we tried to go a new way.'[16] In the intervening decades, Otto's career had first faltered, after postmodernism began to reject overtly technological design, but then had been recognised as a great influence on the high-tech architects who had grown up and out of that era. Otto's attitude to his own more ambitious earlier projects reflects his struggles and the chastened attitudes of later times:

> I was a close friend of Bucky Fuller, and we debated the idea of large domes. But why should we build very large spaces when they are not necessary? We can build houses which are two or three kilometers high and we can design

---

16   Frei Otto interview in *Icon* magazine, No. 23, May 2005.

halls spanning several kilometers and covering a whole city, but we have to ask what does it really make? What does society really need?[17]

This is a far cry from the confidence and excitement with which these very same ambitious proposals were greeted at the time, when they appeared to be the logical next development:

> In the future the main concern of architecture will no longer be the individual building, but the overall system comprising integrated building complexes. Giant envelopes exist as an idea; the prerequisites for their construction are fulfilled in principle. It will probably not be very long before present day society formulates specific structural problems which can best, or exclusively be solved by the construction of vast enclosing structures of this kind.[18]

But now some strange developments have been occurring, emanating from the technology companies of the American West. Until recently, the industries of Silicon Valley treated architecture with almost total indifference, housing their workers in massive suburban campuses of little or no architectural interest or import, taking on the cast-off shells of earlier industries. Recently, however, they have begun to look to prestige architecture to help fulfil their missions. Facebook hired global superstar Frank Gehry to design their headquarters, and Apple built a massive new campus building designed by Norman Foster, a gigantic ring-shaped office, a slick technocratic doughnut, almost like a beached space station. More remarkably, Amazon built themselves a new headquarters in Seattle, the centrepiece of which was a set of interlocking glazed domes which hark back directly to the iconography of Buckminster Fuller.

And in early 2015, Google revealed preliminary proposals for a gigantic new campus in Mountain View, California, the first new buildings that they have built for themselves. Jointly designed by the studios of Bjarke Ingels and Thomas Heatherwick, global stars who are both under fifty

---

17   Ibid.

18   Roland, *Frei Otto: Structures*, p.138

years old, it promised to be the most experimental of all of the new technology headquarters. Google themselves described the project in terms which are more than a little familiar:

> The idea is simple. Instead of constructing immoveable concrete buildings, we'll create lightweight block-like structures which can be moved around easily as we invest in new product areas ... Large translucent canopies will cover each site, controlling the climate inside yet letting in light and air. With trees, landscaping, cafes, and bike paths weaving through these structures, we aim to blur the distinction between our buildings and nature.[19]

Images that were released as part of this announcement showed buildings remarkably similar to the West German pavilion at Expo 67, with a glazed roof structure draped over a series of giant tent-columns under which various platforms are nestled. Furthermore, along the inside of the skin of the canopies were opening and closing flower-like shading structures, almost identical to those in Buckminster Fuller's Montreal dome. If Google's buildings were developed along these lines, they promised to be an unexpected reappearance of all the ideas of the last futures. Giant envelopes, megastructure, indeterminacy, biospheres – it's almost as if every experimental architectural concept of the late 1960s and '70s had been dusted off and moulded into one project for the most powerful media company in the world.

But something wasn't quite right. The architect's images depicted the projects in the same simplified diagrammatic way that they would for a contemporary art museum, a block of luxury apartments or an office tower, the rich potential of the past turned into another flavour of modern corporate space-making. The visualisations for the project, while grasping a little of the spatial qualities of the envelope, were basically no different to the images one would see for a new landscape park, shopping mall or office block; it's just that they were slightly intermixed. And in the process of becoming a reality, the proposals inevitably became more

---

19 *Rethinking Office Space*, 27 February 2015, at googleblog.blogspot.co.uk/2015/02/rethinking-office-space.html.

conventional, leading to the construction of a series of smaller open-plan office buildings with roofs covered in solar panels, their large open interiors as much furniture showroom as anything else. It's as though the lesson was that despite their power to realise past dreams, their ambitions were not as wild as they would like to think.

Indeed, other developments in the technology industry are fascinating and troubling. Google's corporate dominance has allowed them to become ever more ambitious, and their corporate acquisitions and research and development have moved them heavily into fields such as artificial intelligence, military robotics and life-prolongation, and many other areas that had been largely consigned to futures past. Elsewhere the CEO of Amazon, Jeff Bezos, born in 1964, and the prominent entrepreneur Elon Musk, born in 1971, are both heavy investors in private space travel, and both have called for the revival of the space-colony project, if only to provide a backup space for humanity if the earth-bound population is finally wiped out. It's almost as if the last few years have seen an awakening of the potent and ambitious technocracy of the post-war era, including shadows of the military industrial complex, although this time transcending the power of states and, seemingly, politics itself.

This book began with the hypothesis that the landscape of threats in the contemporary world bore a great resemblance to those which were culturally prominent in the last futures era, but with the fundamental difference that half a century ago, there was a boldness of experiment and belief that although such challenges were difficult, they were within the capabilities of a rapidly changing society. The likes of Google may be dusting off the dreams of that era, but with a vision of the world that is fundamentally contradictory.

Back then, automation was seen almost universally as a rising tide that would set people free from drudgery, but now, the mass automation of intellectual work promised by the algorithms of the technology industry seems much more likely to raise the drawbridge between the wealthy and the masses even further. Instead of people working a few days a week and fulfilling themselves with creative leisure at other times, it appears more likely that people will become more tightly squeezed into the last remaining jobs whose empathy and emotional labour the robots cannot synthesise.

Far from the home becoming something as technical and impermanent as an appliance, the house has become an asset class, whose very permanence has allowed it in parts of the world to become a socially ruinous investment, as solid as ever, yet ever more melted into air. Instead of our being housed in bubbles, the monetary value of our housing continues to bubble ever more erratically. And instead of the modern human becoming a nomad, free to roam within their comfort shells, national walls appear to be growing higher again, with anti-immigrant politics on the rise in the wealthy nations and all the grim historical resonances that suggests.

Finally, instead of living in giant structures balancing the energy needs of cities with the natural world around them, it seems more likely that the lack of action on carbon dioxide emissions, combined with rising inequality across human society, will lead instead to the creation of climate enclaves, fortified cities for the super rich, self-sufficient in energy and food yet totally barricaded off from those outside who will be left to fend for themselves – the ultimate in Sloterdijk's bubbles.

Although there is no question of being able to pick up where the last futures left off, there is clearly a need for more ambitious thinking and action regarding the form of housing and cities, and the very nature of how humans live in space. There is overall a sense that these last futures might have been the final chance to change the world, and even if we see flickers of their reanimation, it will be worth nothing if these new spheres do not include absolutely everyone.

ACKNOWLEDGEMENTS

Thanks are due to many people for helping during the production of this book, but in particular:

Everyone at Verso, including Jeanne Tao, Emilie Bickerton, Mark Martin, Angelica Sgouros, Sophia Hussain and Sarah Shin, with special thanks to Leo Hollis for commissioning and admirable patience in editing.

Those who looked at sections of the book or made suggestions, including Kathryn Murphy, Owen Hatherley, Jim Buckfield, Fred Sharman and Meredith L. Miller.

All of the editors who commissioned writing from me, especially Christopher Turner at *Icon*, Tom Wilkinson at *Architectural Review* and Daniel Trilling at *New Humanist*, who all commissioned articles that expanded upon sections of this book.

All of the universities and institutions that invited me to teach or to lecture during this time.

Elad Levin and everyone at PBPW.

Patrick Lynch and everyone at Lynch Architects.

The staff at the British Library and the RIBA Library.

Jamie, Chantal and all of the Cuthills.

Robert, Wilma and Kathryn Murphy.

Marin Tamm, who made all this work possible.

BIBLIOGRAPHY

Allen, John and Mark Nelson. *Space Biospheres*. Malabar, Florida: Orbit Book Company, 1987.

Alling, Abigail, Mark Nelson and Sally Silverstone. *Life under Glass: The Inside Story of Biosphere 2*. Oracle: Biosphere, 1993.

Anker, Peder. *From Bauhaus to Ecohouse: A History of Ecological Design*. Baton Rouge: Louisiana State University Press , 2010.

Archigram Archival Project, archigram.westminster.ac.uk.

Architects' Journal, vol. 154, July–December 1971.

Architectural Design, vols 37–42, 1967–1972.

Banham, Reyner, ed. *The Aspen Papers: Twenty Years of Design Theory from the International Design Conference in Aspen*. London: Pall Mall Press, 1974.

Banham, Reyner. *Megastructure: Urban Futures of the Recent Past*. London: Thames and Hudson, 1976.

Barbrook, Richard. *Imaginary Futures: From Thinking Machines to the Global Village*. London: Pluto, 2007.

Bateson, Gregory. *Steps to an Ecology of Mind: Collected Essays in Anthropology, Psychiatry, Evolution, and Epistemology*. Chicago; London: University of Chicago Press, 2000.

Baudrillard, Jean. *Utopia Deferred: Writings from Utopie (1967–1978)*. Trans. by Stuart Kendall. New York; London: Semiotext(e), 2006.

Bell, Daniel and Stephen R. Graubard, eds. *Toward the Year 2000: Work in Progress*. Cambridge, Massachusetts; London: MIT Press, 1997.

Bell, Daniel. *The Coming of Post-Industrial Society: A Venture in Social Forecasting*. London: Heinemann Educational, 1974.

Beloff, Michael. *The Plateglass Universities*. London: Secker & Warburg, 1968.

Benjamin, Walter. *The Arcades Project*. Ed. by Rolf Tiedemann. Trans. by Howard Eiland. Cambridge, Massachusetts: Harvard University Press, 2002.

Bonnemaison, Sarah and Christine Macy, eds. *Architecture and Nature: Creating the American Landscape*. London: Routledge, 2003.

Brand, Stewart, ed. *Space Colonies*. Harmondsworth: Penguin, 1977.

Brand, Stewart. *Whole Earth Discipline: Why Dense Cities, Nuclear Power, Transgenic Crops, Restored Wildlands, Radical Science, and Geoengineering Are Necessary*. London: Atlantic, 2010.

Branzi, Andrea. *No-Stop City*: Archizoom Associati. Orléans: HYX, 2006.

Burns, Jim. *Arthropods: New Design Futures*. London: Academy Editions, 1972.

Bulletin of the New Alchemists, Fall 1970, http://www.thegreencenter.net/newalchemy.html.

Carson, Rachel. *Silent Spring*. London: Penguin Classics, 2012.

Coleman, Alice, King's College London Design Disadvantagement Team. *Utopia on Trial: Vision and Reality in Planned Housing*. London: Shipman, 1985.

Commoner, Barry. *The Closing Circle: Confronting the Environmental Crisis*. London: Cape, 1972.

Content. Dir. Chris Petit, Channel 4 Films, 2010.

Crosland, Anthony. *The Future of Socialism*. London: William Pickering, 1994.

Curtis, William J. R. *Denys Lasdun: Architecture, City, Landscape*. London: Phaidon, 1994.

Dahinden, Justus. *Urban Structures for the Future*. Trans. by Gerald Onn. London: Pall Mall Press, 1972.

Dalen, George M. and Clyde R. Tipton Jr., eds. *Creating the Future – Agendas for Tomorrow: International Symposium III, October 28–30, 1974, Expo 74, Davenport Hotel, Spokane, Washington, USA*. Columbus, Ohio: Battelle Memorial Institute, 1974.

Drew, Philip. *Frei Otto: Form and Structure*. London: Crosby Lockwood Staples, 1976.

Drexler, Arthur. *The Architecture of the Ecole des Beaux-Arts*. London: Secker & Warburg, 1977.

Ehrlich, Paul R. *The Population Bomb*. London: Pan Books, 1971.

Ellul, Jacques. *The Technological Society*. Trans. by John Wilkinson. New York: Vintage Books, 1970.

Five Architects: Eisenman, Graves, Gwathmey, Hejduk, Meier. New York: Oxford University Press, 1975.

Fuller, R. Buckminster. *Ideas and Integrities: A Spontaneous Autobiographical Disclosure*. Toronto: Macmillan, 1969.

Galbraith, John Kenneth. *The New Industrial State*. London: Hamish Hamilton, 1967.

Glendinning, Miles and Stefan Muthesius. *Tower Block: Modern Public Housing in England, Scotland, Wales and Northern Ireland*. New Haven: Yale University Press, 1993.

Gruen, Victor. *The Heart of Our Cities: The Urban Crisis: Diagnosis and Cure*. New York: Simon and Schuster, 1964.

Habraken, N. J. *Supports: An Alternative to Mass Housing*. Trans. by Ben Valkenburg. Great Britain: Urban International, 1999.

Hays, K. Michael and Dana Miller, eds. *Buckminster Fuller: Starting with the Universe*. New Haven; London: Yale University Press, 2008.

Henket, Hubert-Jan and Heynen Hilde, eds. *Back from Utopia: The Challenge of the Modern Movement*. Rotterdam: 010 Publishers, 2002.

Hughes, Robert. *The Shock of the New: Art and the Century of Change*. London: Thames and Hudson, 1991.

Icon Magazine, No.23, May 2005.

Jacobs, Jane. *The Death and Life of Great American Cities*. London: Pimlico, 2000.

Jencks, Charles and William Chaitkin. *Current Architecture*. London: Academy Editions, 1982.

Jencks, Charles and Nathan Silver. *Adhocism: The Case for Improvisation*. Cambridge, Massachusetts; London: MIT Press, 2013.

Kahn, Lloyd. *Shelter*. Bolinas, California: Shelter, 1973.

Kahn, Lloyd et al. eds. *Domebook 2*. Bolinas, California: Pacific Domes, 1972.

Kaye, Michael S. *The Teacher Was the Sea: The Story of Pacific High School*. New York: Links, 1972.

Kenneally, Rhona Richman and Johanne Sloan, eds. *Expo 67: Not Just a Souvenir*. Toronto: University of Toronto Press, 2010.

Kirk, Andrew G. *Counterculture Green: The Whole Earth Catalog and American Environmentalism*. Lawrence, Kansas: University Press of Kansas, 2007.

Kohlmaier, Georg and Barna von Sartory. *Houses of Glass: A Nineteenth-Century Building Type*. Trans. by John C. Harvey. Cambridge, Massachusetts; London: MIT Press, 1986.

Landau, Royston. *New Directions in British Architecture*. New York: George Braziller, 1968.

Lasdun, Denys and Partners. *A Language and a Theme: The Architecture of Denys Lasdun & Partners*. London: RIBA Publications, 1976.

London County Council. *The Planning of a New Town: Data and Design Based on a Study for a New Town of 100,000 at Hook, Hampshire*. London County Council, 1961.

Maki, Fumihiko. *Fumihiko Maki*. London; New York: Phaidon, 2009.

Maniaque-Benton, Caroline. *French Encounters with the American Counterculture, 1960–1980*. Burlington, Vermont: Ashgate, 2011.

Marcuse, Herbert. *One-Dimensional Man: Studies in the Ideology of Advanced Industrial Society*. London: Ark, 1986.

McLuhan, Marshall. *Understanding Media: The Extensions of Man*. London: Ark, 1987.

Meadows, Donella H., Dennis L. Meadows, Jørgen Randers and William W. Behrens III. *The Limits to Growth: A Report for the Club of Rome's Project on the Predicament of Mankind*. New York: Universe Books, 1972.

Mumford, Lewis. *The Myth of the Machine*. London: Secker & Warburg, 1967.

Muthesius, Stefan. *The Postwar University: Utopianist Campus and College*. New Haven: Yale University Press, 2001.

O'Neill, Gerard K. *The High Frontier*. London: Corgi, 1978.

Pawley, Martin. *Terminal Architecture*. London: Reaktion, 1998.

Phillips, Ian. *From 21st Century Leisure to 20th Century Holiday Catastrophe: The Isle of Man Summerland Fire Disaster*. http://www.birmingham.ac.uk/schools/gees/people/profile.aspx?ReferenceId=9695.

Poole, Robert. *Earthrise: How Man First Saw the Earth*. New Haven; London: Yale University Press, 2008.

Reider, Rebecca. *Dreaming the Biosphere: The Theater of All Possibilities*. Albuquerque: University of New Mexico Press, 2009.

Ritter, Katharina et al., eds. *Soviet Modernism 1955–1991: Unknown History*. Zurich: Park Books, 2012.

Roland, Conrad. *Frei Otto: Structures*. Trans. by C. V. Amerongen. London: Longman, 1972.

Rydell, Robert W. *World of Fairs: The Century-of-Progress Expositions*. Chicago; London: University of Chicago Press, 1993.

Safdie, Moshe. *Beyond Habitat*. Ed. by John Kettle. Cambridge, Massachusetts; London: MIT Press, 1970.

Schumacher, E. F. *Small Is Beautiful: A Study of Economics as if People Mattered*. London: Abacus, 1976.

Scott, Felicity D. *Architecture or Techno-utopia: Politics after Modernism*. Cambridge, Massachusetts; London: MIT Press, 2007.

Sloterdijk, Peter. *In the World Interior of Capital: Towards a Philosophical Theory of Globalization*. Trans. by Wieland Hoban. Cambridge: Polity Press, 2013.

Sloterdijk, Peter. *Bubbles: Spheres Volume 1: Microspherology*. Trans. by Wieland Hoban. Los Angeles: Semiotext(e), 2011.

Smith, C. Ray. *Supermannerism: New Attitudes in Post-Modern Architecture*. New York: Dutton, 1977.

Tafuri, Manfredo. *Architecture and Utopia: Design and Capitalist Development*. Trans. by Barbara Luigia La Penta. Cambridge, Massachusetts; London: MIT Press, 1976.

Tange, Kenzo. *Kenzo Tange, 1946–1969: Architecture and Urban Design*. Ed. by Udo Kultermann. London: Pall Mall Press, 1970.

Toffler, Alvin. *Future Shock*. London: Pan Books, 1972.

Traffic in Towns: A Study of the Long Term Problems of Traffic in Urban Areas. London: Her Majesty's Stationary Office, 1963.

Turner, Fred. *From Counterculture to Cyberculture: Stewart Brand, the Whole Earth Network, and the Rise of Digital Utopianism*. Chicago: University of Chicago Press, 2006.

Wiener, Norbert. *Cybernetics: or Control and Communication in the Animal and the Machine*. New York: John Wiley & Sons, 1948.

Wiener, Norbert. *The Human Use of Human Beings: Cybernetics and Society*. London: Eyre & Spottiswoode, 1950.

Wigley, Mark. *Constant's New Babylon: The Hyper-Architecture of Desire*. Rotterdam: Witte de With, Center for Contemporary Art/010 Publishers, 1998.

Winner, Langdon. *The Whale and the Reactor: A Search for Limits in an Age of High Technology*. Chicago; London: University of Chicago Press, 1986.

ILLUSTRATION CREDITS

INDEX